THE AFRICAN COLONY

STUDIES IN THE RECONSTRUCTION

BY

JOHN BUCHAN

Copyright © 2013 Read Books Ltd.
This book is copyright and may not be
reproduced or copied in any way without
the express permission of the publisher in writing

British Library Cataloguing-in-Publication Data
A catalogue record for this book is available from the
British Library

John Buchan

John Buchan, first Baron Tweedsmuir of Elsfield, was born in Perth, Scotland in 1875. In his youth, his father immersed him in the history, legends and myths of Scotland, and he was an avid reader, stating some years later that John Bunyan's *The Pilgrim's Progress* was a "constant companion" to him. Buchan's education was uneven, but at the age of seventeen he obtained a scholarship to study classics at Glasgow University, where he began to write poetry. His first work, *The Essays and Apothegms of Francis Lord Bacon*, was published in 1894, and a year later he enrolled at Oxford University to study law.

In 1900, Buchan moved to London, and two years later accepted a civil service post in South Africa. In the years leading up to World War I, he worked at a publishers, and also wrote *Prester John* (1910) – which later became a school reader, translated into many languages – as well as a number of biographies. In 1915, Buchan become a war correspondent for *The Times*, and published his most well-known book, the thriller *The Thirty-Nine Steps*. After the war he became a director of the news agency Reuters.

Over the course of his life, Buchan would eventually publish some one hundred books, forty or so of which were novels, mostly wartime thrillers. In the latter part of his life he worked in politics, serving as Conservative MP for the Scottish universities and Lord High Commissioner of the Church of Scotland (1933-34). In 1935, Buchan moved to Canada, where he became the thirty-fifth Governor General of Canada. He died in 1940, aged 64.

TO THE
HONOURABLE
HUGH ARCHIBALD WYNDHAM,
IN MEMORY OF
OUR AFRICAN HOUSEKEEPING.

"The greatest honour that ever belonged to the greatest Monarkes was the inlarging their Dominions, and erecting Commonweales."—Captain John Smith.

CONTENTS

INTRODUCTORY ....Page 1

PART 1. THE EARLIER MASTERS

I. PRIMITIVE SOUTH AFRICA ....Page 13

II. THE GENTLEMEN-ADVENTURERS ......Page 30

III. THE GREAT TREK ....Page 47

IV. THE BOER IN SPORT ....Page 65

V. THE BOER IN ALL SERIOUSNESS ....Page 75

PART II. NOTES OF TRAVEL

VI. EVENING ON THE HIGH VELD ....Page 97

VII. IN THE TRACKS OF WAR ....Page 112

VIII. THE WOOD BUSH ....Page 134

IX. ON THE EASTERN VELD ....Page 151

X. THE GREAT NORTH ROAD ....Page 169

XI. THE FUTURE OF SOUTH AFRICAN SPORT
.... Page 193

PART III. THE POLITICAL PROBLEM

XII. THE ECONOMIC FACTOR ....Page 217

XIII. THE SETTLEMENT OF THE LAND ....Page 290

XIV. THE SUBJECT RACES ....Page 322

XV. JOHANNESBURG ....Page 351

XVI. CONSTITUTIONAL QUESTIONS ....Page 366

XVII. THE POLICY OF FEDERATION ....Page 391

XVIII. THE ARMY AND SOUTH AFRICA ....Page 414

XIX. THE FUTURE OUTLOOK ....Page 434

INTRODUCTORY.

On the last day of May 1902 the signature at Pretoria of the conditions of peace brought to an end a war which had lasted for nearly three years, and had among other things destroyed a government, dissolved a society, and laid waste a country. In those last months of fighting some progress had been made with the reconstruction—at least with that not unimportant branch of it which is concerned with the machinery of government. A working administration had been put together, new ordinances in the form of proclamations had been issued, departments had been created and the chief appointments made, the gold industry was beginning to set its house in order, refugees were returning, and already political theories were being mooted and future parties foreshadowed. But it is from the conclusion of peace that the work of resettlement may fairly be taken to commence. Before that date the restrictions of war limited all civil activity; not till the shackles were removed and the civil power left in sole possession does a fair field appear either for approval or criticism.

It is not my purpose to write the history of the reconstruction. The work is still in process, and a decade later it may be formally completed. Fifty years hence it may be possible to look back and discriminate on its success or failure. The history when it is written will be an interesting book. It will among other matters deal with the work of repatriation, one of the most curious and quixotic burdens ever borne by a nation, and one, I believe, to which no real parallel can be found. It will concern itself with the slow and difficult transference from military to civil government, the renascence of the common law, the first revival of trade and industry, the restitution of prisoners, and the return of refugees—all matters of interest and novel precedents in our history. It will recognise more clearly than is at present possible the problems which faced South Africa at the time, and it will be in the happy position of judging from the high standpoint of accomplished fact. But in the meantime, when we have seen barely eighteen months of reconstruction, history is out of the question. Yet even in the stress of work it is often sound policy for a man to halt for a moment and collect his thoughts. There must be some diagnosis of the problem before him, the end to which his work is directed, the conditions under which he labours. While it is useless to tell the story of a task before it is done, it is often politic to re-examine the difficulties and to get the mind clear as to what the object of all this strife and expense of money and energy may be. Ideals are all very well in their way, but they are apt to become very dim lamps unless often replenished from the world of facts and trimmed and adjusted by wholesome criticism.

Such a modest diagnosis is the aim of the present work. I have tried in the main to state as clearly as I could the outstanding problems of South African politics as they appear to one observer. I say "in the main," because I am aware that I have been frequently led against my intention to express an opinion on more than one such problem, and in several cases to suggest a policy. I can only plead that it is almost impossible to keep a statement of a case uncoloured by one's own view of the solution, and that it is better to give frankly a judgment, however worthless, than to allow a bias to influence insensibly the presentation of facts. For such views, which are my own, I claim no value; for facts, in so far as they are facts, I hope I may beg some little attention. They are the fruit of first-hand, and, I trust, honest observation. Every statement of a case is, indeed, a personal one, representing the writer's own estimate rather than objective truth, but in all likelihood it is several degrees nearer the truth than the same writer's policies or prophecies. South Africa has been in the world's eye for half a century, and in the last few years her problems have been so complex that it has been difficult to separate the permanent from the transitory, or to look beyond the mass of local difficulties to the abiding needs of the sub-continent as a whole. Colonial opinion has been neglected at home; English opinion has been misunderstood in the colonies. It may be of interest to try to estimate her chief needs and to understand her thoughts, for it is only thus that we can forecast that future which she and she alone must make for herself.

Every one who approaches the consideration of the politics of a country which is not his own, and in which he is at best a stranger, must feel a certain diffidence. On many matters it is impossible that he should judge correctly. What seems to him a simple fact is complicated, it may be, by a thousand unseen local currents which no one can allow for except the old inhabitant. For this reason an outside critic will be wrong in innumerable details, and even, it is probable, in certain broad questions of principle. But aloofness may have the qualities of its defects. A critic on a neighbouring hill-top will be a poor guide to the flora and fauna of the parish below; but he may be a good authority on its contours, on the height of its hills and the number of its rivers, and he may, perhaps, be a better judge of the magnitude of a thunderstorm coming out of the west than the parishioner in his garden. The insistence of certain South African problems, familiar to us all, has made any synthetic survey difficult for the South African and impossible for the newspaper reader at home. We have forgotten that it is a country with a history, that it is a land where men can live as well as wrangle and fight, that it has sport, traditions, charm of scenery and weather; and in its politics we are apt to see the problems under a few popular categories, rather as a war of catchwords than the birth-pangs of a people. I have attempted in the following pages to give this synthesis at the expense, I am afraid, of completeness of detail. It is my hope that some few readers may find utility even in an imperfect general survey as a corrective and a supplement to the many able expositions of single problems.

The title begs a question which it is the aim of the later chapters to answer. South Africa is in reality one colony, and it can only be a matter of years till this radical truth is formally recognised in a federation. But some explanation is necessary for the fact that most of the book is occupied with a discussion of the new colonies and with problems which, for the present, may seem to exist only for them. At this moment the settlement of the Transvaal and the Orange River Colony is the most vital South African problem. On their success or failure depends the whole future of the sub-continent. They show, not in embryo, but in the strongest light and the clearest and most mature form, every South African question. On them depends the future wealth of the country and any marked increase in its population. They will be forced by their position to be in the van of South African progress, and to give the lead in new methods of expansion and development. We are therefore fortunate in possessing in the politics of these colonies an isolated and focussed observation-ground, a page where we can read in large clear type what is elsewhere blurred and written over. I do not suppose that this fact would be denied by any of the neighbouring colonies; indeed the tendency in those states is to manifest an undue interest in the affairs of the Transvaal, and to see often, in matters which are purely local, questions of far-reaching South African interest. On the ultimate dominance of the Transvaal opinion naturally differs, and indeed it is a point not worth insisting on, save as a further argument for federation. If South African interests are so inextricably intertwined, it is clearly desirable to have a colony, whose future is obscure but whose wealth and power are at least potentially very great, brought formally into a union where each colony will be one unit and no more, rather than allow it to exist in isolation, unamenable to advice from sister states and wholly self-centred and unsympathetic. It is sufficient justification for the method I have employed if it is admitted that the Transvaal question is the South African problem in its most complete and characteristic form.

A word remains to be said on the arrangement of the chapters. I have tried to write what is a kind of guide-book, not to details, but to the constituents of that national life which is now in process of growth. The reader I have had in mind is the average Englishman who, in seeking to be informed about a country, asks for something more than the dry bones of statistics—*l'homme moyen politique*, who wants a *résumé* of the political problem, some guide to the historical influences which have been or are still potent, an idea of landscape and national character and modes of life. He does not ask for a history, nor does he want a disquisition on this or that question, or a brief for this or that policy, but, being perfectly competent to make up his own mind, he wants the materials for judgment. The first part consists of brief historical sketches, dealing with the genesis of the three populations—native, uitlander, and Boer. The history of South Africa, with all deference to the learned and voluminous works of Dr Theal, can never be adequately written. Her past appears to us in a series of vanishing pictures, without continuity or connection. I have therefore avoided any attempt at a consecutive tale, as I have avoided such topics as the War and the negotiations preceding it, and treated a few historical influences in a brief episodic form. In the second part the configuration of the land has been dealt with in a similar way. A series of short sketches, of the class which the French call "*carnets de voyage*," seemed more suitable than any attempt at the work of a gazetteer. I am so convinced of the beauty and healthfulness of the land that I may have been betrayed into an over-minute description: my one excuse is that in this branch of my task I have had few predecessors.

The third part is highly controversial in character, and is presented with grave hesitation. Many books and pamphlets have informed us on those years of South African history between the Raid and the Ultimatum, and a still greater number have discussed every phase and detail of the war. Another book on so hackneyed a matter may seem hard to justify. It may be urged, however, that the question has taken a wholly different form. Of late years it has been complicated by a division of opinion based not only on political but on moral grounds, an opposition in theories of national duty, of international ethics, of civic integrity. South African policy before the war and during the actual conduct of hostilities was by a considerable section of the English people not judged on political grounds, but condemned or applauded in the one case on moral pretexts and in the other on the common grounds of patriotism. The danger of making the moral criterion bulk aggressively in politics is that the criticism so desirable for all policies is neglected or perfunctorily performed. Matters which, to be judged truly, must be tried by the canons of the province to which they belong, are hastily approved or as hastily damned on some wholly alien test. But with the end of the war and the beginning of civil government it seems to me that this vice must tend to disappear. Whatever our judgment on the past, there is a living and insistent problem for the present. Whatever the verdict on our efforts to meet the problem, it must be based on political grounds. We are now in a position to criticise, if not adequately, at least fairly and on a logical basis. But the old data require revision. The war has been a chemical process which has so changed the nature of the old constituents that they are unrecognisable in a new analysis. I am encouraged to hope that a sketch of the political problem as it has to be faced in South Africa to-day will not be without a certain value to those who desire to inform themselves on what is the most interesting of modern imperial experiments. It is too often assumed in England that the real difficulties preceded war, and that the course of policy, though not unattended with risks, is now comparatively clear and easy. It would be truer to say that the real difficulty has only now begun. I shall be satisfied if I can convince some of my readers that the work to be done in South Africa is exceedingly delicate and arduous, requiring a high measure of judgment and tact and patience; that it is South Africa's own problem which she must settle for herself; and above all, that while the result of success will be more far-reaching and vital to the future of the English race than is commonly realised, the consequences of failure will be wholly disastrous to any vision of Empire.

To my friends in South Africa I owe an apology for my audacity in undertaking to pronounce upon a country of which my experience is limited. Had I not always found them ready to welcome outside criticism, however imperfect, when honestly made, and to hear with commendable patience a newcomer's views, however crude, I should have hesitated long before making the attempt. I have endeavoured to give a plain statement of local opinion, which is expert opinion, and therefore worthy of the first consideration, and, though there are phases of it with which I am not in sympathy, I trust I may claim to have given on many matters the colonial view, when such a view has attained consistency and clearness. But my chief excuse is that while local opinion is still in the making, and politics are still in the flux which attends a reconstruction, the outside spectator may in all modesty claim to have a voice. It may be easier for a man coming fresh to a new world to judge it correctly than for those ex-inhabitants of that older world on whose wreckage the new is built.

PART I.

THE EARLIER MASTERS

CHAPTER I.

PRIMITIVE SOUTH AFRICA.

There are kinds of history which a modern education ignores, and which a modern mind is hardly trained to understand. We can interest ourselves keenly in the first vagaries of embryo humankind; and for savagery, which is a hunting-ground for the sociologist and the folk-lorist, we have an academic respect. But for savagery naked and not ashamed, fighting its own battles and ruling its own peoples, we reserve an interest only when it reaches literary record in a saga. Otherwise it is for us neither literature nor history—a kind of natural event like a thunderstorm, of possible political importance, but of undoubted practical dulness. Most men have never heard of Vechtkop or Mosega, and know Tchaka and Dingaan and Moshesh only as barbarous names. And yet this is a history of curious interest and far-reaching significance: the chronicle of Tchaka's deeds is an epic, and we still feel the results of his iron arguments. The current attitude is part of a general false conception of South African conditions. To most men she is a country without history, or, if she has a certain barbarous chronicle, it is without significance. The truth is nearly at the opposite pole. South Africa is bound to the chariot-wheels of her past, and that past is intricately varied—a museum of the wrecks of conquerors and races, joining hands with most quarters of the Old World. More, it is the place where savagery is most intimately linked with latter-day civilisation. Phœnician,

Arab, Portuguese, Dutch, and English—that is her Uitlander cycle; and a cynic might say that she has ended as she began, with the Semitic. And meantime there were great native conquests surging in the interior while the adventurer was nibbling at her coasts; and when we were busy in one quarter abolishing slavery and educating the Kaffir, in another there were wars more bloody than Timour's, and annihilation of races more terrible than Attila ever dreamed of. We see, before our faces, "the rudiments of tiger and baboon, and know that the barriers of races are not so firm but that spray can sprinkle us from antediluvian seas."

To realise this intricate history and its modern meaning is the first South African problem. No man can understand the land unless he takes it as it is, a place instinct with tradition, where every problem is based upon the wreckage of old strifes. And to the mere amateur the question is full of interest. The history of South Africa can never be written. The materials are lost, and all we possess are fleeting glimpses, outcrops of fact on the wide plains of tradition, random guesses, stray relics which suggest without enlightening. We see races emerge and vanish, with a place-name or a tomb as their only memorial; but bequeathing something, we know not what, to the land and their successors. And at the end of the roll come the first white masters of the land, the Dutch, whom it is impossible to understand except in relation to the country which they conquered and the people they superseded. We have unthinkingly set down one of the most curious side-products of the human family as a common race of emigrants, and the result has been one long tale of misapprehension. It is this overlapping of counter-civilisations, this mosaic of the prehistoric and the recent, which gives South African history its piquancy and its character. It is no tale of old populous cities and splendid empires, no story of developing civilisations and conflicting philosophies; only a wild half-heard legend of men who come out of the darkness for a moment, of shapes warring in a mist for centuries, till the curtain lifts and we recognise the faces of to-day.

Two views have been held on the subject of the present native population. One is that it represents the end of a long line of development; the other that it is the nadir of a process of retrogression. The supporters of the second view point to the growing weakness of all Kaffir languages in inflexions and structural forms, while in the Hottentot-Bushman survival they see a degeneration from a more masculine type. It is impossible to dogmatise on such a matter. Degeneration and advance are not fixed processes, but recur in cycles in the history of every nation. The Bushman, one of the lowest of created types, may well be the original creature of the soil, advancing in halting stages from the palæolithic man; himself practically a being of the Stone Age, and prohibited from further progress by an arid and unfriendly land, and the advent of stronger races. Of the palæolithic man, who 200,000 years ago or thereabout made his home in the river drifts, we have geological records similar to those found in the valleys of the

Somme and the Thames. On the banks of the Buffalo at East London, in a gravel deposit 70 feet above the present river-bed, there have been found rude human implements of greenstone, the age of which may be measured by the time the river has taken to wear down 70 feet of hard greenstone dyke.[1] From the palæolithic it is a step of a few millenniums to the neolithic man, who has left his relics in the shell-heaps and kitchen-middens at the mouth of the same stream—who, indeed, till a few generations ago was an inhabitant of the land. The Bushman was a dweller in the Stone Age, for, though he knew a little about metals, stone implements were in daily use, and, with his kinsmen the Pigmies of Central Africa, he represented a savagery compared with which the Kaffir races are civilised. It is his skull which is found in the shell-heaps by the river-sides. He was a miserable fellow, a true troglodyte, small, emaciated, with protruding chest and spindle legs. He lived by hunting of the most primitive kind, killing game with his poisoned arrows. He had no social organisation, no knowledge of husbandry or stock-keeping, and save for his unrivalled skill in following spoor and a rude elementary art which is shown in the Bushman pictures on some of the rocks in the western districts, he was scarcely to be distinguished from the beasts he hunted. A genuine neolithic man, and therefore worthy of all attention. In other lands his wild contemporaries have gone; in South Africa the elephant, the rhinoceros, and the buffalo survive to give the background to our picture of his life. He himself has perished, or all but perished. The Dutch farmers hunted him down and shot him at sight, for indeed he was untamable. His blood has probably mixed with the Hottentot and the Koranna; and in some outland parts of the Kalahari and the great wastes along the lower Orange he may survive in twos and threes.

Originally he covered all the south-west corner of Africa, but in time he had to retire from the richer coast lands in favour of a people a little higher in the scale of civilisation. The origin of the Hottentots is shrouded in utter mystery, but we find them in possession when the first Portuguese and Dutch explorers reached the coast. They, too, were an insignificant race, but so far an advance upon their predecessors that they were shepherds, owning large herds of sheep and horned cattle, and roaming over wide tracts in search of pasture. They had a tribal organisation, and a certain domesticity of nature which, while it made them an easy prey to warrior tribes, enabled them to live side by side with the Dutch immigrants as herdsmen and house-servants. The pure breed disappeared, but their blood remains in the Cape boy, that curious mixed race part white, part Malay, part Hottentot. Both Bushman and Hottentot, having within them no real vitality, have perished utterly as peoples: in Emerson's words, they "had guano in their destiny," and were fated only to prepare the way for their successors.

For the rest the history of primitive South Africa is a history of the Bantu tribes but for one curious exception. In the districts now included in the general name of

Rhodesia, stretching from the Zambesi to the Limpopo, we find authentic record of an old and mysterious civilisation compared with which all African empires, save Egypt, are things of yesterday. Over five hundred ruins, showing in the main one type, though a type which can be differentiated in stages, are hidden among the hollows and stony hills of that curious country. Livingstone and Baines first called the world's attention to those monuments, and Mr Bent, in his 'Ruined Cities of Mashonaland,' provided the first working theory of their origin. Since that date many savants, from Dr Schlichter to Professor Keane, have elaborated the hypothesis, for in the present state of our knowledge a hypothesis it remains. In those ruins, or Zimbabwes, to use the generic Bantu name, three distinct periods have been traced, and a fourth period, when it is supposed that local tribes began to imitate the Zimbabwe style of architecture. The features of this architecture are simple, and consist chiefly of immense thickness of wall ornamented with a herring-bone, a chess-board, and in a few instances a diaper pattern, enclosures entered by narrow winding passages, and in some cases conical towers similar to the Sardinian *nauraghes*. The discoveries by excavation have not been many, mainly fragments of gold and gold-dust, certain bowls of soapstone and wood ornamented with geometrical patterns and figures which may represent the signs of the zodiac, some curious figures of birds, stone objects which may be *phalli*, and rude stones which may be the sacred *betyli*. It is difficult to judge of the purpose of the buildings. Some suggest forts, some temples, some factories, some palaces:

perhaps they may be all combined, such as we know the early Ionian and Phœnician adventurers built in a new land.

From the remains themselves little light comes, but we have a certain assistance from known history. In early days, before the Phœnicians came to the Mediterranean seaboard, their precursors, the Sabæo-Arabians or Himyarites of South Arabia, were the great commercial people of the East. There was undoubtedly a large trade in gold and ivory with Africa, and all records point to somewhere on the Mozambique coast as the port from which the precious metal was shipped. The only place whence gold in great quantities could have come is the central tableland of Rhodesia, from which it has been estimated that the ancient output was of the value of at least 75 millions. The temple of Haram of Bilkis, near Marib, as described by Müller, has an extraordinary resemblance both in architecture and the relics found in it to the Great Zimbabwe. According to Professor Keane, the Sabæans reached Rhodesia by way of Madagascar, and he finds in the Malagasy language traces of their presence. Ophir he places in the south of Arabia, the emporium to which the gold was brought for distribution; Tarshish, the port of embarkation, he identifies with Sofala; and he finds in Rhodesia the ancient Havilah. Others place Ophir in Rhodesia itself. According to the Portuguese writer Conto, Mount Fura in Rhodesia was called by the Arabs Afur, and some see in the names of Sofala and the Sabi river a reference to Ophir and Sheba. Etymological proofs are always suspicious, save in cases like this where they are merely supplementary to a vast quantity of collateral evidence. When the Phœnicians succeeded to the commercial empire of the Sabæans, they took over the land of Ophir, and to them the bulk of the Zimbabwes are to be attributed. Those later Zimbabwes and the Sardinian *nauraghes*, which are almost certainly Phœnician in origin, have many points of resemblance. The traces of litholatry and phallic worship are Phœnician, the soapstone birds may be the vultures of Astarte, and the rosette decorations on the stone cylinders are found in the Phœnician temple of Paphos and the great temple of the Sun at Emesa.

Such are a few of the proofs advanced on behalf of a hypothesis which is in itself highly probable.[2] It is not a history of generations but of æons, and we cannot tell what were the fortunes of that mysterious land from the days when the Phœnician power dwindled away to the time when the Portuguese discovered the gold mines and framed wild legends about Monomotapa. The most probable theory is that the old Semitic settlers mingled their blood with the people of the land, and as the trade outlets became closed a native tribe took the place of the proud Phœnician merchants. In the words of Mr Selous, "the blood of the ancient builders of Zimbabwe still runs, in a very diluted form, in the veins of the Bantu races, and more especially among the remnants of the tribes still living in Mashonaland and the Barotsi of the Upper Zambesi." The Makalanga, or Children of the Sun, whom Barreto fought, were in the line of succession from the Phœnicians, as the Mashonas are their representatives to-day. In Mashona pottery we can still trace the decorations, which are found on the walls of the Zimbabwes: the people have something Semitic in their features, as compared with other Bantu tribes; they know something of gold-working, a little of astronomy, and in their industries and beliefs have a higher culture than their neighbours. Their chiefs have dynastic names; each tribe has a form of totemism in which some have seen Arabian influences; and in certain matters of religion, such as the sacrifice of black bulls and the observation of days of rest, they suggest Semitic customs. So, if this hypothesis be true, we are presented with a survival of the oldest of civilisations in the heart of modern barbarism. The traveller, who sees in the wilds of Manicaland a sacrifice of oxen to the Manes of the tribe, sees in a crude imitation the rites which the hook-nosed, dark-eyed adventurers brought from the old splendid cities of the Mediterranean, where with wild music and unspeakable cruelties and lusts the votaries of Baal and Astarte celebrated the cycle of the seasons and the mysteries of the natural world—

"Imperishable fire under the boughs Of chrysoberyl and beryl and chrysolite And chrysoprase and ruby and sardonyx."

When the Portuguese first landed in East Africa the chief tribe with which they came in contact was the Makalanga in Mashonaland, ruled by the Monomotapa. But before their power waned they had seen that nation vanquished and scattered by the attacks of fiercer tribes from the north, particularly the Mazimba, in whose name there may lurk a trace of the Agizymba, a country to which, according to Ptolemy, the Romans penetrated. For the last four centuries native South Africa has been the theatre of a continuous *völkerwanderung*, immigrations from the north, and in consequence a general displacement, so that no tribe can claim an ancient possession of its territory. We may detect, apart from the Mashonas, three chief race families among the Bantus—the Ovampas and people of German South Africa; the Bechuanas and Basutos; and the great mixed race of which the Zulus and the Kaffirs of Eastern Cape Colony are the chief representatives. All the groups show a strong family likeness in customs, worship, and physical character. As a rule the men are tall and well-formed, and their features are more shapely than the ordinary negro of West Africa or the far interior. They have a knowledge of husbandry and some skill in metal-working; they have often shown remarkable courage in the field and a kind of rude discipline; and they dwell in a society which is rigidly, if crudely, organised. The Custom of the Ancients is the main rule in their lives, and such law as they possess owes its sanction to this authority. The family is the social unit; and families are combined into clans, and clans into tribes, with one paramount chief at the head, whose power in most instances is despotic, as becomes a military chief. In some of the tribes, notably the Bechuana-Basuto, we find rudiments of popular government, where the chief has to take the advice of the assembled people, as in the Basuto *pitso*, or, in a few cases, of a council of the chief indunas. The chief's authority as lawgiver is absolute, but his judgments are supposed to be only declaratory of ancient custom. Socially the tribes are polygamous, and sexual morality is low, though certain crimes are reprobated and severely punished. The prevailing religion is ancestor-worship, joined with a rude form of natural dæmonism. The ordinary Bantu is not an idolater like the Makalanga, but he walks in terror of unseen spirits which dwell in the woods and rivers,—the ghost of his father it may be, or some unattached devils. Ghost feasts are made at stated times on the graves of the dead; and if the ghost has been whimsical enough to enter the body of an animal, that animal must be jealously respected. Each tribe has its totem—the lion, or the antelope, or the crocodile—from which they derive their descent, one of the commonest features of all primitive societies. There seem traces of a vague belief in a superior deity, who makes rain and thunder and controls the itinerant bands of ghosts—a great ghost, who, if properly supplicated, may intercede with the smaller and more troublesome herd. But abstractions are essentially foreign to the Bantu mind, and his modest Pantheon is filled with the simplest of deities.

No priesthood exists, but it is possible for a clever man to learn some of the tricks of disembodied spirits and frustrate them by his own skill. In this way a class of sorcerers arose, who dealt in big medicine and strong magic. They profess to make rain and receive communications from the unseen, to cure diseases and give increase to the flocks, to expound the past and foretell the future. This powerful class is jealous of amateurs, and does its best to remove inferior wizards; but they are always liable to be annihilated themselves by a powerful chief, who is more bloodthirsty than superstitious. Undoubtedly some of these sorcerers acquire a knowledge of certain natural secrets; they become skilled meteorologists, and seem to possess a crude knowledge of hypnotism. They are also physicians of considerable attainments, and certain native remedies, notably a distillation of herbs, which is used for dysentery in Swaziland, have a claim to a place in a civilised pharmacopœia. This rough science is the only serious intellectual attainment of the Bantu, outside of warfare. They have a kind of music which is extremely doleful and monotonous; they have a rude art, chiefly employed in the decoration of their weapons; but they have no poetry worthy of the name; and their only literature is found in certain simple folk-tales, chiefly of animals, but in a few cases of human escapades and feats of sorcery. The lion is generally the butt of such stories, and the quick wit of the hare and the knavery of the jackal are held up to the admiration of the listeners.[3]

Such are the chief features of Bantu life, and so lived the natives of South Africa up to the early years of last century. But about that time a certain Dingiswayo, being in exile at Cape Town, saw a company of British soldiers at drill, and, being an intelligent man, acquired a new idea of the art of war. When he returned to his home and the chieftainship of the little Zulu tribe, the memory of the soldiers in shakos, who moved as one man, remained with him, and he began to experiment with his army. He died, and his lieutenant Tchaka succeeded to the command of a small but well-disciplined force. This Tchaka was one of those born leaders of men in battle who appear on the stage of history every century or so. He perfected the discipline of his army, armed it with short stabbing spears for close-quarter fighting, and then proceeded to use it as a wedge to split the large loose masses which surrounded him. It was a war of the eagle and the crows. Neighbouring tribes awoke one morning to find the enemy at their gates, and by the evening they had ceased to exist. A wild flight to the north began, and for years the wastes north and east of the Drakensberg were littered with flying remnants of broken clans. All the great deeds of savage warfare—the killing of the Suitors, the fight in the Great Hall of Worms, Cuchulain's doings in the war of the Bull of Cuailgne—pale before the barbaric splendours of Tchaka's slaughterings, the Zulus became the imperial power of South-East Africa, and their monarch's authority was limited only by the length of his impis' reach. By-and-by his career of storm ceases. We find him ruling as a severe and much-venerated king, arbitrary and bloodthirsty but comparatively honest; a huge man, with many large vices and a few glimmerings of virtue. He was succeeded by his brother, the monstrous Dingaan, who was soundly beaten by the Boers in one of the most heroic battles in history; he in turn gave way to his brother Panda, a figure of small note; and the dynasty ended with

Cetewayo and the blood and terror of Isandhlwana and Ulundi.

After Tchaka the man who looms largest in the tale of those wars is Mosilikatse, the founder of the Matabele. The Zulu conquests placed terrible autocrats on the throne, and the marshal who incurred the king's displeasure had to flee or perish. To this circumstance we owe the Angoni in Nyassaland and the empire of Lobengula. About 1817 Mosilikatse with his impi burst into what is now the Orange River Colony, driving before him the feeble Barolong and Bechuana tribes, and established his court at a place on the Crocodile River north of the Magaliesberg, where a pass still bears his name. He began a career of wholesale rapine and slaughter, till, as Fate would have it, he came in contact with the pioneers of the Great Trek. Some hideous massacres were the result, but he had to deal with an enemy against whom his race could never hope to stand. The Boers, under Uys and Potgieter, drove him from his kraal, impounded his ill-gotten cattle, and finally, in a great battle on the Marico River, defeated him so thoroughly that he fled north of the Limpopo and left the country for ever. From the little we know of him he was a cruel and treacherous chief, inferior in strength to Tchaka, as he was utterly inferior to Moshesh in statesmanship. But the men he led had the true Zulu fighting spirit, and in the Matabele, under his son Lobengula, we have learned something of the warriors of Mosilikatse.

A throne which, as with the Zulus and their offshoots, had no strong religious sanction, must subsist either by continued success in battle or a studious statesmanship. Tchaka is an instance of the first; Moshesh, the founder of the Basuto power, is a signal example of the second. The Basutos were driven down from the north by the Zulu advance, and found shelter in the wild tangle of mountains which cradle the infant Orange and Caledon rivers. Moshesh, who had no hereditary claim to a throne, won his power by his own abilities, and on the mountain of Thaba Bosigo established his royal kraal. The name of the "Chief of the Mountain" is written larger even than Tchaka's over South African history, and to-day his people are the only tribe who have any substantive independence. Alone among native chiefs he showed the intellect of a trained statesman, and a tireless patience which is only too rare in the annals of statesmanship. The presence of French missionaries at his court gave him the means of instruction in European ways, and he was far too clever to have any prejudice against so startling a departure from the habits of his race. He watched the dissensions of the rival white peoples, and quietly and cautiously profited by their blunders. He made war against them as a tactical measure, and after an undoubted victory increased his power by making a diplomatic peace. He left his tribe riches and security, and the history of Basutoland since his day is one long commentary on the surprising talents of its founder. How far the credit is his and how far it belongs to his advisers we cannot tell; but we can admire a character so liberal as to accept advice, and a mind so shrewd that it saw unerringly its own advantage. There is none of the wild glamour of conquest about him, but there is a more abiding reputation for a far more intricate work; for, like another statesman, he could make a small town a great city—and with the minimum of expense.

With the death of Moshesh the history of South Africa becomes almost exclusively the history of its white masters. It is an old country, as old as time, the prey of many conquerors, but with it all a patient and mysterious land. Civilisations come and go, and after a millennium or two come others who speculate wildly on the relics of the old. In some future century (who knows?), when the Rand is covered with thick bush and once more the haunt of game, some enlightened sportsman, hunting in his shirt after the bush-veld manner, may clear the undergrowth from the workings of the Main Reef and write a chapter such as this on the doings of earlier adventurers.

[1] An interesting sketch of the palæolithic remains in South Africa is contained in two essays appended to Dr Alfred Hillier's 'Raid and Reform' (1898).

[2] The chief authorities on this curious subject are Mr Bent's 'Ruined Cities of Mashonaland,' Dr Schlichter's papers in the 'Geographical Journal,' Professor Keane's 'Gold of Ophir,' and Dr Carl Peters' 'Eldorado of the Ancients.' Mr Wilmot's 'Monomotapa' contains an interesting collection of historical references

from Phœnician, Arabian, and Portuguese sources; and in 'The Ancient Ruins of Rhodesia,' by Messrs Hall and Neal, there is a very complete description of the ruins examined up to date (1902), and a valuable digest of the various theories on the subject.

[3] There is an account of Bantu life in Dr Theal's 'Portuguese in South Africa.' The same author's 'Kaffir Folk-lore' and M. Casalis' 'Les Bassoutos' contain much information on their customs and folk-lore; while Bishop Callaway's 'Nursery Tales of the Zulus,' M. Jacottet's 'Contes Populaires des Bassoutos,' and M. Junod's 'Chants et Contes des Baronga' and 'Nouveaux Contes Ronga' are interesting collections of folk-tales.

CHAPTER II.

THE GENTLEMEN-ADVENTURERS.

The world's changes, so philosophers have observed, spring from small origins, though their reason and their justification may be ample enough, and exercise the learned for a thousand years. A sailor's tale, a book in an old library, may set the adventurer off on his voyages, and presently empires arise, and his fatherland alters its history. The world moves to no measured tune; everywhere there are sudden breaks, paradoxes, high enterprises which end in smoke, and pedestrian beginnings which issue in the imperial purple. All things have their ground in theory, and by-and-by a dismal post-mortem science will discover impulses which the adventurer never dreamed of. Few lands, even the most remote, are without this variegated history, and the crudest commercial power is built up on the *débris* of romance. South Africa, which is to-day, and to most men, a parvenu country, founded on the Stock Exchange, has odd incidents in her pedigree. Eliminate all the prehistoric guesses, strike out the Dutch, and the Old World has still had its share in her fashioning. Europe may seem only yesterday to have finally sealed her conquest, but she has been trying her hand at it for five hundred years. And the result of the oldest struggle has been a curious story of failure—often heroic, seldom wise, but always fascinating, as such stories must be. It is associated with one of the smallest, and to-day the least enterprising, of European peoples; and it has issued in

Portugal's most notable over-sea possession. Every nation has its holy land of endeavour—England in India, France in Algiers, Russia in Turkestan. Such was South Africa to Portugal; much what Sicily was to the Athenians, the place linked with all her hopes and with her direst misfortunes.

Happily the adventure was not without its chroniclers. The Dominican friar, dos Santos,[4] has sketched for us the empire at its zenith, and de Barros, the Portuguese Secretary for the Indies, has piously narrated its beginnings. But the matter-of-fact histories disguise the real daring of the exploit. The chivalry of Europe in its most characteristic form was carried 8000 miles from home to an unknown land; civilisation of a kind, a Christian church, a code of honour, the rudiments of law and commerce, and the amenities of life, were planted on a narrow malarial seaboard by men who had taken years in the voyage, and had scarcely a hope of return. It is said that a great part of courage lies in having done the thing before, but there was no such ingredient in the valour of those adventurers. Risking all on a dream, they set off on their ten-year excursions, holding an almost certain death as a fair stake in the game. The tenth who survived set themselves cheerfully to transform their discoveries into a national asset. They colonised as whole-heartedly, if not as wisely, as any nation in the world. And in spite of the narrowest and most pragmatic of cultures, they proved themselves singularly adaptable. The Portuguese gentlemen, for whom the Cancioneiros were sung, became Africans in everything but blood, adopting a new land under their old flag, and doing their best to Christianise and colonise it. It was not their fault that the unalterable laws of trade and the destinies of races shattered in time the fabric at which they had laboured.

In 1445, the year in which Diniz Dias is reported to have rounded Cape Verd, the Portuguese were the most daring seamen in Europe. Dwelling on a promontory, they naturally turned their eyes southward and westward, when peace and a moderate wealth gave them leisure for fancies. Those were the days of the foreglow of the Renaissance. Constantinople had not yet fallen, but the spirit of inquiry was abroad, and a fresh wind had blown among scholastic cobwebs. The Church had her share in the revival. A belated missionary, or, as it may be, commercial, zeal stirred the ecclesiastical powers. Fresh lands might be won for the Cross, and fresh moneys to build new abbeys and endow new bishoprics. The merchants of Lisbon and Oporto saw gold in every traveller's tale, and gladly risked a bark on a promising undertaking. There lived, too, at the time a sagacious prince, Henry the Navigator, the son of João I. and Philippa of Lancaster, himself an amateur of colonisation, who set the fashion for courtiers and citizens. So the young Portuguese squire, trained in the pride of his caste, his mind nurtured on chivalrous tales, fired readily at the strange rumours, and found a peaceful life among his vineyards no satisfying career for a man. To him the white sea-wall of the harbour was the boundary of the unknown. Out in the west lay the

Purple Islands of King Juba, the forgotten Atlantis, the lost Hesperides, and dim classical recollections from the monastery school gave authority to his fancies. There were but two careers for a gentleman, arms and adventure, and the latter was for the moment the true magnet. To him it might be given to find the Golden City, the Ophir of King Solomon, or to penetrate beyond the deserts to where Prester John[5] ruled his wild empire in the fear of God. And all the while in Europe men were wrangling over creeds and syllogisms, questioning the powers of the Church, grumbling over dogmas, dying for a few square miles of territory. What wonder if to high-bred, high-spirited youth Europe seemed all too narrow—especially to youth in that south-west corner cut off by the sierras from the world? What mattered desperate peril so long as it had daylight and honour in it? So with hope at his prow and a clear conscience the adventurer set out on his travels.

The first object of Portuguese enterprise was Bilad Ghana, the modern Senegal, which they knew of from Arab geographers. The land route across the Sahara was closed to them, so they were compelled to reach it by sea. It was Henry's dream to make the country a Portuguese dependency, and Christianise it under the iron rule of the Order of the Knights of Jesus Christ,—one of those schemes in which the crusading spirit and a hunger for new territory are subtly blended in the common fashion of the Age of the Adventurers. It was currently believed that the Senegal River rose from a lake near the source of the Nile, and would thus enable the Portuguese to join hands with the Christian monarch of Abyssinia. A special indulgence was obtained from the Pope for all who fought under the banner of the Order of Christ. And so, blessed by the Church, a series of slave-raids began, which were slowly pushed farther south till Cape Verd was reached, and the great turn of the coast to the east began to puzzle the sea-captains. Henry died in 1460, having added, as he believed, a vast territory to the Portuguese Crown, called by the name of Guinea, which is Bilad Ghana corrupted. That the future interests of its discoverer might be properly cared for the new land was divided into parishes, whose chaplains were bound to say one weekly mass for the Iffante's soul. By the time of the death of Affonso V. in 1481 the Portuguese had passed the Niger Delta, discovered the island of Fernando Po, and reached a point two degrees south of the equator. In 1484 Diego Cam reached the mouth of the Congo, and next year set up a marble pillar at Cape Cross to mark his occupation. Another year and Bartolomeo Diaz touched at Angra Pequena, pushed round the Cape, keeping far out to sea, to Algoa Bay; and on returning discovered that Cabo Tormentoso which his king christened Cabo da Boa Esperanza, the first earnest of the hope of the new road to the Indies. Portugal had taken rank as the first of seafaring powers, and, in Politian's words, stood forth as "the trustee of a second world, holding in the hollow of her hand a vast series of lands, ports, seas, and islands revealed by the industry of her sons and the enterprise of her kings." Politian asked that the great story might be written while the materials were yet fresh, but unfortunately Portugal was richer at that time in sea-captains than in men of letters.

On July 8, 1497, Vasco da Gama, the greatest of the world's sailors, left Lisbon on the greatest of all voyages. The circumnavigation of Africa was imposed upon the Archemenid Sataspes as a "penalty worse than death," but to those adventurers death itself was an inconsiderable accident. Five years before Columbus had made his first journey, an enterprise not to be named in the same breath as da Gama's. On Christmas day, having safely passed the Cape, he came to a land of green, tree-clad shores, which he piously christened Natal. He pushed on past the Limpopo and the Zambesi delta to Mozambique, where he found an Arab colony, and to Mombasa, where the chief street still bears his name. He reached Calicut safely on May 20, 1498, ten months and twelve days after leaving Lisbon; and two years later he returned home with one-third of the crew he had sailed with. The Grand Road was now defined; thenceforth it was a trade-route to which commerce naturally turned. No more romantic voyages were ever undertaken, for in those forlorn latitudes Christian and Muslim, East and West, met in war and peace, and creeds and ideas clashed in the strangest disorder. In the expedition of 1500 under Pedro Alvarez Cabral two men were set ashore at Melinda, north of Mozambique, to look for Prester John, and history is silent on the fate of the unfortunate gentlemen. In da Gama's second voyage Nilwa was captured and the Portuguese East African empire began. A fierce enthusiast was this same da Gama, for, meeting with a great ship of the Sultan of Egypt, filled with Muslim pilgrims, he looted it from stem to stern, and sent every pilgrim to Paradise.

After da Gama came Affonso d'Albuquerque, who seized Goa, and established his country's hold on the Malabar coast, and pushing on captured Malacca, the richest of the Portuguese trading stations. He swept all alien navies from the Eastern seas, and established on a sound basis of naval supremacy a great commercial empire. Nothing less than the conquest of Turkey would satisfy him. He dreamed of allying himself with Prester John, and establishing himself on the Upper Nile; and again of raiding Medina, carrying off Muhammad's coffin, and exchanging it for the Holy Sepulchre at Jerusalem. He captured Hormuz on the Persian Gulf, and with it the enormous trade between India and Asia Minor; and he was on the eve of leading an expedition against Aden, which he saw to be the key of the Red Sea, when he was struck down at Goa, and died, like the great seigneur he was, clothed in the robes of his knightly order. Against his expressed wish he was buried at Goa, for the Portuguese believed that, as long as the bones of their intrepid leader lay there, their Empire of the East would stand. So died the foremost of his countrymen, one who may rank with Clive as the greatest of Christian viceroys.

Meantime the East African power had been fully established. Sofala and Mozambique, the chief cities of the coast, had fallen to the Portuguese, and their eyes turned to what they believed to be the fabulously rich hinterlands, where Solomon had won his gold and ivory, and Arab traders had for centuries found their hunting-ground. The Monomotapa, the chief or emperor of the Makalanga, whose Zimbabwe was situated somewhere in what we now know as Mashonaland, took the place of Prester John in their imagination. They pushed up the Zambesi, founding trading stations on the way, which still survive. They found Ophir in every Bantu name, and began that long series of meaningless wars of conquest which in the end shattered their dream of empire. Gold-seeking has never been an enterprise blessed of Heaven; and the Portuguese were more unlucky than most adventurers. They found themselves involved in desperate wars; fever and poison carried off their leaders; and the grandees, like Barreto and Homem, who in cuirasses and velvets held indabas with Makalanga chiefs, got little reward for their diplomacy. Soon the horizon narrowed, boundaries were defined, and the colonist sat down in the coast towns to make a living by legitimate trade.

The chief commercial importance of South-East Africa to the Portuguese was as a port of call on the great trade-route to the Indies. The skins, ivory, and gold, which the country produced, could never vie with the organised exports of Goa and Calicut. So Mozambique and Sofala became rather depots than supply-grounds, at which the great ships anchored and refitted; points of vantage, too, in the endless bickerings with Arab traders. There was a modest commerce with the interior, with

Tete as the chief depot, and Masapa, Luanze, and Bukoto as the up-country stations. Each inland Portuguese trader was also a diplomat. Through him the presents passed from the Portuguese king to the savage "emperors," and, situated as he might be at Masapa, on the very edge of the mountain Fura and the forbidden Makalanga country, his duties were often most delicate and hazardous. The trade as a whole was neither productive nor well managed. The whole empire was undermanned. Portugal was colonising Brazil and West Africa at the time she was sending out her adventurers to the East, and the little kingdom in Europe could not long endure the strain. The sons she sent forth rarely returned; and the estates at home fell out of cultivation for lack of men. Meantime stronger and more fortunate races were appearing in the Eastern waters. The Englishmen Newbery, Candish, and Raymond began the rivalry, and the formidable Dutch followed next, with their northern vigour and commercial aptitudes. In 1595 the first of Linschoten's books was published, and opened up a new world for Dutch enterprise. The Dutch East India Company soon wrested from Portugal her Indian possessions, and in a little her East African ports were mere isolated stations, much harassed by the Netherland fleets, and the Grand Road had become a thing of the past.

But, as commerce declined, a new epoch in the Portuguese history began. The disappearance of trade was followed by the advent of one of the most heroic missionary brotherhoods in history. The Jesuit Gonsalvo de Silveira was the pioneer, and a year after he landed in Africa he was murdered by the Makalanga chief. Some fifty years later the Dominicans joined the Jesuits, and till the beginning of the eighteenth century laboured at their quixotic task. Now and then a chief's son was baptised and attained to some degree of civilisation, but the mass of the people, living among fierce tribal wars, cared little for curious tales of peace. There was no ostentation with those Bishops of This or That *in partibus infidelium*. No churches remain to tell of their work. They lived simply in huts, and died a thousand miles away from their kin, so that their very names are forgotten. In our own day travellers in the Zambesi valley have come to kraals where the people called themselves Christians, and showed a few perverted rites in evidence, the one relic of those forgotten heroes. A few incidents, however, have remained in men's minds. Luiz do Espirito Santa, a prior of Mozambique, on being taken into the presence of the Monomotapa and ordered to make obeisance, stiffened his back, and replied that he did such homage to God alone; for which noble saying he was duly murdered. The Shining Cross, which Constantine saw, appeared also to the friar Manoel Sardinha when he led his forces against the Makalanga. In 1652 the Monomotapa Manuza was received into the Church, an event which was the occasion for a great thanksgiving service at Lisbon, at which the king João IV. attended in state. His son, Miguel, entered the Dominican order, was given the diploma of Master of Theology, and died a vicar of the convent of Santa Barbara in Goa. This barbarian Charles V., the greatest

South African chief of his time, may well be remembered among the few mortals who have voluntarily renounced a crown.

And so the empire, having shipwrecked on a dream of gold and a land where men could not live,[6] dwindled down to isolated forts and stations, and the strenuous creed of the pioneers was softened into the bastard contentment of the disheartened. Miserably and corruptly governed, forgotten by Europe, they forgot Europe in turn, and a strange somnolent life began of half-barbaric, wholly oriental seigneurs, ruling as petty monarchs over natives from whom they were not wholly distinct.[7] Instead of holding the outposts of European culture, they sank themselves into the ways of the soil which their forefathers had conquered. Round Tete and Inhambane and Sofala there grew up great country estates, held on a kind of feudal tenure, where the slack-mouthed grandee idled away his days. Set among acres of orchards and gardens, those dwellings were often noble and sumptuous. Thither came belated travellers, gold-seekers, shipwrecked seamen, wandering friars, men of every nationality and trade, and in the prazo of a de Mattos or a de Mira found something better than the mealie-pap they had been living on in native kraals. Sitting on soft couches, drinking good Madeira, and looking at a copy of a Murillo or a Velasquez on the walls, they may well have extolled those oases in the desert. The grandee had his harem, like any Arab sheikh; he dispensed death cruelly and casually among his subjects; but as a rule he seems to have had the virtue of hospitality, and welcomed gladly any traveller with tales of the forgotten world. Fierce Bantu wars have left few traces of those pleasant demesnes; but to the new-comer the land where they once existed has still a quaint air of decadent civilisation. Coming down from the high tableland of the interior, which is the most strenuous land on earth, through the mountain glens which, but for vegetation, might be Norway, one enters a country of bush and full muddy rivers, a country of dull lifeless green and a pestilent climate. But as one draws nearer the coast, where glimpses of gardens appear and white-walled estancias, and rivers spread into lagoons with spits of yellow sand and Arab boatmen, and, last of all, the pale blue Indian Ocean stretches its sleepy leagues to the horizon, there comes a new feeling into the scene, as of something old, not new, decaying rather than undeveloped, which, joined with the moist heat, makes the place

"A land In which it seemèd always afternoon, All round the coast the languid air did swoon, Breathing like one that hath a weary dream."

The tale of this empire, crude and melancholy as it is, provides an instructive commentary on current theories of colonisation. From Tyre and Sidon down to the last Teutonic performance, there is surely sufficient basis to generalise on; but no two theorists are agreed upon the laws which govern those racial adventures. The only approach to a dogma is the theory that to colonise is to decentralise—that before a vigorous life can begin over-sea the runners must be cut which bind the colony to the homeland. France fails, we say, because a Frenchman away from home cannot keep his mind off the boulevards; he is for ever an exile, not a settler. Britain succeeds because her sons find a land of their adoption. But the converse is equally important, though too rare in its application to be often remembered. No race can colonise which cannot decentralise its energy; but equally no race can colonise which can wholly decentralise its sentiment and memory. Portugal failed for this reason chiefly, that the Portuguese forgot Portugal. Few peoples have been so adaptable. The white man's pride died in their hearts. They were ready to mix with natives on equal terms.[8] Now concubinage is bad, but legitimate marriage with half-castes is infinitely worse for the *morale* of a people. And since Nature to the end of time has a care of races but not of hybrids, this tolerant, foolish, unstable folk dropped out of the battle-line of life, and sank from conquerors to resident aliens, while their country passed from an empire to a vague seaboard. "A people scattered by their wars and affairs over the whole earth, and home-sick to a man," wrote Emerson of the English, and it is the trait of the true colonist. It is as important to remember "sweet Argos" as it is to avoid a womanish *heimweh*. For a colony is a sapling, bound by the law of nature to follow the development of the parent tree. A parcel of Englishmen on the Australian coast have no significance without England at their back, to give them a tradition of manners and government, to be their recruiting-ground, to hold out at once a memory of home and an ideal of polity. Wars of separation may come, but a colony is still a colony: it may have a different colour on the map, but its moral complexion is the same; politically it may be a rival, spiritually it remains a daughter.

The country, too, was wretchedly governed. The Portuguese viceroy, often some impoverished noble, was in the same position as the Roman proconsul, and had to restore his fortunes at the expense of the provincials. Local administration was farmed out to local magnates, another part of the crazy decentralisation which led to catastrophe. There is more in bad government than hardship for the private citizen. It means the weakening of the intellectual and moral nerve of the race which tolerates it. Sound government is not, as revolutionary doctrinaires used to think, the outcome of the grace of God and a flawless code of abstractions. It means a perpetual effort, a keen sense of reality, a constant facing and adjusting of problems. And it is one of the laws of life that this high faculty is inconsistent with extreme luxury and ease. A great governor may be one-fourth voluptuary, but he must be three-parts politician. "Je n'aime pas beaucoup les femmes," was one of Napoleon's self-criticisms, "ni le jeu—enfin rien; je suis tout à fait un être politique." The thin strain of old-world tradition was useless in men who were sheikhs, adventurers, grandees, but never statesmen.

But the ultimate source of weakness was economic. The settlements were unproductive in any real sense. The empire was a chain of forts and depots, and on no side was the ruling power organically connected with the soil. A colony should be built up of farmers and miners and manufacturers, having for its basis the productive energy of the land. To exploit is not to colonise, and on this side there is the most urgent need for decentralisation. The Portuguese lost their European culture, but they remained adventurers and aliens. Their traders bargained for produce, but they never went to the root of the matter and organised production. They had no ranches or plantations, only their trading-booths. Like the Carthaginians, they carried their commerce to the ends of the earth, and left the ends of the earth radically unaffected by their presence. People repeat glibly that trade follows the flag, and that commerce is the basis of empire. And in a sense it is true, for an empire without commercial inter-relations and a solid basis of material prosperity is a house built on the sand. But if the maxim be taken in the sense that commerce is in itself a sufficient imperial bond, it is the most fatal of heresies. The Dutch, in their heyday, had an empire chiefly of forts and factories; and what part has the Dutch empire played in the destinies of mankind? No race or kingdom can endure which is not rooted in the soil, drawing sustenance from natural forces, increasing by tillage and forestry, pasturage and mining and manufacture, the aggregate of the world's production. And the need is as much moral as economic. The trader pure and simple—Tyrian, Greek, Venetian, Dutch, or Portuguese—is too cosmopolitan and adventitious to be the staple of a strong race. He has not the common local affections; he is not knit close enough to nature in his toil. To wrest a living from the avarice of the earth is to form character with the salt and iron of power in it. India, it is true, is a partial exception; but India is a unique case of a long-settled subject people ruled wisely by a race which has sufficient breadth and vitality in its culture to spare time for the experiment. It is to colonies, which must always form the major part of an empire, that the maxim applies; for the former is a native power under tutelage, while the latter is the expansion of the parent country beyond the seas. And this expansion must be more than commercial. The colony must be founded in the soil, its people with each generation becoming more indigenous, and its wealth based on its own toil and enterprise; otherwise it is but such a chain of factories as the Portuguese established, which the proverbial whiff of grape-shot may scatter to-morrow.

[4] There is an English abbreviation of dos Santos in Pinkerton's 'General Collection of Voyages and Travels.' The original work was printed at Evora in 1609.

[5] The Portuguese geographers divided Central Africa into Angola in the west, the kingdom of Prester John in the north (Abyssinia), and the empire of Monomotapa (Mashonaland) in the south. The real Prester John was a Nestorian Christian in Central Asia, whose khanate was destroyed by Genghis Khan about the end of the twelfth century; but the name became a generic one for any supposed Christian monarch in unknown countries.

[6] Purchas wrote, "Barreto was discomfited not by the Negro but by the Ayre, the malignity whereof is the same sauce of all their golden countries in Africa."

[7] One missionary wrote, "They have already lost the knowledge of Christians and thrown away the obligations of Faith" (Wilmot, 'Monomotapa').

[8] Among the Baronga, the Bantu tribe who live around Delagoa Bay, there are some ancient folk-tales, derived from Portuguese sources, in which the heroes have Portuguese names, such as João, Boniface, Antonio. One tale about the king's daughter, who was saved from witchcraft by the courage of a young adventurer called João, is a form of the story of Jack and the ugly Princess, which appears throughout European folk-lore. Cf. M. Junod's 'Chants et Contes des Baronga,' pp. 274-322.

CHAPTER III.

THE GREAT TREK.

Every race has its Marathon into which the historian does not inquire too closely who has a reverence for holy places and a fear of sacrilege. It may be a battle or a crusade, a creed, or perhaps only a poem, but whatever it is, it is part and parcel of the national life, and it is impossible to reach the naked truth through the rose-coloured mists of pious tradition. A Sempach or a Bannockburn cannot be explained by a bare technical history. The spirit of a nation was in arms, the national spirit was the conqueror, and the combatants appear more than mere flesh and blood, walking "larger than human" on the hills of story. This phenomenon has merits which it is hard to exaggerate. It is the basis for the rhetorical self-confidence which is essential to a strong race. It is a fountain from which generous youth can draw inspiration, an old watchword to call the inert to battle. If the race has a literature, it helps to determine its character; if the race has none, it provides a basis for fireside tales. The feeblest Greek at the court of Artaxerxes must have now and then straightened himself when he remembered Salamis. Without such a retrospect a people will live in a crude present, and, having no buttress from the past, will fare badly from the rough winds of life.

To the Boer the Great Trek is the unrecorded but ever-remembered Odyssey of his people. He has a long memory, perhaps because of his very slowness and meagreness of fancy. His life was so monotonous that the tale of how his fathers first came into the land inspired him by its unlikeness to his own somnolent traditions. Besides, he had a Scriptural parallel. The persecuted children of Israel, in spite of the opposition of Pharaoh, had fled across the desert from Egypt and found a Promised Land. The Boer sense of analogy is extremely vivid and extremely inexact. Here he saw a perfect precedent. A God-fearing people, leaving their homes doubtless at the call of the Most High, had fled into the wilds of Amalek and Edom, conquered and dispossessed the Canaanites, and occupied a land which, if not flowing with milk and honey, was at least well grassed and plentifully watered. How keen the sense of Scriptural example was, and how constantly present to the Boer mind was the thought that he was following in the footsteps of Israel, is shown by one curious story. The voortrekkers, pushing out from Pretoria, struck a stream which flowed due north, the first large north-running water they had met. Moreover, it was liable to droughts and floods recurring at fixed seasons. What could it be but the great river of Egypt? So with immense pious satisfaction they recognised it as the Nile, and the Nyl it remains to this day.

The thought of a national exodus comes easily to the Aryan mind,—an inheritance from primeval Asian wanderings. And in itself it is something peculiarly bold and romantic, requiring a renunciation of old ties and sentiments impossible to an over-domesticated race. It requires courage of a high order and a confident faith in destiny. Perhaps the courage needed in the case of the Great Trek was less than in most similar undertakings, because of the cheering Scriptural precedent and the lack of that imagination which can vividly forecast the future. The past history of the Boer, too, prepared him for desperate enterprises. Made up originally of doubtful adventurers from Holland, hardihood grew up in their blood as they pushed northwards from the seacoast. The people of the littoral might be, as Lady Anne Barnard found them, sluggish and spiritless; but the farmers of Colesberg and Graaff-Reinet were in the nature of things a different breed. The true Dutch blood does not readily produce an adventurer, but it was leavened and sublimated by a French Huguenot strain, scions of good families exiled for the most heroic of causes. The coarse strong Dutch stock swallowed them up; the language disappeared, the Colberts became Grobelaars, the Villons Viljoens, the Pinards Pienaars; but something remained of *élan* and spiritual exaltation. Harassed from the north by Griqua and Hottentot bandits, and from the east by Kaffir incursions, they became a hardy border race, keeping their own by dint of a strong arm. The quiet of the great sun-washed spaces entered into their souls. They grew taciturn, ungraceful, profoundly attached to certain sombre dogmas, impatient of argument or restraint, bad citizens for any modern State, but not without a gnarled magnificence of their own. They were out of line with the whole world, far nearer in kinship to an Old Testament patriarch than to the townsfolk with whom they shared the country. All angles and corners, they presented an admirable front to savage nature; but they were hard to dovetail into a complex modern society. They would have made good Ironsides, and would have formed a stubborn left wing at Armageddon, but they did ill with franchises and taxes and paternal legislation.

I will take two savage tales from their history to show what manner of men they were in extremity. A certain Frederick Bezuidenhout, a farmer in the Bruintje Hoogte, and by all accounts a dabbler in less reputable trades, was summoned on some charge before the landdrost of the district, and declined to appear. A warrant was issued for his apprehension, and a party of soldiers sent out to enforce it, whereupon Bezuidenhout took refuge in a cave, and was shot dead in its defence. The fiery cross went round among his relatives; overtures, which were refused, were made to the Kaffir chiefs, and Jan Bezuidenhout, the brother of the dead man, swore to fealty a band of as pretty outlaws as ever dwelt on a border. The insurrection failed; thirty-nine of the insurgents were captured, and five were hanged, and Jan Bezuidenhout himself was shot in the Kaffir country by an advance party of the pursuit. Such is the too famous story of Slachter's Nek. The tale of Conrad de Buys[9] and his doings is wilder but more obscure. A man of great physical strength and the worst character, he was the leader of the sterner desperadoes on the Kaffir border. Through living much in native kraals he had become little better than a savage. He was mixed up in Van Jaarsveld's insurrection, and by-and-by his private crimes exceeded his political by so much that he was compelled to flee into the northern wilds. This first of the voortrekkers is next heard of on the banks of the Limpopo, living in pure barbarism, with a harem of Kaffir wives and an immense prestige among his neighbours. The emigrant party under Potgieter, on their return from Delagoa Bay, found somewhere in the Lydenburg hills two half-breeds who called this ruffian father and acted as interpreters. Conrad peopled the Transvaal with his children, whom he seems to have ruled in a patriarchal fashion, forming a real Buys clan, who still hang together at Marah, in Zoutpansberg. In the Pietersburg Burgher camp during the war there was a Buys location, who strenuously urged their claim to be considered a white people and burghers of the republic.

Such was one element in the race of border farmers—a substratum of desperate lawlessness. But there were other elements, many of them noble and worthy. Their morals were less bad than peculiar; their lawlessness rather an inability to understand restrictions than an impulse to disorder. They had their own staunch loyalties, their own strict code of honour. They had the self-confidence of a people whose dogmatic foundations are unshaken, and who are in habitual intercourse with an inferior race. In a rude way they were kindly and hospitable. They had a courage so unwavering that it may be called an instinct, and the bodily strength which comes from bare living and constant exertion. "Simple" and "pastoral" used to be words of praise. During the late war they became a sneer; but it is well to recognise that while they may comprise the gravest faults they must denote a few sterling virtues.

When Pieter Retief left Graaff-Reinet in 1837, he issued an ingenious proclamation which contains his justification of the Great Trek. He complains of the unnecessary hardships attending the emancipation of the slaves, the insecurity of life and property caused by the absence of proper vagrancy laws, and the disaster certain to attend Lord Glenelg's reversal of British policy on the Kaffir border. Retief was a man of high and conscientious character, and his profession of faith is valuable as showing the view of current politics held by the better class of the voortrekkers. They did not defend slavery—Retief expressly repudiates it; but they objected to the method of its abolition, and the lack of precautions for future public safety which the event demanded. Lord Glenelg's withdrawal from the eastern border to the boundary of the Keiskama and Tyumie rivers, as fixed by Lord Charles Somerset in 1819, appeared to them a flagrant piece of weakness which sooner or later must make life on that border impossible. They saw no hope of redress from the imperial Government, which seemed to be dominated by philanthropic hysteria. It is a grave indictment, and worth examination. The slavery question stands in the foreground. The ocean slave-trade was suppressed in 1807, and the English abolitionists had leisure to turn their minds to South Africa. The first progressive enactment came in 1816, when the registration of slaves and slave-births was made compulsory in every district.

In 1823 a series of laws were passed restricting slave labour on the Sabbath, giving slaves the right of owning property, and limiting the punishments to which they were liable. In 1826 officials were appointed in country districts to watch over slave interests, and see that the protective enactments were carried out. The famous Fiftieth Ordinance of 1828 gave the Hottentots the same legal rights as the white colonists. Meanwhile for years a great missionary agitation for total abolition had been going on, which was powerfully supported by the Whig party in England. The Dutch saw clearly the trend of events, and, in what is known as the "Graaff-Reinet proposals," attempted to procure gradually the emancipation which they realised was bound to come. They proposed, unanimously, that after a date to be fixed by Government all female children should be free at birth, and, by a majority, that all male children born after the same date should also be free. I cannot find in these proposals the insidious attempt to defeat the movement which some writers have discerned: they seem to me to be as fair and reasonable an offer as we could expect a slave-holding class to make. But the British attitude is also perfectly clear. Slave-holding had been condemned as a crime by the national conscience, and there could be no temporising with the evil thing. Here, again, a certain kind of education was necessary to appreciate the point of view. The farmers of Graaff-Reinet had not listened to the harangues of Wilberforce and Fowell Buxton; Zion Chapel and its all-pervading atmosphere of mild brotherly love were not within the compass of their experience. England was right, as she generally is in policies which are inspired by a profound popular conviction; but she could hardly expect men of a very different training to fall in readily with her views. In any case the working out of the policy was attended by many blunders. The Emancipation Act took effect in Cape Colony from the 1st of December 1834. £1,200,000 seems a rather inadequate compensation for 35,000 slaves, and as each claim had to be presented before commissioners in London, the farmer had perforce to employ an agent, who bought up his claims at a discount of anything from 18 to 30 per cent.

The losses from emancipation were chiefly felt in the rich agricultural districts of the colony, such as Stellenbosch, Ceres, and Worcester; the border farmers were not a large slave-owning class, and the lack of cheap labour did not trouble them. But emancipation meant a general dislocation of credit all over the country. A man who in 1833 was counted a rich man was comparatively poor in 1835, and this *peripeteia* had a bad effect on the whole farming class. It was rather the spirit of the Act which the Boers of Graaff-Reinet complained of,—the theory, to them ridiculous, that the black man could have legal rights comparable with the white, and the sense of insecurity which dwellers under such a *régime* must feel. The average Boer was an arbitrary but not an unkind slave-master; he regarded his slaves as part of his *familia*, an enclosure to which the common law should not penetrate. To be limited by statute in the use of what he considered his chattels, to find hundreds of officious gentlemen ready to take the part of the chattels on any occasion against him, were pills too bitter to swallow. Emancipation produced vagrants, and he asked for a stringent vagrancy law which his landrosts could administer. England, refusing naturally to take away with one hand what she had given with the other, declined to expose the emancipated slave to the arbitrariness of local tribunals. Well, argued the farmers, our slaves, being free, have become rogues and vagabonds; they may plunder us at their pleasure and England will take their part: it is time for us to seek easier latitudes.

But the chief factor in Dutch dissatisfaction was undoubtedly Lord Glenelg's limitation of the eastern border line. There is something to be said for the view of that discredited, and, to tell the truth, not very wise statesman. The Boer was a bad neighbour for a Kaffir people. He was always encroaching, spurred on by that nomadic something in his blood—a true Campbell of Breadalbane, who built his house on the limits of his estate that he might "brise yont." A buffer state was apt to become very soon a Boer territory. Better to try and establish a strong Kaffir people, who might attain to some semblance of national life, and under the maternal eye of Britain become useful and progressive citizens. So reasoned Lord Glenelg and his advisers, missionary and official. Unfortunately facts were against him, the chimera of a Kaffir nation was soon dispelled, and ten years later Sir Harry Smith, a governor who did not suffer from illusions, made the eastern province a Kaffir reserve under a British commissioner. The frontier Boer, however, was not in a position to share any sentiment about a Kaffir nation. He saw his cattle looted, his family compelled to leave their newly acquired farm, and a long prospect of Kaffir raids where the presumption of guilt would always be held to lie against his own worthy self. Above all things he saw a barred door. No more "brising yont" for him on the eastern border. Expansion, space, were as the breath of his nostrils, and if he could not have them in the old colony he would seek them in the untravelled northern wilds.

There were thus certain well-defined reasons for the Great Trek in contemporary politics which, combined with distorted memories like Slachter's Nek, made up in Boer eyes a very complete indictment against Pharaoh and his counsellors. But the real reason lay in his blood. Had the British Government been all that he could desire, he would still have gone. He was a wanderer from his birth, and trekking, even for great distances, was an incident of his common life. A pastoral people have few vested interests in land. There are no ancient homesteads to leave, or carefully-tended gardens or rich corn-lands. Their wealth is in their herds, which can be driven at will to other pastures. The Boer rarely built much of a farm, and he never fenced. A cottage, a small vegetable-yard, and a stable made up the homestead on even large farms on the border. There was nothing to leave when he had gathered his horned cattle into a mob, yoked his best team to his waggon, and stowed his rude furniture inside. With his rifle slung on his shoulder, he was as free to take the road as any gipsy. He was leaving the country of the alien, where mad fancies held sway and unjust laws and taxes oppressed him. He was bound for the far lands of travellers' tales, the country of rich grass and endless game, where he could live as he pleased and preserve the fashions of his fathers unchanged. He would meet with fierce tribes, but his elephant-gun, as he knew from experience, was a match for many assegais. There was much heroism in the Great Trek, but there was also for the young and hale an exhilarating element of sport. To them it was a new, strange, and audacious adventure. No predikant accompanied the emigrants. The Kirk did not see the Scriptural parallel, and to a man preferred the treasure in Egypt to the doubtful fortunes of Israel.

The first party consisted of about thirty waggons, under the leadership of Louis Trichard and Jan van Rensburg. They travelled slowly, the men hunting along the route, and outspanned for days, and even weeks, at pleasant watering-places. The main object of those pioneers was to ascertain the road to Delagoa Bay; so they did not seek land for settlement, but pushed on till they came to Piet Potgieter's Rust, a hundred miles or so north of Pretoria, which they thought to be about the proper latitude. Here the party divided. Van Rensburg and his men went due east into the wild Lydenburg country on their way to the coast, and were never heard of again. Trichard waited a little, and then slowly groped his way through the Drakensberg to Portuguese territory. The band suffered terribly from fever; their herds were annihilated by the tsetse fly, of which they now heard for the first time; but in the end about twenty-six survivors struggled down to the bay and took ship for Natal. So ended the adventure of the path-finders. The next expedition was led by the famous Andries Potgieter, and came from the Tarka and Colesberg districts. The little Paulus Kruger, a boy of ten, travelled with the waggons to the country which he was to rule for long. Potgieter settled first in the neighbourhood of Thaba 'Nchu on the Basuto border, and bought a large tract of land from a Bataung chief. Farms were marked out, and a few emigrants remained, but the majority pushed on to the north and east. Some crossed the Vaal, and finding a full clear stream coming down from the north, christened it the Mooi or Fair River; and here in after-days, faithful to their first impression, they planted the old capital of the Transvaal. Potgieter with a small band set off on the search for Delagoa Bay, but he seems to have lost himself in the mountains between Lydenburg and Zoutpansberg. On his return he found that Mosilikatse's warriors had at last given notice of their presence, and had massacred a number of small outlying settlements. So began one of the sternest struggles in South African history.

Potgieter gathered all the survivors into a great laager at a place called Vechtkop, between the Rhenoster and Wilge rivers. The precaution was taken none too soon, for one morning a few days later a huge native army appeared, led by the chief induna of Mosilikatse. The odds, so far as can be gathered, were about a hundred to one, but the little band was undaunted, and Sarel Celliers, a true Cromwellian devotee of the Bible and the sword, called his men to prayer. Then forty farmers rode out from the laager, galloped within range, spread out and fired a volley, riding back swiftly to reload. They did good execution, but forty men, however bold, cannot disperse 5000, and in a little the Matabele were round the laager, and the siege began. The defence was so vigorous that after heavy losses the enemy withdrew, driving with them the little stock which formed the sole wealth of the emigrants.

The glove had been thrown down and there could be no retreat. Midian must be destroyed root and branch before Israel could possess the land. After a short rest Potgieter and Gerrit Maritz began the war of reprisals. With a commando of over 100 men and a few Griqua followers, they forded the Vaal, crossed the Magaliesberg, and arrived at Mosilikatse's chief kraal at Mosega. The farmers' victory was complete. Over 400 of the Matabele were slain, several thousand head of cattle secured, and the kraal given to the flames. Potgieter returned to found the little town of Winburg in memory of his victory, and, with the assistance of Pieter Retief, to frame a constitution for the nascent state. But Mosilikatse still remained. He had not been present at the *debâcle* of Mosega, and while he remained on the frontier there was no security for life and property. New recruits had come up from the south, including the redoubtable family of Uys, the horses were in good condition, all had had a breathing-space; so a new and more formidable expedition started in search of the enemy. They found him on the Marico, and for nine days fought with him on the old plan of a charge, a volley, and a retreat. Then one morning there was no enemy to fight; a cloud of dust to the north showed the line of his flight; Mosilikatse had retired across the Limpopo. Whereupon the emigrants proclaimed the whole of the late Matabele territory—the Transvaal, the Orange River Colony, and a portion of Bechuanaland—as theirs by the right of conquest.

So runs the tale of the Great Trek,—rather an Iliad than an Odyssey, perhaps, and a very bloodthirsty Iliad, too. To most men it must seem a noble and spirited story. Whatever the justice of the emigrants' grievances, they conducted themselves well in their self-imposed exile. Potgieter and his men were indeed rather exceptional specimens of their race, and they were strung to the highest pitch by Christian faith and the unchristian passion of revenge. They relapsed, when all was over, to a somewhat ordinary type of farmer, which seems to bear out the general conception of the Boer character—that, while it is capable of high deeds, it is powerful by sudden effort rather than by sustained and strenuous toil. The experiment which began so well should have ended in something better than two bourgeois republics. There are some who see in the tale nothing more than an unwarranted invasion of native territory, and a cruel massacre of a brave race. No view could be more unjust. The Matabele had not a scrap of title to the country, and had not dwelt in it more than a few years. The real owners, if you can talk of ownership at all, were the unfortunate Bataungs and Barolongs, whom the emigrants befriended. The Matabele were indeed as murderous a race of savages as ever lived, and their defeat was a moral as well as a political necessity. It is well to protect the aborigine, but when he is armed with a dozen assegais and earnestly desires your blood, it is safer to shoot him or drive him farther afield. That the Boers were guilty of atrocities in those fierce wars is undoubted, and, if some tales be true, unpardonable. But there are excuses to be made. When a man has seen his child writhing on a spear and his wife mutilated; when he reflects that he stands alone against impossible odds, and has a keen sense, too, of Scriptural parallels,—he may be forgiven if he slays and spares not, and even gives way to curious cruelties. Revenge and despair may play odd pranks with the best men: *tout comprendre c'est tout pardonner.*

What, then, is the proper view to take of this footnote to the world's history, this Marathon of an unimaginative race? It is possible to see in it only an attempt of a half-savage people to find elbow-room for their misdeeds. The voortrekkers, it has been said, fled the approach of a mild and enlightened modern policy, invaded a land which was not theirs, slaughtered a people who had every right to resist them, and created for themselves space to practise their tyranny over the native, and perpetuate their exploded religious and political creed in a retrograde society. It is easy to say this, as it is easy to explain the doings of the Pilgrim Fathers as a flight from a too liberal and tolerant land to wilds where intolerance could rule unchecked. With the best will in the world to scrutinise Dutch legends, the Great Trek seems to me just that legend which can well support any scrutiny. For it was first and foremost a conflict between civilisations. There were strong and worthy men among the voortrekkers, as there were estimable people among their opponents. The modern political creed, based on English constitutionalism, stray doctrines of the French Revolution, and certain economic maxims from Bentham and Adam Smith, is, in spite of minor differences, common to the civilised world. This was the creed which was forced upon the Border Dutch, and, having received no education in the axioms on which it was based, they unhesitatingly rejected it, and clung to their old Scriptural feudalism. When two creeds come into conflict, the older and weaker usually goes under. But in this case the men on the losing side were of a peculiar temper and dwelt in a peculiar country. They took the bold path of carrying themselves and their creed to a new land, and so extended its lease of life for the better part of a century. Let us take the parallel of the American Civil War. The North fought for the cause of the larger civic organism and certain social reforms which were accidentally linked to it. The South stood for the principle of nationality, and for certain traditions of their own particular nationality. Roughly speaking, it was the same conflict; but the Southern creed perished because there was no practicable hinterland to which it could be transplanted. Had there been, I do not think its most stubborn opponents would have denied admiration to so bold an endeavour to preserve a national faith.

The Great Trek set its seal upon the new countries. The Orange River Colony and the Transvaal are still in the rural places an emigrant's land. The farmhouse is the unit; the country dorps are merely jumbles of little shanties to supply the farmers' wants. The place-names, with the endless recurrence of simple descriptive epithets like Sterkstroom or Klipfontein, or expressions of feeling like Nooitgedacht or Welgevonden, still tell the tale of the first discoverers. There is no obscurity in the nomenclature, such as is found in an old land where history has had time to be forgotten. Any farm-boy will tell you how this river came to be named the Ox-Yoke or that hill the Place of Weeping. It has made the people a solemn, ungenial folk, calculating and thrifty in their ways, and given to living in hovels which suggest that here they have no continuing city. Perhaps, as has been said, no performance, however stupendous, is worth loss of geniality; and the finer graces of life have never had a chance on the veld. There is gipsy blood in their veins, undying vagabondage behind all their sleepy contentment. The quiet of the old waggon journeys, when men counted the days on a notched stick that they might not miss the still deeper quiet of the Sabbaths, has gone into the soul of a race which still above all things desires space and leisure. It is this gipsy endowment which made them born warriors after a fashion; it is this which gives them that apathy in the face of war losses which discomfits their sentimental partisans. Britain in her day has won many strange peoples to her Empire; but none, I think, more curious or more hopeful than the stubborn children of Uys and Potgieter.

[9] In Lichtenstein's 'Travels in South Africa' (1803-6) there is an interesting and comparatively favourable account of Buys in his Cape Colony days.

CHAPTER IV.

THE BOER IN SPORT.

It is a fair working rule of life that the behaviour of a man in his sports is a good index to his character in graver matters. With certain reservations the same holds true of a people. For on the lowest interpretation of the word "sport," the high qualities of courage, honour, and self-control are part of the essential equipment, and the mode in which such qualities appear is a reflex of the idiosyncrasies of national character. But this is true mainly of the old settled peoples, whose sports have long lost the grim reality in which they started. To a race which wages daily war with savage nature the refinements of conduct are unintelligible; sport becomes business; and unless there is a hereditary tradition in the matter the fine manners of the true hunter's craft are notable by their absence.

It is worth while considering the Boer in sport, for it is there he is seen at his worst. Without tradition of fair play, soured and harassed by want and disaster, his sport became a matter of commerce, and he held no device unworthy in the game. He hunted for the pot, and the pot cast its shadow over all his doings. His arms were rarely in the old days weapons of precision, and we can scarcely expect much etiquette in the pursuit of elephant or lion in a bush country with a smooth-bore gun which had a quaint trajectory and a propensity to burst. The barbarous ways which he learned in those wild games he naturally carried into easier sports. Let us admit, too, that the Boer race has produced a few daring and indefatigable hunters, who, though rarely of the class of a Selous or a Hartley, were yet in every way worthy of the name of sportsmen. I have talked with old Boers from the hunting-veld, and in their tales of their lost youth there was a fervour which the commercial results of their expeditions did not explain. But the fact remains that to an Englishman the Boers, with a few exceptions, are not a sporting race—they are not even a race of very skilful hunters. They came to the land when game was abundant and they thinned it out; but the manner of this thinning was as prosaic as the routine of their daily lives.

One advantage the Boer possessed in common with all dwellers in new lands—he was familiar from childhood with gun and saddle, and had to face the world on his own legs from his early boyhood. In this way he acquired what one might call the psychological equipment of the hunter. Any one who has hunted in wild countries will remember the first sense of strangeness, the feeling that civilisation had got too far away for comfort, which is far more eerie than common nervousness. To this feeling the Boer was an utter stranger. It was as natural for him to set a trap for a lion before returning at nightfall, or to go off to the hunting-veld for four winter months, as it was to sow in spring and reap in autumn. And because it was an incident of his common life he imported into it a ridiculous degree of domesticity. On his farm he shot for the pot; on his winter treks with stock to the bush-veld and the wilder hunting expeditions for skins and horns he carried his wife and family in his buck-waggon, built himself a hut in the wilds, and reproduced exactly the life of the farm. It was easy to reproduce anywhere, for it was simplicity itself. Mealie-meal, coffee, and some coarse tobacco were his supplies, and fresh meat when game fell to his gun. So it is not to be wondered at if hunting became to him something wholly destitute of romance and adventure, an affair like kirk and market, where business was the beginning and the end.

But besides the Boer who farmed first and hunted afterwards, there was the Boer who hunted by profession. The class is almost extinct, but in outlying farms one may still meet the old hunter and listen to his incredible tales. Some were men of the first calibre, the pioneers of a dozen districts, men of profound gravity and placid temper, who rarely told the tale of their deeds. But the common hunter is above all things a talker. Like the Kaffir, he brags incessantly, and a little flattery will lead him into wild depths. He lies to the stranger, because he cannot be contradicted; he lies to his friends, because they are connoisseurs in the art and can appreciate the work of a master. Boer hunting tales, therefore, should be received with extreme caution. They would often puzzle an expert lawyer, for they are full of minute and fallacious particulars, skilfully put together, and forming as a rule a narrative of single-hearted heroism. I have listened to a Boer version of a lion-hunt, and I have heard the facts from other members of the same party; and the contrast was a lesson in the finer arts of embroidery. But this society had its compensations. Those men live on the outer fringe of Boerdom; they have no part in politics and few ties to the civilised society of Pretoria; and the result is that race hatred and memory of old strifes have always had a smaller place in their hearts. Without the virtues of their countryman, they are often free from his more unsocial failings.

It is as a big-game hunter that he has acquired his reputation, and by big game he meant the lion and the elephant, animals which he had to go farther afield and run greater risks to secure. The old race of elephant-hunters were a strong breed, men in whom courage from long experience had become a habit; and certainly they had need of it with their long-stocked cumbrous flint-locks, which might put out a man's shoulder in the recoil. They knew their business and took no needless risks, for elephant-hunting is a thing which can be learned. Save in thick bush, there is little real danger; and if the hunter awaits a charging elephant, a point-blank shot at a few yards will generally make the animal swerve. Mr Selous, whose authority is beyond question, has drawn these men as they appeared to him in Mashonaland—skilful shikarris, but jealous, uncompanionable, often treacherous as we count honour in sport; and Oswell's story is the same. The lion, which, in spite of tales to the contrary, remains one of the two most dangerous quarries in the world, was a different affair to them. There was little commercial profit from shooting him, and they had no other motive to face danger. Nor can we blame them, for a charging lion to a man with an uncertain gun means almost as sure destruction as a shipwreck in mid-ocean. The Boer hunter shot him for protection, rarely for sport. Very few of the lions killed on the high veld fell to rifles; a trap-gun set near a drinking-place was the ordinary way of dealing with them. Mr Ericsen, the most famous of Kalahari pioneers, who brought many herds of Ovampa and Damara cattle across the desert, used to tell this story of Boer prowess in lion-hunting. He was travelling with a party of Boer hunters, and one night a lion killed one of the oxen. The men were in a fury, and urged Mr Ericsen to follow, bragging that each of them was prepared to tackle the beast single-handed. Mr Ericsen said that he was no hunter, but promised to let them have his dogs and natives to follow up the spoor in the morning. But when the morning came the party had silently dispersed, mortally afraid lest they should be expected to fulfil their promises. In the long list of South African big-game hunters the names are mostly English,—Gordon-Cumming, Byles, Hartley, Oswell, Sharpe, Selous, Francis, John Macdonald,—and the reason does not wholly lie in the inability and disinclination of the Boer to bring his deeds from the rhetoric of talk to the calmer record of print.

At other four-footed game, from the buffalo to the duiker, the Boer was generally a fair shot, in some cases a good shot, but very rarely a great shot. Reputation in marksmanship was very much a matter of accident. A happy fluke with them, as with natives, might make a reputation for life, though the man in question shot badly ever afterwards. The number of Boer marksmen of the first rank could be counted on the ten fingers. On the other hand, the nature of their life produced a very high average. The Boer boy shot from the day he could hold a rifle, and there were few utter failures among them. To be sure, it was not pretty shooting. His first business was to get the game, and if he could do it by sitting on a tree near the stream and killing at twenty yards, he did it gladly. When he went hunting he reflected that his cartridges cost him 3d. apiece, and were all that stood between him and starvation; so very naturally he became as poky a shot as the English gamekeeper who is sent out to kill for the table. If a hunter took out 500 cartridges and brought back 120 head of game, he was reckoned a good man at his work. To this, of course, there were exceptions, such as old Jan Ludig, who once in Waterberg shot five gnu (who travel in Indian file) within seven miles. The name of Mr Van Rooyen, too, familiar to all Matabele hunters, shows what the Dutch race can produce in the way of marksmanship and veld-craft. In one branch of the chase they were consummate masters. The Boer method of stalking is an art by itself, for it is really a kind of driving, by showing oneself at strategic points till the game is forced into suitable ground. In open country they also followed with great success the method of riding down. Mounted on a good shooting pony, the hunter galloped alongside a herd till he was within reasonable distance; then in a trice he was on the ground, had selected his animal, and fired—all within a few seconds. This was a risky game for a large party, owing to the very rude etiquette which prevailed on the subject of shooting in your neighbour's direction; and I have heard of many seriously wounded and even killed by their companions' shots. Still another way was to ride alongside an animal and shoot him from the saddle at a few paces' distance. This was called "brandt" or "burning," and required a firm seat and a very steady eye.

Birds were thought little of, except by some of the more advanced farmers and by sportsmen from the towns. The country is full of many excellent sporting birds: guineafowl, quail, francolin, duck, geese, and several kinds of partridge and bustard; but though a few farmers shot wildfowl on their dams, the average Boer was a poor shot with a gun, and when he did use one he liked to take his birds sitting. A hunter might kill a bird neatly with a rifle, which he would miss at shorter range with a shot-gun. This fashion is quickly passing. Many farmers possess excellent guns of the latest pattern; and I have known Boers who could hold their own with credit in Norfolk or Perthshire. As shooting is becoming more of a sport and less of a business, etiquette is growing up; and the Boer is learning to spare does and ewes and take pleasure in hard shots, where his father would have slaughtered casually and walked long and far to spare his cartridges. The new order is bringing better manners, but nothing can restore the noble herds of game which fell unlamented and unnoted under the old *régime*.

Other sports were scarcely considered. He rarely fished, leaving the catching of yellow-fish, tiger-fish, and barbel to the Kaffirs; and when he did, his rod and tackle were neolithic in their simplicity. I have never seen a Boer rod which had any of the proper attributes of a rod, and he used to profess scorn for a man with a greenheart or a split-cane as for one who would stipulate for an elegant spade before digging potatoes. Sometimes in a village or among neighbouring farmers flat-races would be got up; but the Boer pony was bred more for endurance than for speed, and a small selling-plate meeting was about the limit of his horse-racing. I have never seen or heard of a Boer steeplechase. On the other hand, he had a wonderful skill, as our army discovered, in riding at full speed over a breakneck country,—a skill due, perhaps, more to veld-craft than to horsemanship. Hunting big game on horseback taught him, as part of the business, to leave much to his horse; and his horse rarely played him false. Whether he was clattering down a stony hillside, or dodging through thick scrub, or racing over veld honeycombed with ant-bear holes, he rode with a loose rein and full confidence in his animal. It is difficult to frame an opinion on his horsemanship. His long stirrups, the easy "tripple" of his horse, and his loose seat make him a type of horseman very different to our cavalryman or Leicestershire master of hounds. But, loose as he sits, he can stick on over most kinds of country, and he is a natural horsemaster of the first order. A Boer knows by instinct how to manage his horse: he never frets him; he rarely ill-treats him; and he can judge to a mile the limits of his endurance.

As a sportsman, then, the Boer is scarcely at his best. He has shown himself dull, sluggish, unimaginative, capable of both skill and endurance, but a niggard in the exercise of either, unless compelled by hunger or hope of gain. Unlike most races, it is in his sports that he shows his most unlovely traits, and that flat incomprehensible side of his character which has puzzled an ornamental world. The truth is that he is, speaking broadly, without imagination and that dash of adventure which belongs to all imaginative men. The noble spurs of the Drakensberg rose within sight of his home; but he would as soon have thought of climbing a peak for the sport or the scenery as of dabbling in water-colours. A dawn was to him only the beginning of the day, a mellow veld sunset merely a sign to outspan; and I should be afraid to guess his thoughts on a primrose by the river's brim, or whatever is the South African equivalent. His religion made him credulous, but his temperament transformed the most stupendous of the world's histories into a kind of Farmer's Almanac, and Eastern poetry became for him a literal record of fact. A friend of mine, travelling with a Boer hunter in the far north, called his attention to the beauty of the starry night, and, thinking to interest his companion, told him a few simple astronomical truths. The Boer angrily asked him why he lied so foolishly. "Do not I read in the Book," he said, "that the world stands on four pillars?" And when my friend inquired about the foundation of the pillars, the Boer sulked for two days. But there is one trait which he shared with all true sportsmen, a love of wild animals. To be sure, the finest reserves of buck were made by new-comers, such as Mr van der Byl's park at Irene and Mr Forbes's at Athole, in Ermelo, both unhappily ruined by the war. But many veld farmers had their small reserves of springbok or blesbok, and permitted no hunting within them. Some did it as a speculation, being always ready to lease a day's shooting to a gun from Johannesburg, and many for the reason that they sought big farms and complete solitude—to pander to a sense of possession. But in all, perhaps, there was a strain of honest pleasure in wild life, a desire to encircle their homes with the surroundings of their early hunting days. In which case, it is another of the anomalies which warn us off hasty generalisations.

CHAPTER V.

THE BOER IN ALL SERIOUSNESS.[10]

The Boer character has suffered by its simplicity. It has, as a rule, been crudely summed up in half a dozen denunciatory sentences, or, in the case of more curious students, it has been analysed and defined with a subtlety for which there is no warrant. A hasty condemnation is not the method for a product so full of difficulty and interest, and a chain of laborious paradoxes scarcely enables us to comprehend a thing which is pre-eminently broad and simple. The Boer has rarely been understood by people who give their impressions to the world, but he has been very completely understood by plain men who have dwelt beside him and experienced his ways in the many relations of life. It is easy to dismiss him with a hostile epigram; easy, too, to build up an edifice of neat contradictions, after the fashion of what Senancour has called "le vulgaire des sages," and label it the Boer character. The first way commends itself to party feeling; the second appeals to a nation which has confessedly never understood its opponents, and is ready now to admit its ignorance and excuse itself by the amazing complexity of the subject. Sympathy, which is the only path to true understanding, was made difficult by the mists of war, and, when all was over, by the exceeding dreariness of the conquered people. There was little romance in the slouching bearded men with flat faces and lustreless eyes who handed in their rifles and came under our flag; National Scouts, haggling over money terms, and the begging tour of the generals, seemed to have reduced honour to a matter of shillings and pence, and dispelled the glamour of many hard-fought battlefields. There is a perennial charm about an *ancien régime*; but this poor *ancien régime* had no purple and fine gold for the sentimental—only a hodden-grey burgess society, an unlovely Kirk, and a prosaic constitution.

And yet the proper understanding of this character is of the first political importance, and a task well worth undertaking for its own sake. Those men are for ever our neighbours and fellow-citizens, and it is the part of wisdom to understand the present that it may prepare against the future. To the amateur of racial character there is the chance of reading in the largest letters the lesson of historical development, for we know their antecedents, we can see clearly the simple events of their recent history, and we have before us a product, as it were, isolated and focussed for observation. Nor can sympathy be wanting in a fair observer,—sympathy for courage, tenacity of purpose, a simple fidelity to racial ideals. No man who has lived much with the people can regard them without a little aversion, a strong liking, and a large and generous respect.

In any racial inquiry there are certain determinant factors which form the axioms of the problem. In the case of a long-settled people these are so intricate and numerous that it is impossible to disentangle more than a few of the more obvious, and we explain development, naturally and logically, rather by the conscious principles which the race assimilated than by the objective forces which acted upon it from the outer world. But in the case of a savage or a backward nation, the history is simple, the ingredients in racial character few and intelligible. The wars of the spirit and the growth of philosophies are potent influences, but their history is speculative and recondite. But the struggle for bare life falls always in simple forms, and physical forces leave their mark rudely upon the object they work on. In this case we have a national life less than a century long, a mode of society all but uniform, a creed short and unsophisticated, an intelligible descent, and a country which stamps itself readily upon its people. Origin, history, natural environment, accidental modes of civilisation, these are the main factors in that composite thing we call character. We can read them in the individual: we can read them writ large in a race which is little more than the individual writ large. In complex societies the composition is a chemical process, the result is a new product, not to be linked with any ingredient; the soul and mind of the populace is something different in kind from the average soul and mind of its units. But in this collection of hardy individualists there was no novel result, and the type is repeated with such scanty variations that we may borrow the attributes of the individual for our definition of the race.

Descent, history, natural environment have laid the foundation of the Boer character. The old sluggish Batavian stock (not of the best quality, for the first settlers were as a rule of the poorest and least reputable class) was leavened with a finer French strain, and tinctured with a little native blood. Living a clannish life in solitude, the people intermarried closely, and suffered the fate of inbreeders in a loss of facial variety and a gradual coarsening of feature. Their history was a record of fierce warfare with savage nature, and the evolution of a peculiar set of traditions which soon came into opposition with imported European ideas. They evolved, partly from the needs of their society and partly from distorted echoes of revolutionary dogma, an embryo political creed, and in religion they established a variant of sixteenth-century Protestantism. Their life, and the vast spaces of earth and sky amid which they lived, strengthened the patriarchal individualism in their blood. The whole process of development, so remote from the common racial experience, produced in the Boer character a tissue of contradictions which resist all attempts at an easy summary. He was profoundly religious, with the language of piety always on his lips, and yet deeply sunk in matter. Without imagination, he had the habits of a recluse and in a coarse way the instincts of the poet. He was extremely narrow in a bargain, and extremely hospitable. With a keen sense of justice, he connived at corruption and applauded oppression. A severe moral critic, he was often lax, and sometimes unnatural, in his sexual relations. He was brave in sport and battle, but his heroics had always a mercantile basis, and he would as soon die for an ideal, as it is commonly understood, as sell his farm for a sixpence. There were few virtues or vices which one could deny him utterly or with which one could credit him honestly. In short, the typical Boer to the typical observer became a sort of mixture of satyr, Puritan, and successful merchant, rather interesting, rather distasteful, and wholly incomprehensible.

And yet the phenomenon is perfectly normal. The Boer is a representative on a grand scale of a type which no nation is without. He is the ordinary backward countryman, more backward and more of a countryman than is usual in our modern world. At one time this was the current view—a "race of farmers," a "pastoral folk"; but the early months of the war brought about a reversal of judgment, and he was credited with the most intricate urban vices. Such a false opinion was the result of a too conventional view of the rural character. There is nothing Arcadian about the Boer, as there is certainly nothing Arcadian about the average peasant. A Corot background, a pastoral pipe, and a flavour of honeysuckle, must be expelled from the picture. To analyse what is grandiloquently called the "folk-heart," is to see in its rude virtues and vices an exact replica of the life of the veld. "Simple" and "pastoral," on a proper understanding of the terms, are the last words in definition.

Let us take an average household. Jan Celliers (pronounced Seljee) lives on his farm of 3000 morgen with his second wife and a family of twelve. His father was a voortrekker, and the great Sarel was a far-out cousin. Two cousins of his mother and their families squat as bywoners on his land, and an orphan daughter of his sister lives in his household. The farmhouse is built of sun-dried bricks, whitewashed in front, and consists of a small kitchen, a large room which is parlour and dining-room in one, and three small chambers where the family sleep. Twelve families of natives live in a little kraal, cultivate their own mealie-patches, and supply the labour of the farm, while two half-caste Cape boys, Andries and Abraham, who attend to the horses, have a rude shanty behind the stable. Jan has a dam from which he irrigates ten acres of mealies, pumpkins, and potatoes. For the rest he has 500 Afrikander oxen, which make him a man of substance among his neighbours, including two spans of matched beasts, fawn and black, for which he has refused an offer of £30 apiece. He is not an active farmer, for he does not need to bestir himself. His land yields him with little labour enough to live on, and a biscuit-tin full of money, buried in the orchard below the fifth apricot-tree from the house, secures his mind against an evil day. But he likes to ride round his herds in the early morning, and to smoke his pipe in his mealie-patch of a late afternoon. He is not fond of neighbours, but it is pleasant to him once in a while to go to Pretoria and buy a cartload of fancy groceries and the very latest plough in the store. As a boy Jan was a great hunter, and has been with his father to the Limpopo and the Rooi Rand; but of late game has grown scarce, and Jan is not the fellow to stir himself to find it. Now and then he shoots a springbok, and brags wonderfully about his shots, quite regardless of the presence of his sons who accompany him. These sons are heavy loutish boys, finer shots by far than Jan, for they have that infallible eyesight of the Boer youth. They, too, are idle, and are much abused by their mother, when she is wide awake enough to look after them. The daughters are plump and shapeless, with pallid complexions inside their sun-bonnets, and a hoydenish shyness towards neighbours. Not that they see many neighbours, though rumour has it that young Coos Pretorius, son of the rich Pretorius, comes now and then to "opsitten" with the eldest girl. Jan believes in an Old Testament God, whom he hears of at nachtmaals, for the kirk is too far off for the ordinary Sabbath-day's journey; but he believes much more in a spook which lives in the old rhinoceros-hole in the spruit, and in his own amazing merits. He is sleepily good-natured towards the world, save to a Jew storekeeper in the town who calls himself on the sign above his door the "Old Boer's Friend," and on one occasion cheated him out of £5. But Jan has also had his triumphs, notably when he induced a coal prospector to prospect in an impossible place and leave him, free of cost, an excellent well. When war broke out Jan and three of his sons, sorely against their will, went out on commando. Two of the boys went to Ceylon, one fell at Spionkop, and Jan himself remained in the field till the end, and came back as proud as a peacock to repatriation rations. His womenfolk were in the Middelburg Burgher camp, where they acquired a taste for society which almost conquered their love for the farm. At any rate, it was with bitter complaints that they sat again under a makeshift roof, with no neighbours except the korhaan and a span of thin repatriation oxen. Jan did not enjoy war. At first he was desperately afraid, and only the strangeness of the country and the presence of others kept him from trekking for home. By-and-by he found amusement in the sport of the thing, and realised that with caution he might keep pretty well out of the way of harm. But in the guerilla warfare of the last year there was no sport, only stark unrelieved misery. Sometimes he thought of slipping over to the enemy and surrendering; often he wished he had been captured and sent to Ceylon with his boys; but something which he did not understand and had never suspected before began to rise in his soul, a wild obstinacy and a resolve to stand out to the last. Once in a night attack he was chased by two mounted infantrymen, and turned to bay in a narrow place, shooting one man and wounding the other badly. He did his best for the sufferer before making off to the rendezvous, an incident which has appeared in the picture papers (Jan is depicted about eight feet high, with a face like Moses, whereas he really is a broken-nosed little man), and which shows that he had both courage and kindness somewhere in his slow soul. But he gladly welcomed peace; he had never cared greatly for politics, and had an ancestral grudge against the Kruger family; and when he had assured himself that, instead of losing all, he would get most of his property back, and perhaps a little for interest, he became quite loyal, and figured prominently on the local repatriation board. He takes the resident magistrate out shooting, and has just sold to the Government a fraction of his farm at an enormous profit.

Such is an ordinary type of our new citizens. If we look at him the typical countryman stands out clear from the mists of tortuous psychology. It is an error, doubtless, to assume that the primitive nature is always simple; it is often bewilderingly complex. An elaborate civilisation may produce a type which can be analysed under a dozen categories; while the savage or the backwoodsman may show a network of curiously interlaced motives. But the man is familiar. We know others of the family; we have met him in the common relations of life; he stands before us as a concrete human being.

His most obvious characteristic is his mental sluggishness. Dialectic rarely penetrates the chain-armour of his prejudices. He has nothing of the keen receptive mind which, like a sensitive plant, is open to all the influences of life. His views are the outcome of a long and sluggish growth, and cling like mandrakes to the roots of his being. He makes no deductions from ordinary events, and he never follows a thing to its logical conclusion. His blind faith requires a cataclysm to shake it, and to revise a belief is impossible for him save under the stress of pain. Death and burning towns may reveal to him a principle, but unless it is written large in letters of blood and fire it escapes his stagnant intelligence. Change is painful to all human creatures, but such coercion of change is doubly painful, since he has no scheme of thought into which it can fit, and it means, therefore, the upturning of the foundations of his world. But the countryman, while he holds tenaciously his innermost beliefs, has a vast capacity for doing lip-service to principles which he does not understand. He sees that certain shibboleths command respect and bring material gain, so he glibly adopts them without allowing them for a moment to encroach upon the cherished arcana of his faith. Hence comes the apparent inconsistency of many simple folk. The Boer had a dozen principles which he would gladly sell to the highest bidder; but he had some hundreds of prejudices which he held dearer (almost) than life. His principles were European importations, democratic political dogmas, which he used to excellent purpose without caring or understanding, moral maxims which bore no relation to his own ragged and twisted ethics. The mild international morality which his leaders were wont to use as a reproach to Britain seems comically out of place when we reflect upon the high-handed international code, born of filibustering and Kaffir wars, which he found in the Scriptures and had long ago adopted for his own. His political confession of faith, which the framers of his constitution had borrowed from Europe and America, with its talk of representation and equal rights and delegated powers, contrasted oddly with the fierce individualism which was his innermost conviction, and the cabals and "spoils to the victor" policy which made up his daily practice. His religion had a like character. In its essentials it was the same which a generation or two ago held sway over Galloway peasants and Hebridean fishermen; but the results were very different. The stern hard-bitten souls who saw the devil in most of the works of God, and lived ever under a great Taskmaster's eye, had no kinship with the easy-going sleek-lipped Boer piety. The Boer religion in practice was a judicious excerpt from the easier forms of Christianity, while its theory was used to buttress his self-sufficiency and mastery over weaker neighbours. His political creed may be stated shortly as a belief in his right to all new territories in which he set foot, his indefeasible right to control the native tribes in the way he thought best, a denial of all right of the State to interfere with him, but an assertion of the duty of the State to enrich him. To these cardinal articles liberty, equality, and fraternity were added as an elegant appendage before publication. So, too, in his religion: God made man of two colours, white and black, the former to rule the latter till the end of time; God led Israel out of Egypt and gave to them new lands for their inalienable heritage; any Egyptian who followed was the apportioned prey of the chosen people, and it was a duty to spoil him; this beneficent God must therefore be publicly recognised and frequently referred to in the speech of daily life, but in the case of the Elect considerable latitude may be allowed in the practice of the commandments,—such may fairly be taken as the ordinary unformulated Boer creed. But, as the statement was too short and bare, all the finer virtues had to be attached in public profession.

A countryman lives in a narrow world which he knows intimately, but beyond is an unexplored region which he knows of by hearsay and fears. He is not naturally suspicious. Among his fellows he is often confiding to a fault, and a little acquaintance with a dreaded object will often result in a revulsion to contempt. The Boer has in a peculiar degree this characteristic of rural peoples. He has an immense awe of an alien Power while he does not know it, but once let it commit itself to some weakness, and the absence of all mental perspective changes the exaggerated awe into an equally exaggerated condescension. This truth is written clear over the whole history of England in Africa. A lost battle, a political withdrawal, a wavering statesman, have had moral effects of incalculable significance. The burgher who opposed us with terror and despair became at the first gleam of success a screeching cock-of-the-walk, and this attitude, jealously fostered, obscured the world to him for the rest of his days. In our threats he saw bluster, in our kindness he read weakness, in our diplomacy folly; and he went out at last with the fullest confidence, which three years of misery have scarcely uprooted. This is one side of the parochial mind; the other is the suspicion which became his attitude to everything beyond his beacons. It is not the proverbial "slimness"; that graceful quality is merely the rustic cunning which he thought the foundation of business, a quality as common on Australian stock-runs and Scottish sheep-farms. His suspicion was his own peculiar possession, born of his history and his race, and, above all, of his intercourse with native tribes. He did not give his confidence readily, as who would if he believed that the world was in league against him? New ideas, new faces, new inventions were all put on his black list. Like Mr By-ends, he found his principles easy and profitable, and was resolved to stick to them. Two forces, however, tended to undermine his distrust. One was his intense practicality. If his principles ceased to be profitable, he was prepared, against the grain, to consider emendations. The second was his crude pleasure in novelties, the curious delight of a child in a mechanical toy. A musical box, a portrait of Mr Kruger which, when wound up, emitted the Volkslied, or the latest variety of mealie-crusher, were attractions which he had no power to resist.

At the root of all his traits lies a meagre imagination. In religion he turns the stupendous tales of Scripture into a parish chronicle, with God as a benevolent burgomaster and Moses and the prophets as glorified landrosts. In politics no Boer since President Burgers saw things with a large vision, and his rhetorical dreams were folly to his countrymen. The idea of a great Afrikander state, very vigorously held elsewhere in South Africa, had small hold on the ordinary population of the Republics, save upon sons of English fathers or mothers, half-educated journalists, and European officials. In the wars which he waged he saw little of the murky splendour which covers the horrors of death. The pageantry of the veld was nothing to him, and in the amenities of life he scarcely advanced beyond bare physical comfort. He had neither art nor literature. If we except Mr Reitz's delightful verses, which at their happiest are translations of Burns and Scott, he had not even the songs which are commonly found among rural peoples. His nursery tales and his few superstitions were borrowed from the Kaffir. On one side only do we discern any trace of imaginative power. Somehow at the back of his soul was the love of the wilds and the open road—a call which, after years of settled life, had still power to stir the blood of the old hunter. He was not good at pictorial forecasts, but he had one retrospect stamped on his brain, and this hunger for old days was a spark of fire which kept warm a corner of his being.

The typical countryman he remains, typical in his limitations and the vices which followed them. The chief was his incurable mendacity. Truth-speaking is always a relative virtue, being to some men an easy habit, and to others of a livelier fancy a constant and strenuous effort. The Boer is not brutal, he is eminently law-abiding and sober, and kindly in most of the relations of life. He has the rustic looseness in sexual morals, and in the remoter farmhouses this looseness often took the form of much hideous and unnatural vice. But the cardinal fault, obvious to the most casual observer, is a contempt for truth in every guise. Masterful liars, who have held their own in most parts of the world, are vanquished by the systematic perjury of the veld. The habit is, no doubt, partly learned from the Kaffir, a fine natural professor of the art; but to its practice the Boer brought a stolid patience, an impassive countenance, and a limited imagination which kept him consistent. He bragged greatly, since to a solitary man with a high self-esteem this is the natural mode of emphasising his personality on the rare occasions when he mixes with his fellows. He lied in business for sound practical reasons. He lied at home by the tacit consent of his household. The truest way to outwit him, as many found, was to tell him the naked truth, since his suspicion saw in every man his own duplicity. But because he is a true countryman, when once he has proved a man literally truthful he will trust him with a pathetic simplicity. There were Englishmen in the land before the war, as there are Englishmen to-day, whose word to the Boer mind was an inviolable oath.

So far I have described the average Boer failings with all the unsympathetic plainness which a hostile observer could desire. But there is a very different side to which it is pleasant to turn. If he has the countryman's faults strongly developed, he has also in a high degree the country virtues. Simplicity is not an unmixed blessing; but it is the mother of certain fine qualities, which are apt to be lost sight of by a sophisticated world. He could live bare and sleep hard when the need arose; and if he was sluggish in his daily life it was the indolence of the sleepy natural world and not the enervation of decadence. Because his needs were few he was supremely adaptable: a born pioneer, with his household gods in a waggon and his heart turning naturally to the wilds. The grandeur of nature was lost on him; but there is a certain charm in the way in which he brought all things inside the pale of his domesticity. His homely images have their own picturesqueness, as when he called the morning star, which summoned him to inspan, the *voorlooper*, or "little boy who leads out the oxen." It is the converse of sublimity, and itself not unsublime. His rude dialect, almost as fine as lowland Scots for telling country stories, is full of metaphors, so to speak, in solution, often coarse, but always the fruit of direct and vigorous observation. In short, he had a personality which stands out simply in all his doings, making him a living clear-cut figure among the amorphous shades of the indoor life.

Wild tales and judicious management from Pretoria succeeded in combining him temporarily into a semblance of a state and a very formidable reality of an army; but at bottom he is the most dogmatic individualist in the world. His allegiance was never to a chief or a state, but to his family. The family was generously interpreted, so that distant relations came within its fold. This clannishness has not been sufficiently recognised; but it is a real social force, and of great importance to a survey of Boer society. In the country farms, with their system of bywoners, a whole cycle of relations lived, all depending upon the head of the household for their subsistence. When sons or daughters married they lived on in the homestead, and as their children grew up and married in turn they squatted on a corner of the farm. The system led to abuses, notably in the ridiculous subdivision of land and the endless servitudes and burdens imposed on real estate; but it relieved the community of any need for orphanages and workhouses. The Boer's treatment of orphans does him much credit. However poor, a family would make room for orphaned children, and there was no distinction in their usage. It is a primitive virtue, a heritage from the days when white folk were few in numbers: a little family in the heart of savagery, bound together by a common origin and a common fear.

But his chief virtue was his old-fashioned hospitality. A stranger rarely knocked at his gates in vain. You arrived at a farmhouse and asked leave to outspan by the spruit. Permission was freely granted, and in a little girls came out with coffee for the travellers. An invitation to supper usually followed, and there is no better fare in the world than a chicken roasted by a Boer housewife and her home-made sausages. Then followed slow talk over deep-bowled pipes, and then good-night, with much handshaking and good wishes. And so all over the veld. The family might be wretchedly poor, but they dutifully and cheerfully gave what they had. In the early months of peace it was a common thing to come on a Boer family living in a hut of biscuit tins or a torn tent, with scanty rations and miserably ragged clothes. But those people, in most cases, set the little they had gladly before the stranger. The Boer, who will perjure himself deeply to save a shilling, will part with a pound's worth of entertainment without a thought.

And, as a host, he has a natural dignity beyond praise. A placid life, backed by an overwhelming sense of worth, is a fine basis for good manners. Boastfulness and prejudice may come later, but the first impression is of an antique kindliness and ease. The veld has no nerves, no uneasy consciousness of inferiority, least of all the cringing friendliness of the low European. The farmer, believing in nothing beyond his ken, makes the stranger welcome as a harmless courier from a trivial world. No contrast can be more vivid than between the nervous, bustling cosmopolitans who throng the Rand and the silent veld-dwellers. The Boer type of countenance is not often handsome; frequently it is flat and expressionless, lustreless grey eyes with small pupils, and hair growing back from chin and lip. But it is almost always the embodiment of repose, and in the finer stock it sometimes reaches an archaic and patriarchal dignity. The same praise cannot be given to the *jeunesse dorée* of the Afrikander world, who acquired the smattering of an education and migrated to the towns. Ignorant, swaggering, mentally and bodily underbred, they form a distressing class of people who have somehow missed civilisation and hit upon the vulgarity of its decline. They claim glibly and falsely the virtues which their fathers possessed without advertisement. Much of the bad blood and spurious nationalism in the country comes from this crew, who, in partnership with the worst type of European adventurer, have done their best to discredit their nation. The true country Boer regards them much as the silent elder Mirabeau and Zachary Macaulay must have regarded their voluble sons—with considerable distrust, a little disfavour, and not a little secret admiration for a trick which has no place in his world.

Understanding is the only basis of a policy towards this remarkable section of our fellow-citizens—understanding, and a decent abstinence from subtleties. We used to flatter our souls that we created our Empire in a fit of absent-mindedness, and in all our troubles convinced ourselves that we were destined to "muddle through." But there are limits to this policy of serene trust in Providence, and it is rather our duty to thank God we have taken so few falls, and brace our minds to forethought and prudence. The Boer is the easiest creature in the world to govern. He is naturally law-abiding, and he has an enormous respect for the accomplished fact. True union may take long, but the nominal amalgamation which is necessary for smooth government already exists. We must understand how slow he is to learn, how deep his pride is, how lively his suspicions. Spiritually he will be a slow pupil, but with proper care politically he may be a ready learner. He has a curiously acute sense of justice, which makes him grumble at compulsion, but obey, and end by applauding. He is also quick to realise what is competent and successful in administration. He will give everything a fair trial, waiting, watching, and forming his slow mind; and if a thing is a practical fiasco, he will laugh at it in the end. The practical is the last touchstone for him. He is not easily made drunk with the ideals of ordinary democracy; an efficient government, however naked of adornments, will always command his respect, and the fool, though buttressed with every sublime aspiration, will find him adamant. To a government which can estimate the situation soberly and face it manfully he is a simple problem. But he will be a hard critic of weakness, and when once his laggard opinions are formed it will be a giant's task to shake them. The war has broken his old arrogance, and he now waits to make up his mind on the new *régime*. We shall get justice from him from the start—laborious justice and nothing more. If we fail, all the honesty of purpose on earth will not save us; for to the Boer good intentions may preserve a man's soul in another world, but they cannot excuse him in this one. There is much practical truth in Bunyan's parable when he makes Old Honest come "from the town of Stupidity," which town "lieth four degrees *beyond* the City of Destruction."

If the Boer is once won to our side we shall have secured one of the greatest colonising forces in the world. We can ask for no better dwellers upon a frontier. If the plateaux of our Central and East African possessions are to be permanently held by the white man, I believe it will be by this people who have never turned their back upon a country which seemed to promise good pasture-land. Other races send forth casual pioneers, who return and report and then go elsewhere; but the Boer takes his wife and family and all his belongings, and in a decade is part of the soil. In the midst of any savagery he will plant his rude domesticity, and the land is won. With all her colonising activity, Britain can ill afford to lose from her flag a force so masterful, persistent, and sure.

[10] The word "Boer" is used in this chapter to denote the average country farmer in the new colonies, and not the educated Dutch of the towns.

PART II.

NOTES OF TRAVEL

CHAPTER VI.

EVENING ON THE HIGH VELD.

We leave the broken highway, channelled by rains and rutted by ox-waggons, and plunge into the leafy coolness of a great wood. Great in circumference only, for the blue gums and pines and mimosa-bushes are scarcely six years old, though the feathery leafage and the frequency of planting make a thicket of the young trees. The rides are broad and grassy as an English holt, dipping into hollows, climbing steep ridges, and showing at intervals little side-alleys, ending in green hills, with the accompaniment everywhere of the spicy smell of gums and the deep rooty fragrance of pines. Sometimes all alien woodland ceases, and we ride through aisles of fine trees, which have nothing save height to distinguish them from Rannoch or Rothiemurchus. A deer looks shyly out, which might be a roebuck; the cooing of doves, the tap of a woodpecker, even the hawk above in the blue heavens, have nothing strange. Only an occasional widow-bird with its ridiculous flight, an ant-heap to stumble over, and a clump of scarlet veld-flowers are there to mark the distinction. Here we have the sign visible of man's conquest over the soil, and of the real adaptability of the land. With care and money great tracts of the high-veld might change their character. An English country-house, with deer-park and coverts and fish-ponds, could be created here and in many kindred places, where the owner might forget his continent. And in time this will happen. As the rich man pushes farther out from the city for his home, he will remake the most complaisant of countries to suit his taste, and, save for climate and a certain ineradicable flora and fauna, patches of Surrey and Perthshire will appear on this kindly soil.

With the end of the wood we come out upon the veld. What is this mysterious thing, this veld, so full of memories for the English race, so omnipresent, so baffling? Like the words "prairie," "moor," and "down," it is easy to make a rough mental picture of. It will doubtless become in time, when South Africa gets herself a literature, a conventional counter in description. To-day every London shopboy knows what this wilderness of coarse green or brown grasses is like; he can picture the dry streams, the jagged kopjes, the glare of summer, and the bitter winter cold. It has entered into patriotic jingles, and has given a *mise-en-scène* to crude melodrama. And yet no natural feature was ever so hard to fully realise. One cannot think of a monotonous vastness, like the prairie, for it is everywhere broken up and varied. It is too great for an easy appreciation, as of an English landscape, too subtle and diverse for rhetorical generalities—a thing essentially mysterious and individual. In consequence it has a charm which the common efforts of mother-earth after grandiloquence can never possess. There is something homely and kindly and soothing in it, something essentially humane and fitted to the needs of human life. Climb to the top of the nearest ridge, and after a broad green valley there will be another ridge just the same: cross the mountains fifty miles off, and the country will repeat itself as before. But this sameness in outline is combined with an infinite variety in detail, so that we readily take back our first complaint of monotony, and wonder at the intricate novelty of each vista.

Here the veld is simply the broad green side of a hill, with blue points of mountain peeping over the crest, and a ragged brown road scarred across it. The road is as hard as adamant, a stiff red clay baked by the sun into porphyry, with fissures yawning here and there, so deep that often it is hard to see the gravel at the bottom. A cheerful country to drive in on a dark night in a light English cart, but less deadly to the lumbering waggons of the farmer. We choose the grass to ride on, which grows in coarse clumps with bare soil between. Here, too, are traps for the loose rider. A conical ant-heap with odd perforations, an ant-bear hole three feet down, or, most insidious of all, a meerkat's hole hidden behind a tuft of herbage. A good pony can gallop and yet steer, provided the rider trusts it; but the best will make mistakes, and on occasion roll over like a rabbit. Most men begin with a dreary apprenticeship to spills; but it is curious how few are hurt, despite the hardness of the ground. One soon learns the art of falling clear and falling softly.

The four o'clock December sun blazes down on us, raising hot odours from the grass. A grey African hare starts from its form, a meerkat slips away indignantly, a widow-bird, coy and ridiculous like a flirtatious widow, flops on ahead. The sleepy, long-horned Afrikander cattle raise listless eyes as we pass, and a few gaudy butterflies waver athwart us. Otherwise there is no sound or sight of life. Flowers of rich colours—chrysanthemums, gentians, geraniums—most of them variants of familiar European species, grow in clumps so lowly that one can only observe them by looking directly from above. It is this which makes the veld so colourless to a stranger. There are no gowans or buttercups or heather, to blazon it like a spring meadow or an August moorland. Five yards off, and nothing is visible but the green stalks of grass or a red boulder.

At the summit of the ridge there is a breeze and a far prospect. The road still runs on up hill and down dale, through the distant mountains, and on to the great pastoral uplands of Rustenburg and the far north-west. On either side the same waving grass, now grey and now green as the wind breathes over it. Below is a glen with a gleam of water, and some yards of tender lawn on either bank. Farmhouses line the sides, each with its dam, its few acres of untidy crop land, and its bower of trees. Beyond rise line upon line of green ridges, with a glimpse of woods and dwellings set far apart, till in the far distance the bold spurs of the Magaliesberg stand out against the sky. A thin trail of smoke from some veld-fire hangs between us and the mountains, tempering the intense clearness of an African prospect. There is something extraordinarily delicate and remote about the vista; it might be a mirage, did not the map bear witness to its reality. It is not unlike a child's conception of the landscape of Bunyan, a road running straight through a mystical green country, with the hilltops of the Delectable Mountains to cheer the pilgrim. And indeed the land is instinct with romance. The names of the gorges which break the mountain line—Olifants' Poort, Crocodile Poort, Commando Nek—speak of war and adventure and the far tropics beyond these pastoral valleys. The little farms are all "Rests" and "Fountains," the true nomenclature of a far-wandering, home-loving people. The slender rivulet below us is one of the topmost branches of the great Limpopo, rising in a marsh in the wood behind, forcing its way through the hills and the bush-veld to the north, and travelling thence through jungles and fever-swamps to the Portuguese sea-coast. The road is one of the old highways of exploration; it is not fifty years since a white man first saw the place. And yet it is as pastoral as Yarrow or Exmoor; it has the green simplicity of sheep-walks and the homeliness of a long-settled rustic land. In the afternoon peace there is no hint of the foreign or the garish; it is as remote as Holland itself from the unwholesome splendours of the East and South.

No landscape is so masterful as the veld. Broken up into valleys, reclaimed in parts by man, showing fifty varieties of scene, it yet preserves one essential character. For, homely as it is, it is likewise untamable. There are no fierce encroachments about it. A deserted garden does not return to the veld for many years, if ever. It is not, like the jungle, the natural enemy of man, waiting for a chance to enter and obliterate his handiwork, and repelled only by sleepless watching. Rather it is the quiet spectator of human efforts, ready to meet them half-way, and yet from its vastness always the dominant feature in any landscape. Its normal air is sad, grey, and Quakerish, never flamboyant under the brightest sun, and yet both strenuous and restful. The few red monstrosities man has built on its edge serve only to set off this essential dignity. For one thing, it is not created according to the scale of man. It will give him a home, but he will never alter its aspect. Let him plough and reap it for a thousand years, and he may beautify and fructify but never change it. The face of England has altered materially in two centuries, because England is on a human scale,—a parterre land, without intrinsic wildness. But cultivation on the veld will always be superimposed: it will remain, like Egypt, ageless and immutable—one of the primeval types of the created world.

But, though dominant, it is also adaptable. It can, for the moment, assume against its unchangeable background a chameleon-like variety. Sky and weather combine to make it imitative at times. Now, under a pale Italian sky, it is the Campagna—hot, airless, profoundly melancholy. Again, when the mist drives over it, and wet scarps of hill stand out among clouds, it is Dartmoor or Liddesdale; or on a radiant evening, when the mountains are one bank of hazy purple, it has borrowed from Skye and the far West Highlands. On a clear steely morning it has the air of its namesake, the Norwegian fjelds,—in one way the closest of its parallels. But each phase passes, the tantalising memory goes, and we are back again upon the aboriginal veld, so individual that we wonder whence arose the illusion.

A modern is badly trained for appreciating certain kinds of scenery. Generations of poets and essayists have so stamped the "pathetic fallacy" upon his soul that wherever he goes, unless in the presence of a Niagara or a Mount Everest, he runs wild, looking for a human interest or a historical memory. This is well enough in the old settled lands, but on the veld it is curiously inept. The man who, in Emerson's phrase, seeks "to impress his English whim upon the immutable past," will find little reward for his gymnastics. Not that there is no history of a kind—of Bantu wars, and great tribal immigrations, of wandering gold-seekers and Portuguese adventurers, of the voortrekker and the heroic battles in the wilds. But the veld is so little subject to human life that had Thermopylæ been fought in yonder nek, or had Saint Francis wandered on this hillside, it would have mastered and obliterated the memories. It has its history; but it is the history of cosmic forces, of the cycle of seasons, of storms and suns and floods, the joys and sorrows of the natural world.

"Lo, for there among the flowers and grasses Only the mightier movement sounds and passes; Only winds and rivers, Life and death."

Men dreamed of it and its wealth long ago in Portugal and Holland. They have quarrelled about it in London and Cape Town, fought for it, parcelled it out in maps, bought it and sold it. It has been subject for long to the lusts and hopes of man. It has been larded with epithets; town-bred folk have made theories about it; armies have rumbled across it; the flood of high politics has swept it. But the veld has no memory of it. Men go and come, kingdoms fall and rise, but it remains austere, secluded, impenetrable, "the still unravished bride of quietness."

As one lives with it the thought arises, May not some future civilisation grow up here in keeping with the grave country? The basis of every civilisation is wealth—wealth to provide the background of leisure, which in turn is the basis of culture in a commercial world. Our colonial settlements have hitherto been fortuitous. They have fought a hard fight for a livelihood, and in the process missed the finer formative influences of the land. When, then, civilisation came it was naturally a borrowed one—English with an accent. But here, as in the old Greek colonies, we begin *de novo*, and at a certain high plane of life. The Dutch, our forerunners, acquired the stamp of the soil, but they lived on the barest scale of existence, and were without the aptitude or the wealth to go farther. Our situation is different. We start rich, and with a prospect of growing richer. On one side are the mining centres—cosmopolitan, money-making, living at a strained pitch; on the other this silent country. The time will come when the rich man will leave the towns, and, as most of them are educated and all are able men, he will create for himself a leisured country life. His sons in turn will grow up with something autochthonous in their nature. For those who are truly South Africans at heart, and do not hurry to Europe to spend their wealth, there is a future, we may believe, of another kind than they contemplate. All great institutions are rooted and grounded in the soil. There is an art, a literature, a school of thought implicit here for the understanding heart,— no tarnished European importation, but the natural, spontaneous fruit of the land.

As we descend into the glen the going underfoot grows softer, the flinty red clay changes to sand and soon to an irregular kind of turf. At last we are on the stream-bank, and the waving grasses have gone. Instead there is the true meadow growth, reeds and water-plants and a species of gorgeous scarlet buck-bean; little runnels from the farm-dams creep among the rushes, and soon our horses' feet are squelching through a veritable bog. Here are the sights and sounds of a Hampshire water-meadow. Swallows skim over the pools; dragon-flies and bees brush past; one almost expects to see a great trout raise a sleepy head from yonder shining reach. But there are no trout, alas! none, I fear, nearer than Natal; only a small greenish barbel who is a giant at four to the pound. The angler will get small satisfaction here, though on the Mooi River, above Potchefstroom, I have heard stories of a golden-scaled monster who will rise to a sea-trout fly. As we jump the little mill-lades, a perfect host of frogs are leaping in the grass, and small bright-eyed lizards slip off the stones at our approach. But, though the glen is quick with life, there is no sound: a deep Sabbatical calm broods over all things. The cry of a Kaffir driver from the highroad we have left breaks with an almost startling violence on the quiet. The tall reeds hush the stream's flow, the birds seem songless, even the hum of insects is curiously dim. There is nothing for the ear, but much for the eye and more for the nostril. Our ride has been through a treasure-house of sweet scents. First the pines and gum-trees; then the drowsy sweetness of the sunburnt veld; and now the more delicate flavour of rich soil and water and the sun-distilled essences of a thousand herbs. What the old Greek wrote of Arabia the Blessed might fitly be written here, "From this country there is a smell wondrous sweet."

Lower down the glen narrows. The stream would be a torrent if there were more water; but the cascades are a mere trickle, and only the deep green rock-pools, the banks of shingle, and the worn foot of the cliff, show what this thread can grow to in the rains. A light wild brushwood begins, and creeps down to the very edge of the stream. Twenty years ago lions roamed in this scrub; now we see nothing but two poaching pariah dogs. We pass many little one-storeyed farms, each with a flower-garden run to seed, and some acres of tangled crops. All are deserted. War has been here with its heavy hand, and a broken stoep, empty windows, and a tumbled-in roof are the marks of its passage. The owners may be anywhere—still on commando with Delarey, in Bermuda or Ceylon, in Europe, in camps of refuge, on parole in the towns. Great sunflowers, a foot in diameter, sprawl over the railings, dahlias and marigolds nod in the evening sunshine, and broken fruit-trees lean over the walks. Suddenly from the yard a huge aasvogel flaps out—the bird not of war but of unclean pillage. There is nothing royal in the creature, only obscene ferocity and a furtive greed. But its presence, as it rises high into the air, joined with the fallen rooftrees, effectively drives out Arcady from the scene. We feel we are in a shattered country. This quiet glen, which in peace might be a watered garden, becomes suddenly a desert. The veld is silent, but such secret nooks will blab their tale shamelessly to the passer-by.

The stream bends northward in a more open valley, and as we climb the ridge we catch sight of the country beyond and the same august lines of mountain. But now there is a new feature in the landscape. Bushes are dotted over the far slope, and on the brow cluster together into something like a coppice. It is a patch of bush-veld, as rare on our high-veld as are fragments of the old Ettrick forest in Tweeddale. Two hundred miles north is the real bush-veld, full of game and fevers, the barrier between the tropical Limpopo and these grassy uplands. Seen in the splendour of evening there is a curious savagery about that little patch, which is neither veld nor woodland, but something dwarfish and uncanny. That is Africa, the Africa of travellers; but thus far we have ridden through a countryside so homely and familiar that we are not prepared for a foreign intrusion. Which leads us to our hope of a new civilisation. If it ever comes, what an outlook it will have into the wilds! In England we look to the sea, in France across a frontier, even in Russia there is a mountain barrier between East and West. But here civilisation will march sharply with barbarism, like a castle of the Pale, looking over a river to a land of mists and outlaws. A man would have but to walk northward, out of the cities and clubs and the whole world of books and talk, to reach the country of the oldest earth-dwellers, the untamable heart of the continent. It is much for a civilisation to have its background—the Egyptian against the Ethiopian, Greek against Thracian, Rome against Gaul. It is also much for a race to have an outlook, a far horizon to which its fancy can turn. Even so strong men are knit and art is preserved from domesticity.

We turn homeward over the long shoulders of hill, keeping to the track in the failing light. If the place is sober by day, it is transformed in the evening. For an hour the land sinks out of account, and the sky is the sole feature. No words can tell the tale of a veld sunset. Not the sun dipping behind the peaks of Jura, or flaming in the mouth of a Norwegian fiord, or sinking, a great ball of fire, in mid-Atlantic, has the amazing pageantry of these upland evenings. A flood of crimson descends on the world, rolling in tides from the flagrant west, and kindling bush and scaur and hill-top, till the land glows and pulsates in a riot of colour. And then slowly the splendour ebbs, lingering only to the west in a shoreless, magical sea. A delicate pearl-grey overspreads the sky, and the onlooker thinks that the spectacle is ended. It has but begun; for there succeed flushes of ineffable colour,—purple, rose-pink, tints of no mortal name,—each melting imperceptibly into the other, and revealing again the twilight world which the earlier pageant had obscured. Every feature in the landscape stands out with a tender, amethystine clearness. The mountain-ridge is cut like a jewel against the sky; the track is a ribbon of pure beaten gold. And then the light fades, the air becomes a soft mulberry haze, the first star pricks out in the blue, and night is come.

Here is a virgin soil for art, if the art arises. In our modern history there is no true poetry of vastness and solitude. What there is is temperamental and introspective, not the simple interpretation of a natural fact. In the old world, indeed, there is no room for it: a tortured, crowded land may produce the aptitude, but it cannot give the experience. And the new lands have had no chance to realise their freshness: when their need for literature arose, they have taken it second-hand. The Australian poet sings of the bush in the rococo accents of Fleet Street, and when he is natural he can tell of simple human emotions, but not of the wilds. For the chance of the seeing eye has gone. He is not civilised but de-civilised, having borrowed the raiment of his elder brother. But, if South African conditions be as men believe, here we have a different prospect. The man who takes this country as his own will take it at another level than the pioneer. The veld will be to him more than a hunting-ground, and the seasons may be viewed from another than a commercial standpoint. If the art arises, it will be an austere art—with none of the fatuities of the picturesque, bare of false romance and preciosities, but essentially large, simple, and true. It will be the chronicle of the veld, the song of the cycle of Nature, the epic of life and death, and "the unimaginable touch of time." Who can say that from this land some dew of freshness may not descend upon a jaded literature, and the world be the richer by a new Wordsworth, a more humane Thoreau, or a manlier Senancour?

Once more we are in the wood, now a ghostly place with dark aisles and the windless hush of evening in the branches. The flying ants are coming out of the ground for their short life of a night. The place is alive with wings, moths and strange insects, that go white and glimmering in the dusk. The clear darkness that precedes moonrise is over the earth, so that everything stands out clear in a kind of dark-green monochrome. Something of an antique dignity, like an evening of Claude Lorraine, is stealing into the landscape. Once more the veld is putting on an alien dress, till in this fairyland weather we forget our continent again. And yet who shall limit Africa to one aspect? Our whole ride has been a kaleidoscope of its many phases. Hot and sunburnt, dry grasses and little streams, the red rock and the fantastic sunset. And on the other side the quiet green valleys, the soothing vista of blue hills, the cool woods, the water-meadows, and the twilight. It is a land of contrasts—glimpses of desert and barbarism, memories of war, relics of old turmoil, and yet essentially a homeland. As the phrase goes, it is a "white man's country"; by which I understand a country not only capable of sustaining life, but fit for the amenities of life and the nursery of a nation. Whether it will rise to a nation or sink to a territory rests only with its people. But it is well to recognise its possibilities, to be in love with the place, for only then may we have the hope which can front and triumph over the many obstacles.

The first darkness is passing, a faint golden light creeps up the sky, and suddenly over a crest comes the African moon, bathing the warm earth in its cold pure radiance. This moon, at any rate, is the peculiar possession of the land. At home it is a disc, a ball of light; but here it is a glowing world riding in the heavens, a veritable kingdom of fire. No virgin huntress could personify it, but rather some mighty warrior-god, driving his chariot among trampled stars. It lights us out of the wood, and on to the highroad, and then among the sunflowers and oleanders of the garden. The night air is cool and bracing, but soft as summer; and as we dismount our thoughts turn homeward, and we have a sudden regret. For in this month and at this hour in that other country we should be faring very differently. No dallying with zephyrs and sunsets; but the coming in, cold and weary, from the snowy hill, and telling over the peat-fire the unforgettable romance of winter sport.

December 1901.

CHAPTER VII.

IN THE TRACKS OF WAR.

I.

We left Klerksdorp in a dust-storm so thick and incessant that it was difficult to tell where the houses ended and the open country began. The little town, which may once have been a clean, smiling place, has been for months the *corpus vile* of military operations. A dozen columns have made it their destination; the transport and supplies of the whole Western Army have been congested there, with the result that the town lands have been rubbed bare of grass, the streets furrowed into dust-heaps, and the lightest breeze turned into a dust-tornado. Our Cape carts rattled over the bridge of the Schoon Spruit—"Caller Water," as we might translate it in Scots, but here a low and muddy current between high banks—and, climbing a steep hill past the old town of Klerksdorp, came out of the fog into clearer veld, over which a gale of wind was blowing strongly. The desert was strewn with empty tins, which caught the sun like quartz; stands of barbed wire were everywhere on the broad uneven highway; little dust devils spouted at intervals on to the horizon. The place was like nothing so much as a large deserted brick-field in some Midland suburb.

There is one feature of the high veld which has not had the attention it deserves—I mean the wind. Ask a man who has done three years' trekking what he mostly complains of, and he will be silent about food and drink, the sun by day and the frost by night, but he is certain to break into picturesque language about the wind. The wind of winter blows not so unkindly as persistently. Day and night the cheek is flaming from its buffets. There is no shelter from scrub or kopje, for it is a most cunning wind, and will find a cranny to whistle through. Little wrinkles appear round blinking eyes, the voice gets a high pitch of protest, and a man begins to walk sideways like a crab to present the smallest surface to his enemy. And with the wind go all manner of tin-cans, trundling from one skyline to another with a most purposeful determination. Somewhere—S.S.W. I should put the direction—there must be a Land of Tin-cans, where in some sheltered valley all the *débris* of the veld has come to anchor.

About ten o'clock the wind abated a little, and the road passed into a country of low hills with a scrub of mimosa thorn along the flats. The bustard, which the Boers have so aptly named "korhaan" or scolding cock, strutted by the roadside, a few hawks circled about us, and an incurious secretary-bird flapped across our path. The first water appeared,—a melancholy stream called Rhenoster Spruit,—and the country grew hillier and greener till we outspanned for lunch at a farmhouse of some pretensions, with a large dam, a spruit, and a good patch of irrigated land. The owner had returned, and was dwelling in a tent against the restoration of his homestead. A considerable herd of cattle grazed promiscuously on the meadow, and the farmer with philosophic calm was smoking his pipe in the shade. Apparently he was a man of substance, and above manual toil; for though he had been back for some time there was no sign of getting to work on repairs, such as we saw in smaller holdings. Fairly considered, this repatriation is a hard nut for the proud, indolent Boer, for it means the reversal of a life's order. His bywoners are scattered, his native boys refuse to return to him; there is nothing for the poor man to do but to take pick and hammer himself. Sooner or later he will do it, for in the last resort he is practical, but in the meantime he smokes and ponders on the mysteries of Providence and the odd chances of life.

In the afternoon our road lay through a pleasant undulating land, with green patches along the streams and tracts of bush relieving the monotony of the grey winter veld. Every farmhouse we passed was in the same condition,—roofless, windowless, dams broken, water-furrows choked, and orchards devastated. Our way of making war may be effective as war, but it inflicts terrible wounds upon the land. After a campaign of a dozen bloody fights reconstruction is simple; the groundwork remains for a new edifice. But, though the mortality be relatively small, our late methods have come very near to destroying the foundations of rural life. We have to build again from the beginning; we have to face questions of simple existence which seem strange to us, who in our complex society rarely catch sight of the bones of the social structure. To be sure there is hope. There is a wonderful recuperative power in the soil; the Boer is simpler in habits than most countrymen; and it is not a generation since he was starting at the same rudiments. Further, our own settlers will have the same beginnings, and there is a chance of rural communities, Boer and British, being more thoroughly welded together, because they can advance *pari passu* from the same starting-point. But to the new-comer the situation has a baffling oddness. It seems strange to be doling out the necessaries of life to a whole community, to be dealing with a society which must have been full of shades and divisions like all rural societies, as a featureless collection of units. Yet it is probable that the Boers themselves are the last to realise it. The people who crowded to the doors of the ruined farms as we passed were on the whole good-humoured, patient, and uncomplaining. They had set about repairing the breaches in their fortunes, crudely but contentedly. At one farm we saw a curious Arcadian sight in this desert which war had made. Some small Boer children were herding a flock of sheep along a stream. A little girl in a sunbonnet was carrying a lamb; two brown, ragged, bare-legged boys were amusing themselves with a penny whistle. To the children war and reconstruction alike can only have been a game; and hope and the future are to the young.

From Klerksdorp to Wolmaranstad the distance is some fifty miles, and it was almost nightfall before we descended with very weary cattle the long hill to our outspan. The country was one wide bare wold, the sky a soft glow of amber; and there was nothing between amber earth and amber sky save one solitary korhaan, scolding in the stillness. I do not know who the first Wolmarans may have been, but he built a stad very like a little Border town—all huddled together and rising suddenly out of the waste. The Makasi Spruit is merely a string of muddied water-holes, but in the darkness it might have been the "wan water" of Liddel or Yarrow. We camped in one of the few rooms that had still a roof, and rid ourselves of the dust of the road in an old outhouse in the company of a facetious monkey and a saturnine young eagle. When we had warmed ourselves and dined, I began to like Wolmaranstad, and, after a moonlight walk, I came to the conclusion that it was a most picturesque and charming town. But Wolmaranstad, like Melrose, should be seen by moonlight; for in the morning it looked little more than a collection of ugly shanties jumbled together in a dusty patch of veld.

II.

On the 12th of August, in the usual dust-storm, we started for Lichtenburg. There is no highroad, but a series of wild cross-country paths merging constantly in farm-roads. No map is quite reliable, and local information is fallacious. The day being the festival of St Grouse, we shot conscientiously all morning with very poor success. The game was chiefly korhaan, and he is a hard bird to get on terms with. About the size of a blackcock, and as slow on the wing, he looks an easy mark; but if stalked, he has a habit of rising just out of range, and repeating the performance till he has lured you a mile from your waggon, when he squawks in triumph and departs into the void. The orthodox way is to ride round him in slowly narrowing circles—a ruse which seems to baffle his otherwise alert intelligence. The country was rolling veld dotted with wait-a-bit thorn-bushes; the farmhouses few but large; the roads heavy with sand. In one hill-top farm, well named Uitkyk, we found an old farmer and his son-in-law, who invited us to enter. The place was in fair order, being out of the track of columns, tolerably furnished, and with the usual portrait of the Reverend Andrew Murray on the wall. The farmer had no complaints to make, being well-to-do and too old to worry about earthly things; but the son-in-law, a carpenter by trade, was full of his grievances. The neighbourhood, being in ruins, was crying for his services, he said, but there was no material in the country to work with. Building material was scarce in Johannesburg and Pretoria; how much scarcer it must be in Wolmaranstad! This just complaint was frequent on our journey; for the Transvaal, served by its narrow-gauge single-line railways choked with military traffic, is badly equipped with the necessaries of reconstruction, and many willing workmen have to kick their heels in idleness.

We outspanned at midday near some pools of indifferent water, which our authorities had enthusiastically described as an abundant water-supply. There was a roofless farm close by, where a kind of hut of biscuit-tins had been erected, in which a taciturn young woman was nursing a child. There was also a boy of about sixteen in the place who had coffee with us, and took us afterwards to stalk korhaan with a rifle. He was newly home from commando, full of spirit and good-humour, and handled longingly the rifle which the law forbade him to possess. All afternoon we passed roofless farmhouses crowded with women and children, and in most cases the farmer was getting forward in the work of restoration. Dams and water-furrows were being mended, some kind of roof put on the house, waggons cobbled together, and in many cases a good deal of ploughing had been done. The country grew bleaker as we advanced, trees disappeared, huge wind-swept downs fell away on each side of the path, and heavy rain-clouds came up from the west. The real rains begin in October, but chill showers often make their appearance in August, and I know nothing more desolate than the veld in such a storm. By-and-by we struck the path of a column, ploughed up by heavy gun-carriages, and in following the track somehow missed our proper road. The darkness came while we were yet far from our outspan, crawling up a great hill, which seemed endless. At the top a fine sight awaited us, for the whole country in front seemed on fire. A low line of hills was tipped with flame, and the racing fires were sweeping into the flats with the solid regularity of battalions. A moment before, and we had been in Shelley's

"Wide, grey, lampless, deep, unpeopled world";

now we were in the midst of light and colour and elfish merriment. To me there is nothing solemn in a veld-fire—nothing but madness and fantasy. The veld, so full at other times of its own sadness, the

"Acerbo indegno mistero della cose,"

becomes demented, and cries an impish defiance to the austere kings who sit in Orion. The sight raised our spirits, and we stumbled down the long hillside in a better temper. By-and-by a house of a sort appeared in the valley bottom, and a dog's bark told us that it was inhabited. To our relief we found that we had actually struck our outspan, Korannafontein, having approached it from the opposite side. The Koranna have long since gone from it, and the sole inhabitant was a Jew storekeeper, a friendly person, who assisted us to doctor our very weary horses. The ways of the Jew are past all finding out. Refuse to grant him a permit for himself and goods, and he says nothing; but he is in occupation months before the Gentile, unless that Gentile comes from Aberdeen. Our friend had his store stocked, and where he got the transport no man knows. He spoke well of the neighbourhood, both of Boer and native. The natives here, he said, are civilised. I asked him his definition of civilisation. "They speak Dutch," he said,— an answer worth recording. We camped for the night behind what had once been the wool-shed. The floor of the tent was dirty, and, foolishly, I sent a boy to "mak skoon." He made "skoon" by digging up dust with a shovel and storing it in heaps in different corners. About midnight the rain fell heavily, and a little later a great wind rose and put those dust-heaps in circulation. I awoke from dreams of salmon-fishing with a profound conviction that I had been buried under a landslip. I crawled hastily through a flap followed by a stream of dust, and no ventilation could make that tent habitable, so that in the morning we awoke with faces like colliers, and throats as dry as the nether millstone.

From Korannafontein to Lichtenburg is something over forty miles, so we started at daybreak and breakfasted at a place called Rhenosterput, where some gentleman sent a Mauser bullet over our heads to remind us of his presence. The country was downland, very full of Namaqua partridge and the graceful spur-winged plover, a ranching country, for the streams had little fall and less water. At midday we outspanned at a pretty native village called Rooijantjesfontein, with a large church after the English village pattern, and a big dam lined with poplars. The life of a commercial missionary, who bought a farm when land was cheap and had it cultivated by his congregation, is a pleasant one: he makes a large profit, spends easy days, and returns early to his native Germany. It is a type I have little patience with, for it discredits one of the most heroic of human callings, and turns loose on society the slim Christian native, who brings Christianity and civilisation alike into discredit. We were now out of the region of tracks and on the main road to Lichtenburg, and all afternoon we travelled across the broad shallow basin of the Hartz River with our goal full in view on a distant hill-top. Far off on our right we saw a curious sight—a funeral waggon with a train of mourners creeping slowly across the veld. The Boers, as we heard from many sources, are exhuming the dead from different battle-fields, and bringing them, often from great distances, to the graveyards on their own homesteads. An odd sombre task, not without its grandeur; for to the veld farmer, as to the old Roman, there are Lares and Penates, and he wishes at the last to gather all his folk around him.

III.

Lichtenburg, as I have said, stands on a hill-top, but when one enters he finds a perfect model of a Dutch village. The streets are lined with willows and poplars, and seamed with water-furrows, and all the principal buildings surround a broad village green on which cattle were grazing. Seen in the morning it lost nothing of its attractiveness; and it dwells in my memory as a fresh clean place, looking over a wide upland country,—a place where men might lead honest lives, and meet the world fearlessly. It has its own relics of war. The court-house roof and walls are splashed with bullets, relics of Delarey's fight with the Northumberland Fusileers. General Delarey is himself the principal inhabitant. He owns much land in the neighbourhood, and his house stands a few miles out on the Mafeking road. From this district was drawn all that was most chivalrous and resolute in the Boer forces; and the name of their leader is still a synonym with lovers of good fighting men for the finest quality of his race.

The Zeerust road is as bad going for waggons as I have ever seen. It runs for miles through a desert where the soil is as black as in Lancashire, and a kind of coaly dust rises in everlasting clouds. We started late in the day, so that sunset found us some distance from water, in a featureless country. We were to outspan at the famous Malmani Oog—the eye of the Malmani; but a fountainhead is not a good goal on a dark night to ignorant travellers. Shortly after dusk we rode on ahead to look for the stream. Low slopes of hills rose on all sides, but nowhere could we see a gleam or a hollow which might be water. The distance may have been short, but to a hungry and thirsty man it seemed endless, as one hill after another was topped without any result. We found a fork in the road, and took the turn to the left as being more our idea of the way. As it happened we were trekking straight for the Kalahari Desert, and but for the lucky sound of a waggon on the other road might have been floundering there to-day. We turned aside to ask for information, and found we were all but at the Oog, which lay in the trees a hundred yards off. The owner of the waggon was returning to Lichtenburg with a sick wife, whom he had taken to Zeerust for a change. He had been a road surveyor under the late Government, had served on Delarey's staff, and had been taken prisoner. A quiet reserved man with dignified manners, he answered our questions without complaint or petulance. There is something noble in travel when pursued in this stately leisure. The great buck-waggon, the sixteen solemn oxen lumbering on, the master walking behind in the moonlight, have an air of patriarchal dignity, an elder simplicity. I suppose fifteen to twenty miles might be a good day's march, but who shall measure value by miles? It is the life for dreams, for roadside fires, nights under the stars, new faces studied at leisure, good country talk, and the long thoughts of an unharassed soul. Let us by all means be up and doing, setting the world to rights and sounding our own trumpet; but is the most successful wholly at ease in the presence of great mountains and forests, or men whose lives share in the calm cycle of nature?

The night in tents was bitterly cold, and the morning bath, taken before sunrise in the springs of Malmani, was the most Arctic experience I have ever met. We left our drivers to inspan and follow, and set off down the little stream with our guns. There are hours which live for ever in the memory—hours of intense physical exhilaration, the pure wine of health and youth, when the mind has no thoughts save for the loveliness of earth, and the winds of morning stir the blood to a heavenly fervour. No man who has experienced such seasons can be other than an optimist. Dull nights in cities, heartless labours with pen and ink, the squalid worries of business and ambition, all are forgotten, and in the retrospect it is those hours which stand up like shining hill-tops—the type of the pure world before our sad mortality had laid its spell upon it. It is not pleasure—the word is too debased in human parlance; nor happiness, for that is for calm delights. Call it joy, that "enthusiasm" which is now the perquisite of creeds and factions, but which of old belonged to the fauns and nymphs who followed Pan's piping in the woody hollows of Thessaly. I have known and loved many streams, but the little Malmani has a high place in my affections. The crystal water flowed out of great reed-beds into a shallow vale, where it wound in pools and cataracts to a broad ford below a ruined mill. Thence it passed again into reed-beds fringed with willows and departed from our ken. There was a bamboo covert opposite full of small singing birds; the cries of snipe and plover rose from the reed-beds, and the fall of water, rarest of South African sounds, tinkled like steel in the cold morning air. We shot nothing, for we saw nothing; the glory of the scene was all that mortal eye could hold at once. And then our waggons splashed through the ford, and we had perforce to leave it.

We took a hill road, avoiding the detour by Malmani Drift, and after some hours in a country of wooded glens, came into the broad valley of the Klein Marico. The high veld and its scenery had been left far behind. Something half tropical, even in this mid-winter, was in the air of those rich lowlands. After the bleak uplands of Lichtenburg it was pleasant to see good timber, the green of winter crops, and abundant runnels of water. The farm-houses were larger and in fair repair,—embowered, too, in orange-groves, with the golden fruit bright among the glossy leaves. Blossom was appearing in every orchard; new and strange birds took the place of our enemy the korhaan; and for the first time on our journey we saw buck on the slopes. The vale was ringed with stony tree-clad hills like the Riviera, and in the hot windless noon the dust hung in clouds about us, so that, in spite of water and greenery, my impression of that valley is one of thirst and discomfort. Zeerust[11] is a pretty village close under the hills, with tree-lined streets,—a prosperous sleepy place, with no marks of the ravages of war. The farmers, too, are a different stock from the high-veld Boers; they get their living more easily, and in their swarthy faces and slouching walk one cannot read the hard-bitten spirit which inspired the men of Botha and Delarey. They seemed on good terms with their new masters. We attended a gymkhana given by the South African Constabulary, and the Dutch element easily predominated in the crowd which watched the races. A good-humoured element, too, for the men smoked and criticised the performances in all friendliness, while their womenkind in their Sunday clothes thronged to the marquees for tea.

[11] Zeerust is a type of the curious truncated Boer nomenclature, being a corruption of Coetzee's Rust.

IV.

The Rustenburg road runs due east through a fine defile called Klein Marico Poort, and thence in a country of thick bush for twenty miles to the ford of the Groot Marico. We started before dawn, and did not halt for breakfast till the said ford, by which time the sun was high in the heavens and we were very hot, dusty, and hungry. Lofty wooded hills rose to the north, and not forty miles off lay the true hunting-veld, with koodoo, water-buck, and hippopotamus. Bird life was rich along the road—blue jays, rollers, and the handsome malicious game-bird which acts as scout to the guinea-fowl, and with his harsh call informs them of human presence. The farms were small and richly watered, with laden orange-groves and wide ruined verandahs. The people of Zeerust had spoken with tears in their eyes of the beautiful condition of this road, but we found it by far the worst in our travels. It lay deep in sand, was strewn with ugly boulders, and at one ford was so impossible that we had to make a long detour over virgin veld. The Great Marico, which, like all streams in the northern watershed, joins the Limpopo, and indeed forms its chief feeder, is a muddy tropical water, very unlike the clear Malmani. Beyond it the country becomes bare and pastoral again, full of little farms, to which the bulk of the inhabitants had returned. It was the most smiling country we had seen, for bush-veld has an ineradicable air of barbarism, but a green open land with white homesteads among trees is the true type of a settled country. Apricot blossom lay like a soft haze on the landscape. The young grass was already springing in the sheltered places, the cold dusty winds had gone, and a forehint of spring was in the calm evening.

We spent the night above the Elands River, a very beautiful full water, almost on the site of the battle. The Elands River fight seems to have slipped from the memory of a people who made much of lesser performances; but to soldiers it is easily the Thermopylæ of the war. Five hundred or so of Australians of different regiments, with a few Rhodesians, were marching to join another force, when they were cut off at Elands River by 3000 Boers. They were invited to surrender, and declined. A small number took up a position beside the stream; the remainder held a little ridge in the centre of the amphitheatre of hills. For several days they toiled at dug-outs—terrible days, for they were shelled continually from the whole rim of the amphitheatre. One relieving force from the west retired in despair; a relieving force from the east was deceived by false heliograms, and went away, believing the work accomplished. Then came the report that they had surrendered; and then, after some fifteen days, they were found by Lord Kitchener, still holding the forlorn post. It was a mere sideshow, but to have been there was worth half the clasps in the campaign. More shells were fired into that little place than into Mafeking, and the courage of the few by the river who passed up water in the night to their comrades is beyond praise. The Colonials will long remember Elands River. It was their own show: without generalship or orders, against all the easy traditions of civilised warfare, the small band followed the Berserker maxim, and vindicated the ancient dignity of arms. In the morning we went over the place. The dug-outs were still mostly intact, and in a little graveyard beneath rude crosses slept the heroic dead.

A few miles farther on and the summit of a ridge was reached, from which the eye looked over a level valley to the superb western line of the Magaliesberg. Straight in front was the cleft of Magata's Nek, beyond which

Rustenburg lay. The western Magaliesberg disappoints on closer acquaintance. The cliffs prove to be mere loose kranzes, the glens are waterless, the woods are nothing but barren thorn. But seen from afar in the clear air of dawn, when the darkness is still lurking in the hollows and the blue peaks are flushed with sunrise, it is a fairyland picture, a true mountain barrier to an enchanted land. Our road swung down a long slope to the Coster River, where we outspanned, and then through a sandy wilderness to the drift of the Selons. From this it climbed wearily up to the throat of the nek, a dull tract of country with few farms and no beauties. The nek, too, on closer view has little to commend it, save the prospect that opens on the other side. The level green plateau of Rustenburg lay before us, bounded on the north by a chain of kopjes, and on the south by the long dark flanks of the Magaliesberg as it sweeps round to the east. A few miles and the village itself came in sight, with a great church, as at Wakkerstroom, standing up like some simple rural cathedral over the little houses. Rustenburg was always the stronghold of the straitest sect of the Boers; and in the midst of the half-tropical country around, this sweep of pasture, crowned with a white kirk, had something austere and Puritan in its air,—the abode of a people with their own firm traditions, hostile and masterful towards the world. The voortrekker having fought his way through the Magaliesberg passes, outspanned his tired oxen on this pleasant upland, and called it his "city of rest." And it still looks its name, for no orchards and gardens can make it otherwise than a novelty in the landscape—

sober, homely, and comforting, like some Old Testament Elam where there were twelve wells of water and threescore and ten palm-trees, or the "plain called Ease" wherein Christian "walked with much content."

V.

We took up our quarters at a farm a little way south of the town in the very shadow of the mountains. It was a long, low, rambling house called Boschdaal, with thick walls and cool passages. All around were noble gum-trees; a clear stream ran through the garden, which even at this season was gay with tropical flowers; and the orchard was heavy with oranges, lemons, and bananas. A little conical hill behind had a path made to its summit, whence one had a wide prospect of the Magaliesberg and the whole plateau. There were sheer cliffs in the background, with a waterfall among them; and between them and the house were some miles of park-like country where buck came in the morning. The rooms were simply but pleasantly furnished; the walls a forest of horns; and the bookcases full of European classics, with a great abundance of German story-books for children, telling how wicked Gretchen amended her ways, or little Hans saved his pennies. Altogether a charming dwelling-place, where a man might well spend his days in worthy leisure, shooting, farming, gardening, and smoking his pipe in the evening, with the sunset flaming over the hills.

We spent two nights in Rustenburg, visiting in the daytime a horse depot to which a number of brood mares had been brought for winter grazing, and paying our respects to a neighbouring chief, Magata, who lives in a *stad* from which many town councils might learn a lesson of cleanliness and order. The natives are as rich as Jews from the war, owning fine spans of oxen and Army Service Corps waggons, and altogether disinclined to stir themselves for wages. This prosperity of the lower race must be a bitter pill for the Boer to swallow, as he drives in for his rations with a team of wretched donkeys, and sees his former servants with buck-waggons and cattle. We watched strings of Burghers arriving at the depot, and at night several fires in the neighbouring fields told of their outspans. Most of them were polite and communicative: a very few did their business in sulky silence. There was one man who took my fancy. Originally he must have been nearly seven feet high, but a wound in the back had bent him double. He had long black hair, and sombre black eyes which looked straight before him into vacancy. He had a ramshackle home-made cart and eight donkeys, and a gigantic whip, of which he was a consummate master. A small boy did his business for him, while he sat hunched up on his cart speaking hoarsely to his animals, and cracking his whip in the air,—a man for whom the foundations of the world had been upset, and henceforth, like Cain, a dweller apart.

On the third morning we started regretfully, for Pretoria was only two days distant. This was the pleasantest stage in our journey: the air was cool and fine, the roads good, water abundant, and a noble range of mountains kept us company. This is the tobacco-land of the Transvaal, whence comes the Magaliesberg brand, which has a high reputation in South Africa. There are no big farms but a great number of small holdings, richly irrigated and populous—the stronghold of Mr Kruger in former times, for he could always whistle his Rustenburgers to his will. Now and then a pass cleft the mountain line on our right, and in the afternoon we came in sight of the great gap through which the Crocodile River forces its passage. Farther east, and at a higher altitude, lay Silikat's Nek, which is called after Mosilikatse. It was approaching sunset as we crossed Commando Nek, which is divided from Crocodile Poort by a spur of mountain, and looked over the Witwatersberg rolling south to the Rand and the feverish life of cities. High up on a peak stood a castellated blockhouse, looking like a peel tower in some old twilight of Northumbrian hills, and to the left and right the precipitous cliffs of the Magaliesberg ran out to the horizon. At the foot of the pass we forded the Magalies River, a stream of clear water running over a bed of grey-blue stones, and in another half-hour we had crossed the bridge of the Crocodile and outspanned on the farther bank.

The rivers unite a mile away, and the cleft of the Poort to which the twin streams hurried stood out as black as ink in the moonlight. Far up on the hillside the bush was burning, and the glare made the gorge like the gate of a mysterious world, guarded by flames and shadows. This Poort is fine by daylight, but still not more than an ordinary pass; but in the witching half-light it dominated the mind like a wild dream. After dinner we set out over the rough ground to where a cliff sank sheer from the moonlight into utter blackness. We heard the different notes of the two rivers—the rapid Magalies and the sedater Crocodile; and then we came to the bank of the united stream, and scrambling along it found ourselves in the throat of the pass. High walls of naked rock rose on either hand, and at last, after some hard walking, we saw a space of clear star-sown sky and the land beyond the mountains. I had expected a brawling torrent; instead, I found a long dark lagoon sleeping between the sheer sides. In the profound silence the place had the air of some underground world. The black waters seemed to have drowsed there since the Creation, unfathomably deep—a witch's caldron, where the savage spirits of the hills might show their faces. Even as we gazed the moon came over the crest: the cliff in front sprang into a dazzling whiteness which shimmered back from the lagoon below. Far up on the summit was a great boulder which had a far-away likeness to an august human head. As the light fell on it the resemblance became a certainty: there were the long locks, the heavy brows, the profound eyes of a colossal Jove. Not Jove indeed, for he was the god of a race, but that elder deity of the natural man, grey-haired Saturn, keeping his ageless vigil, quiet as a stone, over the generations of his children. Forgotten earth-dwellers, Mosilikatse and his chiefs, Boer commandos, British yeomanry,—all had passed before those passionless eyes, as their successors will pass and be forgotten. And in the sense of man's littleness there is comfort, for it is part of the title of our inheritance. The veld and the mountains continue for ever, austerely impartial to their human occupants: it is for the new-comer to prove his right to endure by the qualities which nature has marked for endurance.

August 1902.

CHAPTER VIII.

THE WOOD BUSH.

Some thirty miles east of Pietersburg, the most northerly railway station in the Transvaal, the Leydsdorp coach, which once a-week imperils the traveller's life, climbs laboriously into a nest of mountains, and on the summit enters an upland plateau, with shallow valleys and green forest-clad slopes. Twenty miles on and the same coach, if it has thus far escaped destruction, precipitously descends a mountain-side into the fever flats which line the Groot Letaba and the Letsitela. The Leydsdorp road thus cuts off a segment of a great irregular oblong, which is bounded on the south by the spurs of the Drakensberg, which the Boers call the Wolkberg or Mountain of Cloud, and on the north divided by the valley of the Klein Letaba from the Spelonken. It is a type of country found in patches in the de Kaap mountains, and in parts of Lydenburg; but here it exists in a completely defined territory of perhaps 700 square miles, divided sharply from high veld and bush veld. The average elevation may be 5000 feet, and, though cut up into valleys and ridges, it preserves the attributes of a tableland, so that on all sides one can journey to an edge and look down upon a wholly different land. But the geographical is the least of its distinctions. The climate has none of the high-veld dryness or the low-veld closeness, but is humid and sharp and wholesome all the year round. Mists and cool rains abound, every hollow has its stream, and yet frost is rarely known. Its vegetation, the configuration of its landscape, the soil itself, are all things by themselves in South Africa. Fever, horse-sickness, and most cattle diseases are unknown. It is little explored, for till quite lately the native tribes were troublesome, and only the poorer class of Boer squatted on its occupation farms, and, though a proclaimed gold-field for some years, the uitlander who strayed there had rarely an eye for its beauty. The unfortunate man who took his life in his hands and journeyed by coach to Leydsdorp forgot the landscape in the perils of the journey, and in all likelihood forgot most things in fever at the end of it. It remained, therefore, a paradise with a few devotees, a place secret and strange, with a beauty so peculiar that the people who tried to describe it were rarely believed. A delight in the Wood Bush is apt to spoil a man for other scenery. The high veld seems tame and monotonous, the bush veld an intolerable desert, and even the mountain glories of the Drakensberg something crude and barbarous after this soft, rich, and fascinating garden-land.

The mountains come into view a little way from Pietersburg, but there are many miles of featureless high veld to be covered before the foothills are reached. It was midsummer when I first travelled there, and the dusty waterless plains were glazed by the hot sun. The Sand River, filled with acres of fine sand, but not a drop of moisture, was not a cooling object in the scene, and the dusty thorn scrub offered no shade. But insensibly the country changed. Bold kopjes of rose-red granite appeared on the plain, and at a place called Kleinfontein the road turned sharply south, and we were confronted with a noble line of crags running out like a buttress from the mountains. At Smith's Drift the road swerved east again, and a long valley appeared before us running up into the heart of the hills. A clear stream came down it, and the sides were dotted in bush-veld manner with redwood and sikkelboom and syringa, and a variety of thorns, of which the Kaffir waak-en-beetje and the knopjes-doorn were the prettiest. Occasionally the dull green of the olivienhout appeared, and when the bush ceased aloes raised their heads among the rocks. Everywhere the mimosa was in bloom, and the afternoon air was laden with a scent like limes. Towards the top the valley flattened out into upland meadows, little farms appeared dotted on the hillsides, and the yellow mimosa blossom on the slopes was so indistinguishable from gorse that in the half-light I could have sworn I was among Cumberland fells, and not on the edge of the tropics and 300 miles from the sea. We assisted a Boer farmer to slay a pig, had coffee afterwards with his family, and slept the sleep of the just on a singularly hard piece of ground under a magnificent sky of stars, being roused once to give a drink to a belated member of the S.A.C.

Shortly after dawn next day we toiled to the top of a long hill, and entered the Wood Bush. A high blue ridge—the Iron Crown mountain behind Haenertsburg—rose before us, which changed with the full light to a dazzling green, studded in the kloofs with patches of dark forest. Glimpses of other forest-crowned hills appeared in the turnings of the path; and when we had exhausted the horizon we had time to look at the roadside. It was a perfectly new country. The soil was as red as Devonshire, the steep sides oozed with little runnels of water. Thickly grassed meadows of the same dazzling yet delicate green fell away to the little hollows, where copses took their place, and now and then a small red farm showed in a group of alien gum-trees. It was so novel as to be almost unbelievable. And then in the meadows little shrubs like dwarf hazels appeared, which on closer view showed themselves as tree-ferns,—old gnarled veterans and young graceful saplings. The herbage, too, was gay with flowers, as gay as an English meadow save that for daisies there were patches of tall arums and lilies, and for buttercups a superb golden-belled campanula. I am no botanist and am not ashamed of it, but on that morning I regretted a wasted youth and many unprofitable hours given to the classics. By-and-by we descended on the little township of Haenertsburg, a cluster of rondhavels and the tents of an S.A.C. post. On leaving we crossed a torrent, the Bruderstroom, which later becomes the Groot Letaba and flows through miles of feverish deserts to join the Olifants and thence to the Limpopo. It was a true highland stream, with deep dark-blue pools, and great swirls of icy grey water sweeping round crags or stretching out into glistening shallows. On the high veld it would be dignified by the name of river, and be shorn and parcelled into a thousand water-furrows. But here it was but one of many, for every hollow had its limpid stream slipping out of sight among the tall grasses.

Beyond Haenertsburg the Iron Crown mountain comes into full view, with its green sides scarred and blackened in places with the works of gold-seekers. To the left rose the crags of the Wolkberg, and far behind the blue lines of the Drakensberg itself. To the north the true Wood Bush country appeared, an endless park laid out as if by a landscape gardener, with broad dales set with coppices, and little wood-covered hills. "A park-like country," is the common travellers' phrase for the bush veld; but there the grass is rank and ugly, the trees isolated thorns, and the whole land flat and waterless. Here was a true park, like Chatsworth or Windsor, so perfectly laid out that one could scarcely believe that it was not a work of man. For surely a park is properly man's work, a flower of civilisation, which nature aids but rarely contrives. Yet when she does contrive, how far is the result beyond our human skill! For an exception the mountain-tops were free from mist; the land lay bathed in a cool morning light, and the scent of a thousand aromatic herbs—wormwood, southernwood, a glorified bog-myrtle, musk, and peppermint—rose from the wayside. Bracken was as plentiful as on a Scots moor, and the old familiar fragrance was like a breath of the sea. We breakfasted in a water-meadow, where a spring of cold water stole away through a forest of tree-ferns, arums, giant orchises, and the tall blue agapanthus. As we smoked our morning pipes and watched a white eagle and a brace of berghaans circling in the blue, I vowed that here at last had been found the true Hesperides.

A few miles on and we were on the farther edge. At a place called Skellum Kloof the road dips sharply over the crest, and down three break-neck miles to the Groot Letaba. Behind lay the green garden-land; in front, a hundred miles of broken country, fading in the far distance into misty flats. The little range of the Murchison hills ran out at right angles; away to the north the peaks of Majajie's mountains, with the Spelonken beyond, blocked the horizon. As far as the eye could see, the faint blue line of the Rooi Rand, the Portuguese border, was just distinguishable from the sky, with the fingers of the little Lebombo breaking the thin line to the south. One forgot the weary miles of swamp and fever that lay between, and saw only a glorious sunlit plain, which might have been full of clear rivers and vineyards and white cities, instead of thorn and Kaffir huts and a few ugly mining shanties. The Wood Bush on its eastern side is a series of soft green folds, with the superb evergreen forest in every kloof. At first sight the woods look like hazel copses, and you plunge gaily in to your disaster. Below Skellum Kloof is a little wooded glen, into which I descended for water, and at one time there were doubts of my ever emerging again. The place was matted with monkey-creepers, mosses, huge ferns, and a thick undergrowth around the trunks of great trees. Yellowwoods, 200 feet high, essenwood, sneezewood, stinkwood, most of them valuable timber-trees, and all with a glossy dark foliage, rose out of the jungle to the confusion of the poor inhabitant below. I noticed some giant royals, some curious orchids, and quantities of maidenhair fern and the graceful asparagus creeper. But soon I noticed little beyond the exceeding toilsomeness of the passage. Every step had to be fought for, the place was hot to suffocation, and I was in mortal fear of snakes. Also, I had no desire to meet a bushbuck ram, than whom no fiercer fellow for his size exists, at close quarters in his native haunts. I kept down-hill, listening for water, and by-and-by rolled over a red scaur into an ice-cold pool, which was the only pleasing thing in the forest. Happily in returning I struck a native path, and reached open country in greater comfort. Two boys who had been sent to find me—Basutos, and, like all Basutos, fools in a thick wood— succeeded in getting lost themselves, and had to be searched for.

Hereabouts, when my ship comes home, I shall have my country house. There is a piece of flat land, perhaps six acres square, from which a long glen runs down to the Letaba. There I shall have my dwelling. In front there will be a park to put England to shame, miles of rolling green dotted with shapely woods, and in the centre a broad glade in which a salmon-river flows in shallows and falls among tree-ferns, arums, and bracken. There may be a lake, but I am undecided. In front I shall have a flower-garden, where every temperate and tropical blossom will appear, and in a sheltered hollow an orchard of deciduous trees, and an orange plantation. Highland cattle, imported at incredible expense, will roam on the hillsides. My back windows will look down 4000 feet on the tropics, my front on the long meadow vista with the Iron Crown mountain for the sun to set behind. My house will be long and low, with broad wings, built of good stone and whitewashed, with a thatched roof and green shutters, so that it will resemble a *prazo* such as some Portuguese seigneur might have dwelt in in old times. Within it will be cool and fresh, with stone floors and big fireplaces, for the mists are chill and the winds can blow sharply on the mountains. There will be good pictures and books, and quantities of horns and skins. I shall grow my own supplies, and make my own wine and tobacco. Rides will be cut in the woods, and when my friends come to stay we shall drive bushbuck and pig, and stalk tiger-cats in the forest. There will be wildfowl on my lake, and Lochleven trout in my waters. And whoever cares to sail 5000 miles, and travel 1500 by train, and drive 50 over a rough road, will find at the end of his journey such a palace as Kubla Khan never dreamed of. The accomplishment is difficult, but not, I trust, impossible. Once upon a time, as the story goes, a Dutchman talked with a predikant about the welfare of his soul. "You will assuredly be damned," said the predikant, "and burn in hell." "Not so," said the Dutchman. "If I am so unfortunate as to get in there, I shall certainly get out again." "But that is folly and an impossibility," said the predikant. "Ah," said the other with confidence, "wait and see: I shall make a plan." *Ek sal 'n plan maak*—this must be my motto, and I shall gratefully accept all honourable suggestions.

The country is full of wealth—mines, agriculture, forestry, and pasturage. The presence of payable gold, both in quartz and banket, is undoubted, and some improvement in the roads, possibly a light railway, and the completion of the Selati line may provide for the rise of Haenertsburg from a very little dorp into a flourishing township. There is magnificent pasturage for stock, for cattle diseases are few and horse-sickness is unknown. It has been said that one acre in the Wood Bush will carry an ox, and though this is an exaggeration, it is certain that the rich herbage will maintain three or four times the head of stock which can be run on the high veld. The grass in spring is very early, and in the worst part of winter the forests can be resorted to, so that hand-feeding is almost unknown. The grass is sour veld, but any extensive pasturing would soon bring it into the sweet veld class. Once it were properly grazed down, it would be also a natural sheep country of high value. The soil is a clayey red loam, and the moist climate provides perfect conditions for most seed crops. Tobacco would thrive well—as well perhaps as on the lower slopes along the Groot Letaba, where Mr Altenroxel produces excellent pipe tobacco and a respectable cigar. It is a paradise for vegetables, and all hardy fruits and a few sub-tropical ones could be made to flourish in the rich straths. It is a land for small holdings, save for a few larger farms on the hill-tops, and here might arise a community of British settlers, making a new England out of a country which already possesses the climate of the West Highlands and the configuration of a Sussex park.

At Skellum Kloof we descended from the uplands to an elevation of about 2000 feet, a type of scenery halfway between the wholesome high veld and the pernicious flats of the Lower Letaba. I take that descent to be all but the worst in the Transvaal, second only to the appalling cliff over which the road from Lydenburg drops to the Olifants. The grades are so steep that with a waggon it is necessary to outspan all animals but the two wheelers, and lock the wheels tightly. With a two-wheeled Cape cart to attempt it is to court destruction. Just at the foot is an awesome corner, and then a straight slope to the Letaba, a stream about the size of the Spean and not unlike it. There is a fine salmon pool below the ford, in which I swam circumspectly, being in dread of stray crocodiles. The valley has nothing of that raw unfinished look so common in South African landscapes. The peaks rise in noble contours from long stretches of forest and Kaffir tillage. As we crossed, the mist drooped over the hills and we ascended the far side to our camp in a heavy persistent rain. The whole country was full of crying waters, and but for the clumps of wild bananas and the indescribable African smell, we might have been climbing to a Norwegian saeter after a long day's fishing.

All night it rained in torrents, and next morning—New Year's Day—dawned in the same driving misty weather. We could not see twenty yards, and the long sloppy grass and thick red mud of the roads made bad going even for Afrikander ponies. We sent our heavy transport back, and, carrying little more than a dry shirt and a toothbrush, struck down a track which follows the eastern ridge of the valley. The vegetation was as dense as any jungle, and swishing through the reeds and ducking the low branches of trees soaked us to the skin in a few minutes. But in spite of discomfort it was a fascinating ride. The heavy tropical scents which the rain brought out of the ground, the intense silence of the drooping mists and water-laden forests, the clusters of beehive Kaffir huts in the hollows, all made up a world strange and new to the sight and yet familiar to the imagination. This was the old Africa of a boy's dream, and there is no keener delight than to realise an impression of childhood. Yet, though the air blew sharp, there was something unwholesome in it. Fever lurked in the comely glens, and the clear reaches of the Letaba were not the honest, if scanty, waters of the high veld. The pungent penetrating smell of the herbs we trod underfoot had an uncanniness in it as if all were simples and antidotes—a faint medicinal flavour like the ante-chamber of a physician.

Krabbefontein, which we reached at mid-day, is a very beautiful clearing in the woods on the left bank of the river and at the foot of the Machubi glen. Mr Altenroxel, the owner, farms on a large scale, and has long been famous for his tropical produce. The luxuriance of the growth is so great as almost to pass belief. Gum-trees grow from 10 to 15 feet in a year; and we saw a bamboo fully 50 feet high whose age was under two years. Huge drying-sheds for tobacco, numerous well-built outhouses and cottages, wholly the work of natives, and a few rondhavels made up the farm-steading.

The time was past for apricots, but the orchard was full of grenadillas, finest of South African fruit, and kei apples; grapes were plentiful; and in a field of pines we destroyed the remnants of our digestion. The owner remained on his farm throughout the war, growing his own supplies, which included tea, sugar, and coffee. His tobacco is the finest brand of Transvaal pipe-tobacco I have smoked, and he exports to the towns boxes of light-flavoured but pleasant cigars, making everything on the farm except the labels. I have rarely seen native workers so intelligent and industrious, and the whole place leaves an impression of strenuous and enlightened toil. In the bungalow we ate our New Year's dinner, washed down by excellent German beer, carried many miles across the hills. If the conversation at table approached the domain of fact at all, the neighbourhood is full of uncanny things. A disgusting variety of tarantula, whose bite means death in half an hour, has his home around the tobacco-sheds; puff-adders abound; and the week before our visit a black mamba had attacked and killed a young Dutch girl. We heard, too, many tales of the eastern hunting-veld, and in the huge dark spaces beyond the rafters we saw the shadowy trophies of former hunting trips.

At daybreak next morning, in a thick drizzle, we started to reascend the mountains. A Kaffir set us on our way, and soon the hills closed in and we were in the long glen of Machubi. Machubi was a Kaffir chief with whom the Boers waged one of their many and most inglorious little wars. When his people were scattered he took refuge in the thick forest at the head of the river which bears his name. After my experience of that kind of forest I do not wonder that the Boers preferred not to fight a hand-to-hand battle in its tangled depths. So, after their fashion, they hired an impi of Swazis, who sat around the wood for three weeks, and ultimately slew the chief—not, however, before he had accounted in single-handed combat for three of his enemies. Mr Altenroxel possesses the old warrior's skull, which, except for the great thickness at the crown of the head, is finely shaped, and all but Caucasian in its lines. For this glen of Machubi I have nothing but praise: high bush-clad mountains, grey corries, streaked with white waterfalls, a limpid hill-stream, and in the flats green patches of Kaffir tillage. But the road—which once was a coach-road!—is pure farce. If there is a peculiarly tangled piece of scrub it dives into it, a really awkward rock and it ascends it, an unfordable reach of an easy stream and it makes straight for it, a swamp and it leads you into the deepest and direst part. We had constantly to dismount and coax our ponies down and up impossible steeps. My little African stallion as a rock-climber was not at his best, and I had some awkward positions to get him out of. One in particular remains in my memory. A very deep river could only be crossed by standing on a stone, leaping to an old log, and thence with a final sprawl to the farther bank. I turned my reins into a halter, went in front, and tried to coax my pony. When at last he did it he all but landed on my chest, and I made the acquaintance of the hardness of every one of his bones before I got him out of the valley.

The road climbs a spur in the fork of two streams, and as one ascends and looks up the narrow twin glens, the old exquisite green of the true Wood Bush takes the place of the sadder colours of the lowlands. The heads of the glens have the form of what are called in the north of England and Scotland "hopes," rounded green cup-shaped hollows; only here all things are on a larger scale, and the evergreen forest takes the place of birch and juniper in the corries. The road wound through wood and bracken, now coming out clear on a knoll, and now sinking to the level of some little stream. The mist which had covered the mountains was clearing, and one after another the green summits came forth like jewels against the pale morning sky. The tropical scents ceased, the sun shone out, and suddenly we were on the neck of the pass with a meadow-land country falling away from our feet. It was still hazy, but as we breakfasted the foreground slowly cleared. Little white roads sped away over the shoulders of hill; a rushing stream appeared in a hollow with one noble waterfall. Still the landscape opened; wood after wood came into being, glistening like emeralds in the dawn; long sweeps of pasture, each with its glimpse of water, carried the eye to where the great Drakensberg, blue and distant, was emerging from the fleecy mists of morning. Once more we were in the enchanted garden-land.

It is easy to describe the awesome and the immense, but it is hard indeed to convey an adequate impression of exceeding charm and richness. Hard, at least, in dull prose. A line of gleaming poetry, such as Herrick's—

"Here in green meadows sits Eternal May,"

or Theocritus's—

πάντ' ὧσδεν θέρεος μάλα πίονος ὧσδε δ' ὀπώρας,

will convey more of the true and intimate charm than folios of elaborated description. The main feature of the place is its sharp distinction from the common South African landscape. The high veld with its vast spaces, the noble mountain ravines, the flats of the bush veld, have all their own charm; but the traveller is plagued with the something unfriendly and austere in their air, as if all thought of human life had been wanting in their creation. They are built on a scale other than ours; man's labour has in the last resort no power to change them. They remain rough, unfinished, eternally strange, a country to admire, but scarcely to adopt and understand. But this garden-ground is wholly human. Natura Benigna was the goddess who presided at its creation, and no roughness enters into the "warm, green-muffled" slopes, the moist temperate weather, and the limpid waters. It is England, richer, softer, kindlier, a vast demesne laid out as no landscape gardener could ever contrive, waiting for a human life worthy of such an environment. But it is more—it is that most fascinating of all types of scenery, a garden on the edge of a wilderness. And such a wilderness! Over the brink of the meadow, four thousand feet down, stretch the steaming fever flats. From a cool fresh lawn you look clear over a hundred miles of nameless savagery. The first contrast which fascinates the traveller is between the common veld and this garden; but the deeper contrast, which is a perpetual delight to the dweller, is between his temperate home and the rude wilds beyond his park wall.

What is to be the fate of it? There is no reason why it should not become at once a closely settled farming country. If the Pietersburg line is looped round between Magatoland and the Spelonken and brought south to meet a line from Leydsdorp, this intervening plateau will have a ready access to markets. The place, too, may become a famous sanatorium, to which the worried town-dwellers may retire to recover health from the quiet greenery. Country houses may spring up, and what is now the preserve of a few enthusiasts may become in time the Simla or Saratoga of the Transvaal. How much, I wonder, will the new-comers see of its manifold graces? Any one can appreciate the mellow air, the restful water-meadows, the profound stillness of the deep-bosomed hills. These are physical matters, making a direct appeal to the simpler senses. But for the rest? It is the place for youth, youth with high spirit and wide horizon, sensitive to scenery and weather, loving wild nature and adventure for their own noble sakes. How much, I wonder, will they see of it all—the people who have the purse to compass health resorts and the constitutions to need them? For here, as in all places of subtle and profound beauty, there is need of the seeing eye and the understanding heart.

"We receive but what we give, And in our life alone does Nature live; Ours is her wedding garment, ours her shroud! And would we aught behold of higher worth Than that inanimate cold world allowed To the poor loveless, ever-anxious crowd, Ah! from the soul itself must issue forth A light, a glory, a fair luminous cloud Enveloping the earth."

I do not think that the place will ever become staled. The special correspondent will not rhapsodise over it—he will find many places better worthy of his genius; the voice of the halfpenny paper will not, I think, be heard in that land. Its appeal is at once too obvious and too subtle: too obvious in its main features to please the common connoisseur, too subtle and remote for the wayfaring man to penetrate. It will remain, I trust, the paradise of a few—a paradise none the less their own because towns and hotels and country houses may have sprung up throughout it. To such it will always appear (as it appeared to us when we took farewell of it from the summit above Haenertsburg and saw the hills and glades sleeping in the mellow afternoon) an old-world Arcadia, a lost classic land which Nature with her artist's humour has created in this raw unstoried Africa.

December 1902-January 1903.

CHAPTER IX.

ON THE EASTERN VELD.

Machadodorp, that straggling village called after a Portuguese commander, is the most easterly outpost of the high veld. A few miles farther and there is a sheer fall into narrow mountain glens, down which the Elands River and the Delagoa Bay Railway make the best of their way to the lowlands. North lies the hill country of Lydenburg, to which the traveller may come in a coach after a day of heart-breaking hills and neck-breaking descents. But south for a good hundred miles sweeps the high veld in a broad promontory from Machadodorp to the Pongola, and on the east to the Swaziland border. It is the highest part of the great central tableland, and a very bleak dwelling-place in winter; but in summer and autumn it has a full share of the curious veld beauty. In particular, being in the line of the Drakensberg, you can come to its edge and look over into the wild tangle of glens which lie between you and the Lebombo hills. Also it is the lake district of South Africa, being full of tarns of all sizes from Lake Chrissie, which is a respectable sheet of water, to the tiniest reed-filled pan. It is the coldest, freshest, and windiest part of the land, a tonic country where the inhabitants are rarely ill, and few doctors can make a living.

The journey to the first outspan from Machadodorp on the Ermelo road is a little monotonous, for you are not yet on the ridge of the high veld, the grass is rank, and the landscape featureless. You are pursued, too, by an unfinished railway, the Machadodorp-Carolina line, and if there is an uglier thing than the raw scar made by earthworks and excavations and uncompleted culverts, I do not know it. The line is being taken over by Government, and the sooner it is laid the better, for at present the richest farming population in the Transvaal are some sixty miles from a rail-head. At the fine stone bridge of the Komati you enter a more pleasing country, with a glimpse to the east of a gap in the hills through which the river enters the broken country. The Komati here is a slow high-veld stream creeping through long muddy pools with the slenderest of currents, but some eight miles down it is a hill torrent. This is one of the paradoxes of the high-veld rivers. Elsewhere it is in their cradle that streams have their "bright speed"; here the infant river must be content to creep like a canal, and lo! when it is almost full grown, it finds itself hurled in cataracts down a mountain valley. Who, seeing the Olifants near Middelburg, can ever believe that it is the same stream which swirls round a corner of the berg north of Ohrigstad; or, watching the sluggish Umpilusi crawling through the high veld, find any kinship between it and the Swaziland salmon-river? It is a romantic career—first a chain of half-stagnant pools, then a cataract, and then a full-grown river, rolling its yellow waters through leagues of bush and jungle to the tropical ocean.

From Everard's store, which is a pleasant outspan among trees, the road climbs steeply to the ridge of the country. A tremendous sweep of veld comes into view, stretching to the west in hazy leagues till the eyes dazzle with the soft contours and infinite lines, and in the east barred at a great distance by a faint blue range, the Ingwenya Mountains. The first pan appeared, no larger than an English mill-dam, and overgrown with reeds which made a patch of darker green against the veld. One had the sensation of being somewhere on the roof of the world, for on every horizon but one the land sloped to a lower altitude, and even on the east the mountains seemed foreshortened, like the masts of a vessel just coming into sight at sea. Presently a little white dorp, Carolina, appeared some miles away on the left, with that curious look of a Pilgrim's Progress village which so many veld townships possess. Then miles on miles of the same green downland, the road now sinking into little valleys with a glimpse of farm-steadings, and now holding the ridge in the centre of the amphitheatre. As the autumn evening fell, and the soft lights bathed the landscape, it became a spectral world, a Tir-an-Oig, in which it was difficult to believe that this rose-coloured slope was not a dream or that purple clump of trees a mirage. Little lochs appeared, some olive-green with rushes, some cold and black with inky waves lapping on dazzling white shores. Water, in Novalis' quaint fancy, is as the eye to a landscape, the one thing generally lacking in the blind infinity of the veld. Strings of wild-geese passed over our heads, and from the meadow bottoms there came the call of ducks and now and then the bark of a korhaan. Curious echoes arose as we passed, for there is something in the geological structure of the country which makes it full of eerie noises. And then, as darkness closed down, a long piece of water appeared, beyond which rose a little hill with two woods of blue gum and a light between them. A nearer view showed a trim cottage, with Kaffir huts around it, the beginnings of a garden, and, even in the dusk, a glimpse of long lines of crops stretching down to the lake. It was the homestead of Florence, which stands on the apex of a large block of Crown land, and is used as the headquarters of the land commissioner of the eastern district.

From Florence to the Swaziland border is some fifty miles as the crow flies, so at dawn our horses were saddled, and, with a mule-cart for provisions, we set out towards the remote hills. The morning had begun in a Scots mist, but by ten o'clock the sky was cloudless, and the intense blue of the lakes, the white shores, and the many patches of marl on the slopes caught the sun with a bewildering glare. The water in the pans is generally brackish, but some few are fresh, and one in particular, about four miles long, has wooded islets and a bold white bluff like a chalk cliff. The names are mostly Scots—Blairmore, Ardentinny, Hamilton,—for the land was first bought and settled by a Glasgow company. They are almost all stock farms, with little irrigation except along the Umpilusi; and many are fenced, efficiently enough, with slabs of stone for uprights. On one farm, Lake Banagher, we rode past a herd of some 300 or 400 blesbok and springbok, which are preserved by Mr Schalk Meyer, the owner. About noon we came into the shallow vale of the Umpilusi, and left it again for a high ridge, whence all afternoon we had a view of rolling country to the south, with the Slaangaapies mountains on the horizon. The great hills in the north of Swaziland were faint but clear, though we were still too high ourselves to see them to advantage. The country began to change, the valleys became almost glens, a great deal of tumbled rock appeared overgrown with bush and bracken, and everything spoke of the beginnings of a mountain country, which, strangely enough, we were approaching from above. In the late afternoon we came to large belts of trees around a ruined farmhouse, and as the sky was beginning to threaten we outspanned for the night. We were not more than half a dozen miles from the Swazi border and in full sight of it—a chain of little kopjes with a hint of faint mountains behind.

The farmhouse was an odd place seen in that stormy dusk. Thick woods of blue-gum and pine surrounded it, and below, also hemmed in by trees, was a lush water-meadow. The house had been a substantial stone building, but it was stripped to the walls, every scrap of woodwork having been used by the troops for fuel. The broken stoep was overgrown with moon-flowers, whose huge white blossoms gleamed uncannily in the shadows. We pushed through the wood and the overgrown paddock to a neglected orchard, where the fruit-trees had lost all semblance of their former selves, and struggled vainly among creepers and high grasses, and thence to the meadow where a little reddish stream trickled through the undergrowth. Owls flitted about like the ghosts of the place, and this relic of war with its moated-grange melancholy had a depressing effect on our spirits. We gladly sought our camp in an old barn on higher ground, where a blazing fire restored us to cheerfulness. The rain never fell, and the morning dawned grey and misty, so that when we set out for the border we had little hope of a view. We passed some Swazi kraals, and got directions from their picturesque occupants. The men are active and tall, and their wives with their curious head-dresses are better to look at than the sluttish native women of the central districts. They are beautiful dancers, and the performance of a body of Swazis in war costume is a thing to remember. The country began to be extremely rocky, and tree-ferns and other specimens of sub-tropical vegetation appeared in the hollows. One glossy-leaved bush bore a berry about the size and shape of a rasp, called by the natives "infanfaan," which had an agreeable sub-acid flavour. A little hill, looking as if it were made of one single gigantic boulder, appeared on the right, and with some scrambling we got our horses to the foot of it. This was Bell's Kop, a famous landmark, and beyond and below was Swaziland.

The morning had cleared, and though the horizons were misty, we saw enough to reward us. The ground fell sharply away from our feet to a green glen studded with trees, down which a white road wound. A hill shut the glen, but over the hill and at a much lower altitude we saw the strath of the Umpilusi, with the river running in wide sweeps with shores of gravel, not unlike the Upper Spey as seen from the Grampians. Beyond were tiers of broken blue hills, rising very high towards the north, where they culminate in Piggs' Peak, but fading southward into a misty land where lay the Lebombo flats. The grey soft air had an intense stillness, a kind of mountain melancholy, but far to the south there was a patch of sunlight on the green hills above Amsterdam. It is a type of view which can be had in all parts of the Drakensberg, from Mont aux Sources frowning over Natal to the Spelonken looking down on the plains of the Letaba—a view to me of infinite charm, for you stand upon the dividing line between two forms of country and two climates, looking back upon the endless prairies and their fresh winds and forward upon warm glens and the remote malarial tropics.

From Bell's Kop we fetched a wide circuit, going to Amsterdam, which was not more than fifteen miles from where we stood, by Florence and Ermelo, a journey of over 100 miles. The afternoon ride was something to remember, for the day had cleared into a bright afternoon with cool winds blowing, and the green ridges had a delicate pastoral beauty, as of sunlit sheep-walks. When we forded the Umpilusi its sluggish pools were glowing with the fires of sunset. Cantering in the hazy twilight of the long slopes was pure romance, and the sounds from a Kaffir kraal, the slow mild-eyed oxen on the road, and the wheeling of wild birds had all the strangeness of things seen and heard in a dream. I know no such tonic for the spirits, for in such a scene and at such a time the blood seems to run more freely in the veins, the mind to be purged from anxious indolence, and the whole nature to become joyous and receptive. Much comes from the air. There is something in those spaces of clear absolute ether, eternally wide, fresh as spring water, pure as winds among snow, which not only sustains but vitalises and rejuvenates the body. There is something, too, in the life. Fine scenery is too often witnessed by men when living the common life of civilisation and enjoying the blessings of a good cook and a not indifferent cellar. But on the veld there is bare living and hard riding, so that a man becomes thin and hard and very much alive, the dross of ease is purged away, and body and mind regain the keen temper which is their birthright.

We outspanned at a Boer farm and dined with the family off home-made bread, *confyt*, and tea. They were very hospitable and friendly, and discussed the war and current politics with all freedom. The walls were adorned with numerous portraits of *British* generals; and the farmer, who had been in Bermuda, displayed with much pride the carvings with which he had beguiled his captivity. One of the sons read assiduously a Dutch translation of one of Mayne Reid's novels, and when he could tear himself from the narrative contributed to the talk some details of his commando-life under Ben Viljoen, for whom, in common with most of the younger Dutch, he had a profound admiration. These people are a strange mixture—so hospitable, that the traveller is ashamed to go near a Boer farm, seeing the straitness of their lives and the generosity with which they give what they have; and yet so squalid that they make little effort to better their condition. This particular farmer owned four large farms, worth in the present market not less than £20,000; the sale of one or a part of one would have given him ample means to buy stock and start again. But he was content to go on as he was, running up a long bill with the Repatriation depot, and grumbling at the high prices for stock compared with what he had been used to pay. The result was that, though he had been back for nine months, I saw no living thing on that farm but a few chickens, six goats, and a spavined horse.

We made the last stage to Florence shortly after sunrise, and arrived at the homestead in time for breakfast. The twenty odd miles to Ermelo were the easy journey of an afternoon. We passed the ruined township of Chrissie, with a roofless kirk and some flourishing plantations of firs. The lake itself lay over some meadows, a pear-shaped piece of water, very shallow, and at its greatest perhaps some six or eight miles round. Yet in spite of its shallowness there is ample depth for a small centre-board; and when the railway is completed and Chrissie becomes a summer sanatorium, there is no reason why a modest kind of yachting should not be enjoyed. For the rest it is a bare road, with outcrops of coal appearing here and there, and the infant Vaal to be crossed, a very mean and muddy little stream. You come on Ermelo with surprise, dipping over the brow of a barren ridge and seeing a cheerful little town beneath you. It suffered heavily in the war, being literally levelled with the ground, but when we passed most of the houses had been cobbled together and new buildings were arising. It lies in a rich mineral tract, and is also the centre of a wide pastoral district, so with improved communications it may very well become a thriving country town. Whoever laid it out showed good judgment in the planting of trees; and in that bare land it is pleasant to come on such a village in a wood. My chief recollection of Ermelo is of a talk with a deputation of neighbouring farmers on the subject of cattle diseases. One admirable old man explained his perplexity. "Formerly," he said, "we used to be told that all diseases came from on High. Now we are told that some are from on High and some are our own fault. But which is which? Personally," he concluded, "I believe that Providence is a good deal to blame for them all."

About noon the following day we set out for Amsterdam. The first part of the road is monotonous, for it follows a straight line of blockhouses in a bleak featureless country. We crossed the inevitable Vaal again, a little larger and perhaps a little dirtier, but not appreciably more attractive. Sometimes we came to a flat moor like Rannoch with faint blue mountains beyond it, but the common type was a succession of ridges without a shade of difference between them. The weather had broken, and dust-coloured showers pursued us over the face of the heavens, till, as we came in sight of the considerable hill of Bankkop, the whole sky behind us had darkened for a wet evening. As we came down from the height, where the colour of the roads told of coal, and entered a green marshy valley, the storm burst on us,—a true African rain which drenches a man in two minutes. We sought shelter in a farmhouse, or rather in a blockhouse in the stackyard, for there was little left of the house except a shanty which the owner had restored for his present accommodation. All evening it rained in solid sheets, and to dinner, a meal cooked under difficulties, the Boer farmer came and talked to us, sitting on a barrel and telling stories of the war. He had the ordinary tale— against the war at the start, compelled to fight, had remonstrated with Louis Botha on his conduct of the Natal campaign, and, grumbling greatly, had followed his leader till he was caught and sent to Ceylon. The Boer discipline must have been a curious growth, and, when we realise the intense individualism of the fighting men, we begin to see the greatness of the achievement of Botha and Delarey in keeping them together at all. Our friend was living in squalid penury, but he was drawing enough in mineral options on his farm to have restocked it and lived in comfort, if he had pleased. There is no doubt in my mind, after such experiences, as to what would have been the wisest and kindest form of repatriation for landowners, had we had the courage to adopt it,—compulsory sale of a portion of the farm, and out of the capital thus supplied the farmer could have bought what he wanted at reasonable prices from Government depots. Such a method would have given the Government more good land, which it urgently wants; it would have saved the endless credit accounts which in the long-run will give trouble both to Boer and Government; and it would have saved the pauperisation into which the Boer is only too ready to sink. There would, of course, have been many exceptions in the case of the very poor and landless classes, but for the landholder it would have been not only the most politic but in his eyes the most intelligible plan.

I shall never forget the night spent in that blockhouse. Every known form of vermin—fleas, bugs, mosquitoes, spiders, rats, and, for all I know, snakes—came out of the holes where they had fasted for months and attacked us. I lay for hours swathed in a kaross, my face tingling, watching through the open square of door a melancholy moon trying to show herself among the rain-clouds, and wishing I had had the wisdom to sleep on the wet veld rather than in that chamber of horrors. Sheer bodily weariness induced a few uneasy hours of sleep, but the first ray of dawn found me thankfully arising. We breakfasted in haste, inspanned hurriedly, and were on the road an hour after sunrise. A long ascent brought us to the ridge of those hills of which Bankkop and Spitzkop are part, an extension of the Drakensberg from Wakkerstroom across the veld to the Swazi border. Then we passed over some very flat meadows to another ridge, from which we had a clear view of the Slaangaapies mountains to the south, and before us to the north-east the long green range of hills above Amsterdam. It was a curious picture for the Transvaal, a line of hills with regular glens and soft contours unbroken by rock or tree, and at the foot in a wood a few white cottages—a reminiscence of Galloway or Tweeddale; and one can well understand how the Scots settlers, who founded the place and gave it its first name of Robburnia after their national poet, saw in the landscape a picture of their home. We skirted the village on the left, and found the farm where we were to outspan. Here heroic measures were taken to get rid of the results of the blockhouse. A large tub was filled with hot water, and a bottle of sheep-dip was emptied into it. In this mixture we wallowed, and emerged from it scarified but clean.

The farm was the property of a Scots gentleman, who in six months had made new water-furrows, built himself a comfortable house, put over 200 acres under crops, and was running a fair head of stock on the hills. In the afternoon we rode with him to Mr Forbes' farm of Athole, some three miles off, which is perhaps the largest private landed estate in one piece in the country. It runs to some 60,000 acres, a huge square tract between two streams, from which is obtained a fine prospect of the Swaziland hills. Mr Forbes, who owns much land across the border, is one of the two or three living Englishmen who know the Swazis best, having for fifty years or more traded, farmed, and mined in their country. Before the war Athole was a great game-preserve, with 3000 blesbok, 2000 springbok, as well as reed-buck, impala, the two rheboks, and a few klipspringer. Now some odd springbok along the stream are almost all that remain. But when Mr Forbes first came to the place eland, koodoo, and hartebeest were the common game, and one could kill a lion on most farms. Of the original Scots settlers, who gave the name of New Scotland to the district, a few still remain, and their farms can be told far off by the neat strips of plantation which make the place like a hillside in Ayrshire. The land was acquired very cheaply from the Government,—one farm, if tales be true, going for a pair of boots, and another for a keg of whisky. The Boers themselves bought the whole tract from the Swazi border to Ermelo, and from the Komati in the north to the Pongola in the south—perhaps 3000 square miles—from the Swazi king for 150 oxen and 50 blankets. As at that time an ox was worth about 30s., it was not a high price, and the Boers still further improved the bargain by declining to pay the blankets. When Mr Forbes came to the place he was visited by a deputation of Swazi chiefs to discuss the subject, and to save trouble gave them the blankets from his own stores.

In Amsterdam next morning I was taken for a prospector, and played the part for a considerable time, to the confusion of an ex-official of the place, who wished to profit by my knowledge, but could make neither head nor tail of my answers. It is a sleepy little town, with not more than half a dozen houses lying pleasantly in gardens, with mountain streams on all sides and pastoral green hills to the east and north. South, where lay our road, are swelling moorlands, flanked by the Slaangaapies and the Swazi hills, and crossed at frequent intervals by clear grey streams. The first of these is the Compies, a few miles from the village, and a more naturally perfect trout-stream I have rarely seen. There were deep blue pools, and long shallow stretches, and little rapids in whose tail one should have been able to get a salmon. When trout become thoroughly acclimatised in the Transvaal, and the proper waters are stocked, he will be a happy man who owns a mile or two of the Compies. As if to intensify the atmosphere of fishing, it began to rain heavily and a cold mist blew up from the south. The long grass became hoar with rain-drops, and the innumerable veld watercourses found their voices after months of dry silence. Still more lipping grey streams, and then the rain ceased as suddenly as it had come, and in a deceptive gleam of sunlight we came into Piet Retief. It is a long, straggling, dingy village lying on two ridges. The mountains on all sides are too far off to be a feature in one's view of it, and save that it is one of the backdoors to Swaziland, there is little of interest for the traveller. At the entrance you pass a monument to Piet Retief, of which only the pedestal is completed—a poor tribute to a great man.

After lunch the rain began again in real earnest, and there was nothing for it but to loiter through the afternoon in waterproofs and hope for a dry morrow. It is not the most cheerful of places, but seen through the pauses of the driving wrack it had a wild charm of its own. In particular the Slaangaapies mountains, a dozen miles off, when by any chance they were visible for a moment, stood out black and threatening, with white cataracts seaming their sides and murky shadows in their glens. The Dutch name means "Snake-monkeys," but the natives call them beautifully "The Mother of Rains." The inhabitants of the district are almost the lowest type in the Transvaal,—poor, disreputable, half-bred, despised by their neighbours and neglected by the late Government. The progressive element in the district is represented by a

German colony, who were originally placed there by the wily Boer as a buffer against the natives, but who throve and multiplied and now own the best farms in the district. The most interesting thing I saw in the place was a large Boer hound, with the hair on the ridge of his back growing in an opposite direction to the rest of his coat. Now this type is rare, and, when found, makes the finest hunting dog in the world, for he will tackle a charging lion, and, indeed, fears nothing created. I had often been advised if I came across such a dog to buy him at any price, but in this case his Dutch owner utterly refused to sell, and I had to depart in envious gloom.

Before daybreak next morning, in a mist which clothed the world like a garment, so that we walked in fleecy vapour, we set off on the sixty miles' journey to Wakkerstroom. The first half is through an exceedingly dreary land. We crossed the Assegai, a finely named but inglorious stream, chiefly remarkable for its rapid flooding, and then for a score of miles we ascended and descended little sandy hills, and saw on each side of the road as far as the edge of the mist the same endless coarse herbage. In fine weather there is the wall of Slaangaapies to give dignity to the landscape; but for us there was only a bank of cloud. Before our mid-day outspan the sky cleared a little, and huge stony blue hills appeared on our left, with bush straggling up their sides and stray sun-gleams on their bald summits. We outspanned for lunch at Vanderpoel's store, which is a couple of huts in a perfectly flat dusty plain with a fine ring of hazy mountains around it. The day became exceedingly hot, still cloudy, but with a dazzle behind the mists which it hurt the eye to look at,—the kind of weather which makes the cheeks flame and tires the traveller far more readily than a clear sun and a blue sky. Again the same hills and dales, but now with a gradually increasing elevation, till when we came to a fine stream falling over a precipice into a meadow and looked back, we saw the Slaangaapies as if from a neighbour hill-top. A curious little peak appeared on the right, with what the Dutch call a *castrol* or saucepan on its head, a perfectly round ring of kranzes which presented the appearance of an extinguisher dropped down suddenly on the summit. It is a common sight in this part of the Berg, where the great original chain of cliffs has been broken and hills lie tumbled about like the *débris* of greater mountains.

At Joubert's Hoogte the road emerges from the glens, and the south opens up into a mazy tangle of hills. It is one of the noblest views in the country; but for us the mist curtailed the perspective, while it greatly increased the mystery. Shapes of mountains floating through a haze have far more fascination for the lover of highlands than a long prospect to a clearly defined horizon. Below lay the broad woody valley of the Upper Pongola, shut off in the east by the spurs of the Slaangaapies. The far mist was flecked with little sun-gleams, which showed now an emerald slope, now the grey and black of a cliff, and now a white flash of water. The air had the intense stillness of grey weather and great height; only the neighing of our horses broke in upon what might have been the first chaos out of which the world emerged. Thence for a few miles we kept on the ridge till we dipped into the hollow of a stream and slowly climbed a long pass where the road clung to the edges of precipitous slopes and wriggled among great rocks. The mist closed down, and but for the feeling in the air which spoke of wider spaces, we could not have told that we had reached the top of Castrol's Nek, the gate of the South-Eastern Transvaal. A Constabulary notice plastered on a weather-worn board was another sign that the place was a known landmark. As soon as we passed the summit the country grew softer. The shoulders of hills seemed greener, and along the little watercourses bracken and a richer vegetation appeared. The evening was falling, and as we slipped down the winding road the white mist faded into deeper and deeper grey, till at last we emerged from it and saw a clear sky above us and hills standing out black and rain-washed against the yellows of sunset. By-and-by in the centre of the amphitheatre of mountains a dozen lights twinkled out, and in a little we were off-saddling very weary horses in the pleasant town of Wakkerstroom.

March-April 1903.

CHAPTER X.

THE GREAT NORTH ROAD.

The romance which is inseparable from all roads belongs especially to those great arteries of the world which traverse countries and continents, and unite different zones and climates, and pass through extreme variations of humankind. For in them the adventurous sense of the unknown, which is found in a country lane among hedgerows, becomes an ever-present reality to the most casual traveller. And it is a peculiarity of the world's roads that this breath of romance blows most strongly on the paths which point to the Pole-star. The Æmilian Way, up which the Roman legions clanked to the battlefields of Gaul and Britain, or that great track which leads through India to the mountains of the north and thence to the steppes of Turkestan, captures the fancy more completely than any lateral traverse of the globe. A way which passes direct through the widest extremes of weather, and is in turn frozen and scorched or blown in sand, has an air of purpose which is foreign to long tracks in the same latitude, and carries a more direct impress of the shaping and audacious spirit of man. Of all north roads I suppose the greatest to be that which runs from the Cape to Egypt, greatest both for its political meaning, the strangeness of the countries to which it penetrates, the difficulties and terrors of the journey, and, above all, for the fact that it is a traverse of the extreme length of a vast and mysterious continent. It has been associated in the south with the schemes of a great dreamer, and in the north with the practical work of a great soldier and a great administrator. Between these two beginnings we all but lose trace of it in wilds of sand and swamp, the dense forests, the lakes and the wild mountains of Equatorial Africa, penetrated at rare intervals by native paths and old hunters' tracks. But to the eye of faith the road is there, marching on with single purpose from one railway head on the veld to another in the Soudanese desert. The men who travel it are hunters and prospectors, a few soldiers, a chance official, and once and again an explorer: but they travel only short stages, and there are few indeed who, like my friend Mr E. S. Grogan, carry their staff and scrip from end to end of it. To the amateur, like the present writer, who goes a little way on it, the thought of this majestic Way gives dignity to the ill-defined sandy track in which he may be floundering, and makes each northern horizon seem like the hill-tops of the Apennines, somewhere behind which, as the pilgrim is confident, lie the towers and pinnacles of Rome. I would recommend as a panacea for cold and comfortless nights on the road that the mind of the traveller should occupy itself with a projected itinerary. He will see the Road running as a hunter's path from the Limpopo to the Zambesi—through thorn scrub and park-land and stony mountain. Then he will travel up the Shiré by Nyassaland and on by Tanganyika to Ruwenzori and the lakes; and if he is not asleep by the time he has seen the sun rise on Albert Nyanza and fought his way through the Dinkas and the mosquitoes of the Nile swamps, then he must be an unquiet man with an evil conscience.

Only a little section of the road runs through the Transvaal. The practical road has indeed been diverted at De Aar in Cape Colony, and in the shape of a railway runs to Rhodesia and the neighbourhood of the Victoria Falls. But to the pilgrim this is a palpable subterfuge, for the straight highway goes through the Transvaal, taking the form of a railway as far as Pietersburg, and then becoming the Bulawayo coach-road for some eighty miles, till it plunges sheer into the bush as a hunter's road and makes for Main Drift on the Limpopo. It is a type of the vicissitudes which the Great Road is made to suffer,—railway, admitted highroad, hunter's path, native track, no road, and then a chain of waterways till it becomes a river, and meets the railway again after 3000 miles of obscurity. With a profound respect for the road, I am constrained to admit that it makes bad going, that it is insufficiently provided with water, that there are no signposts or inns or, for the matter of that, white habitations, that lions do the survey work and wild pigs the engineering, and that it is apt to cease suddenly and leave the traveller to his own devices. But for the eye of Faith, that wonderful possession of raw youth and wise old age, it is as broad and solid as the Appian Way; the wheels of empire and commerce pass over it, and cities, fairer than a mirage, seem to rise along its shadowy course.

Our starting-point was the Repatriation depot at Pietersburg, a large white-walled enclosure, with row upon row of stables and sheds and in the centre a cluster of thatched white dwelling-houses. It has the air of an Eastern caravanserai, for convoys come in and go out all day long, and the news of the Road is brought there by every manner of traveller. Apart from Government work with its endless trains of ox and mule waggons, it is the starting-place for all sorts of prospecting and hunting parties, and farmers from seventy miles round ride in for stock or supplies. If a lion is killed or gold found or a man lost anywhere in the north, word will be brought in to the depot by some Dutch conductor, so that the place is far better supplied with news of true interest than your town with its dozen newspapers. For the essence of news is that it should be vital to one's daily interests, and tidings of a massacre in China is less stimulating to the mind than word of a neighbour's windfall or disaster. I can conceive no more fascinating life than to dwell comfortably on the edge of a savage country from which in the way of one's business all news comes first to one's ears. To control transport is to be the tutelary genius of travel, and in a sense the life of the wilds takes its origin from the little caravanserai which sends forth and welcomes the traveller.

The high veld continues for some thirty miles north of the town before it sinks into bush and a humbler elevation. It is ordinary high veld—bleak, dusty, and in August a sombre grey; but on the east the blue lines, which are the Wood Bush and the Spelonken mountains, and in the far west the thin hills about the Magalakween valley, remind the traveller how near he is to the edge of the central plateau. Ten miles out a crest was reached, and we looked down on a long slope, with high mountains making gates in the distance, and a sharp little hill called Spitzkop set in the foreground. It was a cool hazy day, and in the west the kopjes seemed to swim in an illimitable sea of blue. The land is all part of Malietsie's location, and patches of tillage and an occasional cluster of huts gave it a habitable air. The native girls wear thick rings of brass round their necks, which gives them a straight figure and a high carriage of the head, pleasant to see in a place where people slouch habitually. Malietsie's is one of those Basuto tribes which are scattered over the North Transvaal—not the best type of native, for they are credulous and idle in their raw state, and when Christianised and dwelling near mission-stations, incorrigibly lazy and deceitful. They are also inordinately superstitious. I found that no one of my boys, who were mostly from Malietsie's, would stir ten yards beyond the camp after dark. At first I thought the reason was dread of wild beasts, but I discovered afterwards that it was fear of spooks, particularly of one spook who rolled along the road in the shape of a ball of fire. It is a tribute to the greatness of the North Road that it should have a respectable ghost of its own. In a little we passed the last store, kept by an old Scotsman, who gave us much information about the district. He talked of the Road, the River, and the Mountain, without further designation, which is a pleasing habit of country folk, who give the generic name to the instances which dominate their daily life. The Limpopo was the River, the Zoutpansberg the Mountain, because no other river or mountain had a local importance comparable with these, just as to a Highland gillie his own particular ben is "the hill," just as to Egypt the Nile is not the Nile but "the River." He measured distance, too, by the Road: this place was so many miles down the road, that water-hole so many days' journey up.

We inspanned again in the evening, and in a little turned the flanks of Spitzkop, and coming over a little rise saw a wide plain before us densely covered with dwarf trees. The long line of the Zoutpansberg comes to an abrupt end in a cliff above the Zoutpan. On the west the huge mass of the Blaauwberg also breaks off sharply in tiers of fine precipices. Between the two is a level, from fifteen to twenty miles wide, which is the pass from the high veld to the north. It is a broad gate, but the only one, for to the east the Zoutpansberg is impassable for a hundred miles, and on the west beyond the Blaauwberg the Magalakween valley is a long circuit and a difficult country. The great mountain walls were dim with twilight, but there was day enough left to see the immediate environs of the road. They had a comical suggestion of a dilapidated English park. The road was fine gravel, the trees in the half light looked often like gnarled oaks and beeches, and the coarse bush grass seemed like neglected turf. It is a resemblance which dogs one through the bush veld. You are always coming to the House and never arriving. At every turn you expect a lawn, a gleam of water, a grey wall; soon, surely, the edges will be clipped, the sand will cease, the dull green will give place to the tender green of watered grass. But the House remains to be found, though I have a fancy that it may exist on a spur of Ruwenzori. As it was, we had to put up with a tent and a dinner of curried korhaan, and during the better part of a very cold night some jackals performed a strenuous serenade.

The next morning dawned clear and very chilly, the mountains smoking with mist, and the dust behind our waggons rising to heaven in sharply outlined columns. However cold and comfortless the night, however badly the limbs ache from sleeping on hard ground, there is something in the tonic mornings which in an hour or so dispels every feeling but exhilaration. Water-holes have been made for the post-cart at lengthy intervals, but between there is nothing but rank bush, with flat trees like the vegetation in a child's drawing produced by rubbing the pencil across the paper. Animal life was rich along the road—numerous small buck, a belated jackal or two, the graceful black-and-white birds which country people call "Kaffir queens," korhaan, guinea-fowl, partridge, quantities of bush crows, and an endless variety of hawk and falcon. We left the Road and made a long detour over sandy tracks to visit the Zoutpan, from which the hills get their name, the most famous of Transvaal salt-pans. It is about three miles in circumference, and consisted at this season of caked grey mud, with little water-trenches and heaps of white salt on their banks. A wise law of the late Government forbade the alienation of salt-pans, but for some unknown reason a concession was given over this one, and instead of being the perquisite in winter of the *arme Boeren* it is managed by a Pietersburg syndicate, and as far as I could judge managed very well. The work is done by natives from the mountains who live round a little stream which flows from the berg to the pan, and forms the only fresh water for miles. The day became very hot, and the glare from the pan was blinding to unaccustomed eyes. As we returned to the main road, the noble mass of the Blaauwberg was before us, one of the finest and least known of South African mountains. That curious fiasco, the Malapoch war, was fought there, and Malapoch's people still live in its corries. To a rock-climber it is a fascinating picture, with sheer rock walls streaked with fissures which a glass shows to be chimneys, and I longed to be able to spend a week exploring its precipices. To a mountaineer South Africa offers many attractions, for apart from what may be found in isolated ranges, there are some hundreds of miles of the Drakensberg with thousands of good climbs, and above all the great north-eastern buttress of Mont aux Sources, which to the best of my knowledge has never been conquered.

In the afternoon the country changed, the bush opened out, timber trees took the place of thorn, and long glades appeared of good winter pasture. There was a great abundance of game, and for the first time the paauw appeared, stalking about or slowly flapping across the grass. He is a fine bird to shoot with the rifle, but a hard fellow for a gun, for it is difficult to get within close range; and as a rule at anything over thirty yards he will carry all the shot you care to give him. This park-land lasts for about ten miles, and then at Brak River it ends and a dense thorn scrub begins, which extends almost without interruption to the Limpopo. There we found our relays of mules, and on a dusty patch near the mule-scherm we outspanned for the night. We were nearing the country of big game. A lion had been seen on the Bulawayo road the day before, a little north of the station; and it was a common enough thing to have them reconnoitring the scherm. As soon as darkness fell the cry of wolves began, that curious unearthly wail which is one of the eeriest of veld sounds. Most forcible reminder of all, a hunting party ahead of us had lost a man, who, after wandering for six days in the bush, while his companions gave him up for dead, had come out on the Road and been found by the man in charge of our relays. It was a miracle that he had not lost his reason or perished of thirst and fatigue, for he had neither food nor water with him, and only a little cloth cap to keep off the tropical sun. An old Boer from Louis Trichard, trekking with oxen, camped beside us; and after dining delicately off guinea-fowl I went over to his fire to talk to him. He was a typical back-veld Boer—a great hunter, friendly, without any sort of dignity, a true frontier man, to whom politics mean nothing and his next meal everything. He told me amazing lion stories, in which he always gave the *coup de grâce*, and displayed incredible courage and skill. He showed me with pride a ·400 express bullet which he kept wrapt up in paper—whether as a charm or a souvenir I do not know, for his own weapon was an ancient Martini. His one political prejudice concerned the Jews, whose character he outlined to me with great spirit. They were the opposite of everything implied in the term "oprecht"; but I am inclined to believe that, like many of us, he secretly believed that all foreigners were Jews, and in hugging the prejudice showed himself a nationalist at heart.

The coach-road runs due north to Tuli and Bulawayo, but the Road itself takes a slight bend to the east and follows the course of the mythical Brak River. For miles this stream does not exist—there is not even the slightest suggestion of a bed; and then appears a dirty hole full of greenish, brackish water, and we hail the resurrected river. It is necessary for the traveller to know where such holes lie, for they are the only water in the neighbourhood; and though the Road keeps close to them, there is nothing in the dense thorn bush which lines its sides to reveal the presence of water. I have never seen bleaker bush-land. All day long, through hanging clouds of dust, we crept through the featureless country, the Zoutpansberg and Blaauwberg behind us growing hourly fainter. For the information of travellers, I would say that the first water is at a place called Krokodilgat, the second at a place called Rietgaten, and that after that the Road bends northward away from the river, and there is no water till Taqui is reached. The dust of the track was thick with the spoor of wild cats, wolves, the blue wildebeest, and at rare intervals of wild ostrich. As night fell the bush became very dead and silent, save for the far-away howl of a jackal,—a dull olive-green ocean under a wonderful turquoise sky. We encamped after dark in a little wayside hollow, where we built a large fire and a massive scherm or enclosure of thorns for the animals. There was every chance of a lion, so I retired to rest with pleasant anticipations and a quantity of loaded firearms near my head. But no lion came, though about two o'clock in the morning the mules grew very restless, and a majestic figure (which was indeed no other than the present writer's), armed with a ·400 express, might have been seen clambering about the top of the waggon and straining sleepy eyes into the bush.

We started at dawn next morning, as we had a long journey before water. The thorn bush disappeared and gave place to a more open country, full of a kind of wormwood which gave an aromatic flavour to the fresh morning air. Then came a new kind of bush, the mopani, a wholesome green little shrub, with butterfly-shaped foliage. The leaves of this tree would appear to be for the healing of the nations, for a decoction of them is regarded both as a preventive against and a cure for malaria; and a mopani poultice is a sovereign cure for bruises. Among the spoor on the track was that of a large lion going towards Taqui. There were also to our surprise the spoor and droppings of oxen. When about eleven o'clock we reached the large pits of whitey-blue brackish water which bear that name, we found the reason of both. A shooting party encamped there had had their cattle stampeded in the night, and early in the morning a Dutch hunter who accompanied them had gone out to look for them, and found an ox freshly killed by a lion not a quarter of a mile from the camp. He followed the lion, and wounded him with a long-range shot. When we arrived the search for the lion had begun, and he was found stone-dead a little way on, with his belly distended with ox-flesh and the bullet in his lungs. He was a very large lion, measuring about ten and a-half feet from tip to tip, rather old, and with broken porcupine-quills embedded in his skin. A trap-gun was set, and two nights later a very fine young black-maned lion, about the same size, was found dead a hundred yards from the trap, with a broken shoulder and a bullet in his spine. The remainder of the story shows the Providence which watches over foolish oxen. All were recovered save one, which died of red-water. They went straight back the road they had come; and though the country-side was infested with lions, wolves, and tiger-cats, they reached the mule-scherm at Brak River in safety.

From Taqui the road climbs a chain of kopjes where it is almost overarched with trees, so that a covered waggon has difficulty in getting through. From the summit there is a long prospect of flat bush country running to the Limpopo, with a bold ridge of hills on the Rhodesian side, and far to the east the faint line of mountains which is the continuation of the Zoutpansberg to the Portuguese border. The bush was dotted with huge baobabs, the cream-of-tartar trees which so impressed the voortrekkers in Lydenburg. At this season the branches were leafless, but a good deal of fruit remained, which our native boys eagerly gathered and munched for the rest of the journey. The fruit has a hard shell, and is filled with little white kernels like the sweetmeat called Turkish Delight. They have a faint sub-acid flavour, but otherwise are rather insipid. Their properties are highly salutary, and they are used to purify bad water and to keep the hunters' blood clean in the absence of vegetable food. Their enormous trunks, often forty feet in circumference, are not wood but a sort of fibrous substance, so that a solid rifle bullet fired from short range will go through them. The baobab is indeed less a tree than a gigantic and salutary fungus; but in a distant prospect of landscape it has the scenic effect of large timber. An old Boer in the hunting party we had passed had given us an estimate of the distance to the next water; but, as it turned out, he was hopelessly wrong. It is nearly impossible to get a proper calculation of distance from country-people in South Africa. They are accustomed to calculate in hours, which of course vary in every district according to the nature of the road and the quality of the transport. Six miles an hour is the usual allowance; but when a Dutchman tries to calculate in miles he gets wildly out of his bearings. The hours method still sticks in their mind; and one man solemnly informed us that a certain place was six miles off for horses and ten for mules.

We outspanned for the night without water, and with the accompaniment of scherm and camp fires. Next morning we came suddenly out of the bush to a perfect English dell, where a little clear stream, the first running water we had seen, flowed out of a reed-bed into a rock pool. There were a few large trees and quantities of a

kind of small palm. Under the doubtful shade of a
baobab we breakfasted, and then went up the stream
with our rifles to look for game. There was the usual
superfluity of birds, but we saw no big game except a few
bush-hogs. The stream ceased as suddenly as it began,
and we followed up a dry sandy bed all but overgrown
with a thorn thicket. A mile or so up we came on
another pool, which was evidently the drinking-place of
the bush, for the edges were trodden with the spoor of
pig and monkey and a few large buck. Pig drink during
the day, but the large game come to the water early in the
morning or very late in the evening, and in the heat of
mid-day go many miles into the bush. It was a hot
business ploughing along in the deep sand, and I was
very glad to return to the rock-pool and a bath on a cool
slab of stone. It is a good bush-veld rule to follow the
advice of Mr Jorrocks and sleep where you eat, and in
the shade of the waggon we dozed till the cooler
afternoon. The evening trek was in the old thorn-
country, perfectly featureless, silent, and uninhabited.
Since Malietsie's location we had seen no Kaffirs except
our own and the post-runners, and we were told that this
whole tract of land is almost without natives. Even the
water-holes, some of which are large and permanent,
have failed to attract inhabitants. I am reminded of a
story which has no application, but is worth recording. It
was told to a burgher camp official by an old and deeply
religious Boer, who was greatly pained at the experience.
He fell asleep, he said, one night and dreamed; and, lo
and behold, he was dead and at the gates of Paradise. An
affable angel met him and conducted him to a place

where people were playing games and laughing loudly, and were generally consumed with energy and high spirits. "This," said his guide, "is the Rooinek heaven." "No place for me," said the dreamer; "these folk do not keep the Sabbath, and their noise wearies me." Then he came to another place where there was much beer and tobacco, and roysterers were swilling from long mugs and smoking deep-bowled pipes to the strains of a brass band. "Again this intolerable row," said my friend, "though the tobacco looks good—clearly the German paradise." The next place they came to was a town where thin-faced men were running about buying and selling and screeching market quotations. My friend would not at first believe that this was Paradise at all, but his informant said it was the corner reserved for virtuous Americans. "Take me as soon as possible to the paradise of my own folk," said the dreamer; "I am tired of these uitlander heavens." And then it seemed to him he was taken to a very beautiful country place, with rich green veld, seamed with water-furrows, and huge orchards of peaches and nartjes, and pleasant little houses with broad stoeps. The soul of my friend was ravished at the sight. Clearly, he thought, the Boers are God's chosen folk, and he was about to select his farm when a thought struck him. "But where are all our people?" he asked. "Alas!" said the affable angel, dropping a tear, "it pains me to tell you that they are all in the Other Place."

Our evening outspan was below the kopjes where the copper mines lie, and a few tracks in the veld and an empty tin or two gave warning of human habitation.

These copper mines, which are about to be thoroughly exploited by Johannesburg companies, are old Kaffir workings, and, possibly, from some of the remains, Phœnician. The scenery suddenly became very peculiar,—English park-land, but with a tint of green which I have never seen before, a kind of dull metallic shade like some mineral dye. There were avenues of tolerably high trees, and a sort of natural hedgerow. The grass was short and rich, and but for the odd hue not unlike a home meadow. There were also a number of wood-pigeons of the same metallic green, so that the whole place was a symphony in a not very pleasing colour. Early next morning, leaving our transport behind, we set off for the Limpopo, which is about eight miles off. The thorn thickets appeared again, and the heat as we descended into the valley became oppressive. The altitude of the river is about 1500 feet, which is a descent of nearly 3000 feet from the high veld, and even in winter time the heat is considerable, for the soil is a fine sand, and no breeze penetrates to the wooded valley. I had seen the Limpopo a wild torrent in the passes of the Magaliesberg, and I had seen it a broad navigable river at its mouth; so I was scarcely prepared for the bed of dazzling white sand which here represented the stream. Main Drift is about a quarter of a mile wide, with a bed of bulrushes in the centre, and except for a thin trickle close to the Rhodesian shore it is as dry as the Egyptian desert. But twelve miles higher up it is a full stream with rapids and falls, crocodile and hippo, and some miles down it is a stagnant tropical lagoon. The water is there, but buried below Heaven knows how many feet of rock and sand. Those mysterious African rivers which disappear and return after many miles have a fascination for the mind which cares for the inexplicable. The valley is there, the bulrushes, the shingle, the water-birds, but no river—only a ribbon of white sand, or a few dusty holes in the rock. And then without warning, as the traveller stumbles down the valley, water rises before him like a mirage, and instead of a desert he has a river-side. There is little kinship between the torrent which rushes through Crocodile Poort and this arid hollow, but the great river never loses itself, and though it is foiled and swamped and strained through sand it succeeds in the end, like Oxus in the poem, in collecting all its waters, and pours a stately flood through the low coast-lands to the ocean. Ploughing about in the dry bed under the tropical noontide sun was dreary work, and put us very much in the position of Mr Pliable in the Slough of Despond, when he cried, "May I get out again with my life, you shall possess the brave country alone for me." We saw a number of spur-winged geese, which for some reason the Boers call wild Muscovy, and a heron or two sailing down the blue. A little up stream there was a lagoon in the sand flanked on one side by rocks—a clear deep pool, where a man might bathe without fear of strange beasts. Wallowing in the lukewarm water, the glare exceeded anything I have known—blue water, white rock, and acres and acres of white sand between hot copper-coloured hills.

As we left the river we said farewell to the Road. It showed itself on the Rhodesian side climbing a knoll past a cluster of huts which had once been a police station, but had been relinquished because of the great mortality from fever. Thereafter it was lost among bush and a chain of broken hills. It cared nothing for appearances, being sandy and overgrown and in places scarcely a track at all, for it had a weary way to go before it could be called a civilised road again. There was something purposeful and gallant in the little trail plunging into the wilds, and with regret we took our last look of it and turned our faces southwards.

Our way back lay mostly through dense bush-land, and in the days of hunting and the evenings round the fire I saw much of the life and realised something of the fascination of this strange form of country. It has no obvious picturesqueness, this interminable desert of thorn and sand and rank grass, varied at rare intervals by a raw kopje or a clump of timber. The sun beats on it at mid-day with pitiless force, and if it was hot in the month of August, what must it be at midsummer? The rivers are sand-filled ditches, and the infrequent water is found commonly in brack lagoons; but, dry as it is, it has none of the wholesomeness of most arid countries, generally forming a hotbed of fever. An aneroid which I carried to give a flavour of science to our expedition, put its average elevation at between 1500 and 2000 feet. Agriculture is everywhere impossible, though some of the better timbered parts might make good winter ranching country. But, apart from possible mineral exploitation, the land must remain hunting veld, and indeed is favourably placed for a large-game preserve. The very scarcity of water makes it a suitable dwelling-place for the larger buck, who drink but once a-day; and the difficulty of penetrating such a desert will be an effective agent in preservation. A man walking through it sees nothing for days beyond the dead green of thorn bush, till he comes to some slight ridge and overlooks a round horizon, a plain flat as mid-ocean, crisped with the same monotonous dwarf trees. Hidden away round waterholes there are glades and drives with a faint hint of that softness which to us is inseparable from woodland scenery, but they are so few that they only increase by contrast the sense of hard desolation. The bush is very silent. Its dwellers make no noise as they move about, till evening brings the cries of beasts of prey. The nights in winter are intensely cold, with a sharpness which I found more difficult to endure than the honest frost of the high veld. The noons are dusty and torrid, and the thirst of the bush is a thing not easily coped with. But in three phases this desert took on a curious charm. That South African landscape must be bleak indeed which is not transformed by the mornings and evenings. For two hours after sunrise a chill hangs in the air, light fresh winds blow from nowhere, and the scrub which is so dead and ugly at mid-day assumes clear colours and stands out olive-green and rich umber against the pale sky. At twilight the wonderful amethyst haze turns everything to fairyland, the track shimmers among purple shadows, and every little gap in the bush is magnified to a glade in a forest. I have also a very vivid memory of a view from one of the small ridges in full moonlight. It was like looking from a hill-top on a vast virgin forest, a dark symmetrical ocean of tree-tops with a glimpse of ivory from an open space where the road emerged for a moment from the covert.

There is little danger in hunting here unless you are happy enough to meet a lion and so unfortunate as not to kill with the first shot. But it is very arduous and hot, the clothes become pincushions of thorns, face and hands are scratched violently with swinging boughs, and a man's temper is apt to get brittle at times. In thick bush one can only hunt by spoor, and it is a slow business with a grilling sun on one's back and a few obtuse native boys. The native is usually a good tracker, but he is an unsatisfactory colleague because of the difficulty of communicating with him. For one thing, even in a language which he understands, he does not seem to know the meaning of the note of interrogation. If he is asked if a certain mark is a black wildebeest's spoor, he imagines that his master asserts that such is the case, and politely hastens to agree with him, whereas he knows perfectly well that it is not, and if he understood that he was being asked for information, would give it willingly. The difficulty, too, of hunting by a kind of rude instinct is that when this instinct is at fault he is left utterly helpless, and has no notion of any sort of deductive reasoning. If a native is once lost he is thoroughly lost, though his knowledge of the country may enable him to keep alive when a white man would die. I found also that my boys had so many errands of their own to do in the bush that it was difficult to keep them to their work. They scrambled for baobab fruit; they hunted for wolves' and lions' dung, from which they make an ointment, smeared with which they imagine they can safely walk through the bush at all seasons. The supreme danger of this kind of life is undoubtedly to be lost away from water and tracks. It is a misfortune which any man may suffer, but for any one with some experience of savage country, who takes his bearings carefully at the start and never gets out of touch with them, the danger is very small. In this country there is always some landmark—a kopje, a big tree, and in some parts the distant ranges of mountains—by which, with the sun and some knowledge of the lie of the land, one can safely travel many miles from the camp. For a man on a good horse there is no excuse, here at any rate, for losing himself; for a man on foot heat and fatigue and the closeness of the bush may well drive all calculations out of his head. Apart from other terrors, a night in those wilds is likely to be disturbed from the attentions of beasts of prey, and a man who has not the means of making a scherm or a fire will have to spend a restless night in a tree. To be finally and hopelessly lost is the most awful fate which I can imagine. It is easy to conjure up the details, and many uneasy nights I have spent in such dismal forecasts. First, the annoyance, the hasty pushing through the scrub, believing the camp to be just in front, and lamenting that you are late for dinner. Then the slow fatigue, the slow consciousness that the camp is not there, that you do not know where you are, and that you must make the best of the night in the open. Morning comes, and confidently you try to take your bearings; by this time others are seeking you, you reflect, and with a little care you can find your whereabouts and go to meet them. Then a long hot day, without water or food, pushing eternally through the dull green scrub, every moment leaving confidence a little weaker, till the second night comes, and you doze uneasily in a horror of nightmare and physical illness. Then the spectral awaking, the watching of a giddy sunrise, the slow forcing of the body to the same hopeless quest, till the thorns begin to dance before you and the black froth comes to the lips, and in a little reason takes wing, and you die crazily by inches in the parched silence.

I have said that the bush is without human inhabitants, but every now and then we found traces of other travellers. A dusty pack-donkey would suddenly emerge from the thicket, followed by two dusty and sunburnt men, each with some prehistoric kind of gun. Sometimes we breakfasted with this kind of party, and heard from them the curious tale of their wanderings. They would ask us the news, having seen no white man for half a-year, and it was odd to see the voracity with which they devoured the very belated papers we could offer them. They had been east to the Portuguese border and west to Bechuanaland and north to the Zambesi, pursuing one of the hardest and most thankless tasks on earth. The prospector skirmishes ahead of civilisation. On his labours great industries are based, but he himself gets, as a rule, little reward. Fever and starvation are incidents of his daily life, and yet there is a certain relish in it for the old stager, and I doubt if he would be content to try an easier job which curtailed his freedom. For, if you think of it, there is an undercurrent of perpetual excitement in the life, which is treasure-hunting made a business: any morning may reveal the great reef or the rich pipe, and change this dusty fellow with his tired mules into a nabob. Among the taciturn men who crept out of the bush every type was represented, from Australian cow-punchers to well-born gentlemen from home, whose names were still on the lists of good clubs. One party I especially remember, three huge Canadians, who came in the darkness and encamped by our fire. They had a ramshackle cart and two mules, and the whole outfit was valeted by the very smallest nigger-boy you can imagine. It did one good to see the way in which that child sprang to attention at sunrise, and, clad simply in a gigantic pair of khaki trousers and one side of an old waistcoat, lit the fire, made coffee for his three masters, cooked breakfast, caught and harnessed the mules, and was squatting in the cart, all within the shortest possible time. The Canadians had been all over the world and in every profession, but of all trades they liked the late war best, and made anxious inquiries about Somaliland. They were the true adventurer type,—long, thin, hollow-eyed, tough as whipcord, men who, like the Black Douglas, would rather hear the lark sing than the mouse cheep. After making fierce inroads on my tobacco, and giving me their views on the native question and many incidental matters, they departed into the Western bush, one man cracking the whip and whistling "Annie Laurie," and the other two, with guns, creeping along on the flanks. I took off my hat in spirit to the advance-guard of our people, the men who know much and fear little, who are always a little ahead of everybody else in the waste places of the earth. You can readily whistle them back to the defence of some portion of the Empire or gather them for the maintenance of some single frontier; but when the work is done they retire again to their own places, with their eyes steadfastly to the wilds but their ears always open for the whistle to call them back once more.

August 1903.

CHAPTER XI.

THE FUTURE OF SOUTH AFRICAN SPORT.

The great days of South African sport are over, and there is no disguising the fact. Open any early record, such as Oswell or Gordon-Cumming, and the size and variety of the bag dazzles the mind of the amateur of to-day. Then it was possible to shoot lion in Cape Colony and elephant in the Transvaal, and to find at one's door game whose only habitat is now some narrow region near the Mountains of the Moon. Turn even to the later pages of Mr Selous, and anywhere north of a line drawn east and west through Pretoria, there was such sport to be had as can now be found with difficulty on the Zambesi. The absence of game laws and the presence of many bold hunters have cleared the veld of the vast herds of antelope which provided the voortrekker with fresh meat, and the advance of industry and settlement have driven predatory animals still farther afield. From the Zambesi southward ten or twelve species of antelope may still be found in fair numbers, but the nobler and larger kinds of game, the giraffe, the koodoo, the black wildebeest, the two hartebeests, and the eland, are scarce save in a few remote valleys. The white rhinoceros is almost extinct and the ordinary kind uncommon. The hippopotamus, which is not a sporting animal, is still found in most tropical rivers; wild pigs—both bush-hog and wart-hog—are plentiful in the northern bush; but the graceful zebra is rapidly disappearing. Lion are still fairly easy to come on unawares anywhere north of the

Limpopo, and in the mountains and flats of the north-eastern Transvaal. A few troops of elephant may exist unpreserved in the region between the Pungwe and the Zambesi, a few in Northern Mashonaland, with perhaps one or two in the Northern Kalahari. The war, on the whole, has been on the side of the wild animals, for though large herds of springbok and blesbok were slaughtered by the troops on the high veld, the native, that inveterate poacher, has been restrained from his evil ways by lucrative military employment, so that the northern districts are better stocked to-day than they were five years ago. But the fact remains that South Africa is no longer virgin hunting-veld. The game is disappearing, and, unless every care is taken, will in a few years go the way of the American buffalo. If we are to preserve for South Africa its oldest inhabitants, and keep it as a hunting-ground for the true sportsman, we must bestir ourselves and act promptly. In this, as in graver questions, an intelligent forethought must take the place of the old slackness.

Such a policy must take two forms,—the establishment of good laws for the preservation of game and the regulation of sport, and the formation of game-reserves. The best course would have been to declare a rigid close time for five years, during which no game other than birds and destructive animals should be killed, save in the case of damage to crops. The administrative difficulties, however, in the way of such a heroic remedy were very great, and the code of game laws, now in force in the Transvaal, seems to mark the limit of possible restriction. Under these power is given to declare a close season—a valuable discretionary power, since the season varies widely for different kinds of game—during which no game may be killed, and also to preserve absolutely any specified bird or animal in any specified district up to a period of three years. This would permit the absolute preservation of such animals as the springbok and the blesbok in certain parts of the country where they are scarce, without interfering with sport in other localities where they are plentiful. The ordinary shooting licence for birds and antelope is fixed at £3 for the season; but certain rarer animals have been made special game, and to hunt these permission must be obtained in writing from the Colonial Secretary and a fee paid of £25. The chief of these are the elephant, hippo, rhinoceros, buffalo; the quagga and the zebra; the two hartebeests, the two wildebeests, the roan and the sable antelope, the koodoo, eland, giraffe, and tsessabe. The wild ostrich and that beautiful bird the mahem or crested crane (*Chrysopelargus balearica*) are also included. Provision is made against the sale or destruction of the eggs of game-birds and the sale of dead game in the close season. Under this law the ordinary man, on the payment of a small sum, has during the season the right to shoot over thirty varieties of game-birds and over a dozen kinds of buck, as well as wild pig and lion and tiger-cats, if he is fortunate enough to find them, on most Crown lands and on private lands when he can get the owner's permission,—a tolerably wide field for the sportsman. But restrictive laws are not enough in themselves; it is necessary to provide an equivalent to the sanctuary in a deer-forest, reserves where wild animals are immune at all seasons. The late Government established several nominal reserves, notably on the Lesser Sabi River and in the extreme eastern corner of Piet Retief which adjoins Tongaland; but no proper steps were taken to enforce the reservations. The new Government has strictly delimited the Sabi preserve and appointed a ranger; and certain adjoining land companies between the Sabi and the Olifants have made similar provisions for their own land. But one reserve in one locality is not enough. The true principle is to establish a small reserve and a sanctuary in each district. Part of the Crown lands in Northern Rustenburg, in Waterberg, in Northern and Eastern Zoutpansberg, and especially in the Springbok Flats district, might well be formed into reserves without any real injury to such agricultural and pastoral development as they are capable of. If the greater land companies could be induced to follow suit—and there is no reason why they should not—an effective and far-reaching system of game preservation could be put in force.[12] Finally, something must be done at once to stop native poaching, more especially the depredations of the wretched Kaffir dogs. Officers of constabulary, land inspectors, as well as all owners and lessees of farms, should have the power to shoot at sight any dog trespassing on a game-preserve or detected in the pursuit of game. An increased dog-tax, too, might stop the present system of large mongrel packs which are to be seen in any Kaffir kraal. A stringent Vermin Act, which is highly necessary for the protection of small stock like sheep and goats, would also help to prevent the slaughter of buck by wild dogs and jackals.

But for the big-game hunter, in the old African sense, there is little or nothing left. The day of small things has arisen, and we must be content to record tamely our sport in braces of birds and heads of small buck, where our grandfathers recorded theirs in lion-skins and tusks and broken limbs. Big game there still is, but they are far afield, and have to be pursued at some risk to horse and man from fly and malaria. The lion, as I have said, is still fairly common in the district between Magatoland and the Limpopo, in the continuation of the Zoutpansberg east to the Rooi Rand, down the slopes of the Lebombo, and in the flats along the Lower Letaba, Olifants, and Limpopo. He is frequently met with in most parts of Rhodesia, though his habits are highly capricious, and while a tourist one day's journey from Salisbury may see several, a man who spends six months hunting may never get a shot. Portuguese territory is still a haunt of big game, though the natives are doing their best to exterminate it, for the thick bush and the pestilent climate between the Lebombo and the sea will always make hunting difficult; and the Pungwe and its tributaries still form, at the proper season, perhaps the best shooting-ground south of the Zambesi. The elephant cannot be counted a quarry; and any man who attempts to kill an elephant in South Africa to-day deserves severe treatment, save in such preserves as the Addo Bush and the Knysna forest in Cape Colony, where they are rapidly becoming a nuisance. A few head of buffalo still survive, in spite of rinderpest, in the extreme Eastern Transvaal, as well as in Portuguese territory; and the eland, that noblest and largest of buck, is found along the Portuguese border. Report has it that in some of the Drakensberg kloofs between Basutoland and Natal a few stray eland may also be found. The beautiful antelopes, sable and roan, the exquisite koodoo, the blue wildebeest and the two hartebeests, roam in small herds on the malarial eastern flats, and a few giraffe are reported from the same neighbourhood. The gemsbok, with his lengthy taper horns, has long been confined to the remote parts of the Kalahari.

A big-game expedition will, therefore, in a few years' time still be a possibility in Central South Africa, and with judicious management it may long remain so, for those who can afford the time and the not inconsiderable expense. The best place must remain the country between the Lebombo and the Drakensberg, and north from the Olifants to the Limpopo. Eastern Mashonaland, the Kalahari, and the Pungwe district will be available for those who care to go farther afield. The venue must be chosen according as a man proposes to hunt on horse or on foot. Both forms of sport have their attractions. On the great open flats of the Kalahari and Rhodesia no sport in the world can equal the pursuit of big game with a trained horse—the wild gallop, stalking, so to speak, at racing speed, the quick dismounting and firing, the pursuit of a maimed animal, the imminent danger, perhaps, from a charging buffalo or a wounded lion. This horseback hunting is, as a rule, pursued in a healthy country, every moment is full of breathless excitement, and success requires a steady nerve and a sure seat. But stalking on foot in thick bush makes greater demands on bodily strength and self-possession. The country is rarely wholesome, and in those blazing flats a long daylight stalk will tire the strongest. There is more need, too, for veld-craft, and an intimate knowledge of the habits of game; and when game is found, there is more need for a clear eye and a steady pulse, for a man hunting in veldschoen and a shirt is pretty well at the mercy of a mad animal. But in both forms of sport there is the same lonely freedom, the same wonderful earth, and the same homely and intimate comforts. No man can ever forget the return, utterly tired, in the cool dusk, which is alive with the glimmer of wings, and the sight of the waggon-lantern and the great fire at which the boys are cooking dinner. A wash and a drink—indispensable after a hot day lest a man should overstay his appetite; and then a hunter's meal, which tastes as the cookery of civilisation seldom tastes. There is no reason why a hunter should not live well, far better than in any South African town, for he can count on fresh meat always, and, if he is fortunate, on eggs and fish and fruit. And then the evening pipe in a deck-chair, with the big lantern swinging from a tree, the great fire making weird shadows in the forest, and natives chattering drowsily around the ashes. Lastly, to an early bed in his blankets, and up again at dawn, with another day before him of this sane and wholesome life.

The chief dangers in African hunting, greater far than any from wild animals, are the chances of malaria and the possibility of getting lost. In many trips the first may be absent, but for a keen man it is often necessary to time his expeditions when the grass is short or when he has a chance of having the field to himself, periods which do not always coincide with the healthy season. It is not for anyone to venture lightly on a long hunting trek. But, granted a sound constitution, decent carefulness in matters such as the abstinence from all liquids save at meals, and from alcohol save before dinner, and the rigorous use of a mosquito-curtain, can generally bring a man safely through. The system can be fortified by small and regular doses of quinine, and the camp should be pitched, whenever possible, in some dry and open spot. These may seem foolish precautions to an old hunter whose body has been seasoned with innumerable attacks, but it is wise for one who has not suffered that misfortune to take every means to avoid it. To be lost in the bush is an accident which every man is horribly afraid of, and which may happen any day even to the most cautious, unless he has gone far in the curious lore of the wilds. There are men, of course, who are beyond the fear of it, chosen spirits to whom a featureless plain is full of intricate landmarks, and the sky is a clearer chart than any map. But the common traveller may walk a score of yards or so from the path, look round, see all about him high waving grasses somewhere in which the road is hidden, go off hastily in what seems the right direction, walk for a couple of hours and change his mind, and then, lo! and behold, his nerve goes and he is lost, perhaps for days, perhaps for ever. The ordinary procedure of a hunting trip, tossing for beats in the morning and then scattering each in a different direction, gives scope for such misfortunes. The safest plan is, of course, never to go out without a competent native guide; and, where this precaution is out of the question, the next best is to rely absolutely on some experienced member of the party who can follow spoor, sit down once you have lost your bearings, and wait till he finds you. A time is fixed after which, if a man does not return, it is presumed that he is in difficulties, and a search party is sent out; and naturally it saves a great deal of trouble if a man does not confuse the searchers by constantly going back on his tracks. If the hunter is on horseback he can try trusting his horse, which is said—I have happily never had occasion to prove the truth of the saying—to be able on the second day to go back to its last water. The whole hunting veld is full of gruesome tales of men utterly lost or found too late; and most hunting parties in flat or thickly wooded country come back with a wholesome dread of the mischances of the bush.

For the man who has little time to spare there remain the smaller buck. And such game is not to be lightly despised. The commonest and smallest are the little duiker and steinbok, shy, fleet little creatures which give many a sporting shot and make excellent eating. I suppose there are few farms in any part of South Africa without a few of them, and in some districts they are nearly as common as hares on an English estate. The springbok, a true gazelle, is more local in his occurrence, though large herds still exist in Cape Colony and parts of the Orange River Colony. Fair-sized herds are to be found, too, in the western district of the Transvaal and in certain parts of Waterberg and Ermelo. The blesbok is rather less frequent, though he used to be common enough, but there are numerous small herds in various parts of the country. These four varieties are the stand-by of South African shooting: other buck are to be sought more as trophies than in the ordinary way of sport. The water-buck, with his handsome head, and extremely poor venison, is common along all the sub-tropical and tropical rivers, but to shoot him requires a certain amount of trekking. So with the reed-buck, who haunts the same localities, though he is still found in places so close to the high veld as the southern parts of Marico and the Amsterdam district in the east. The beautiful impala, with his reddish coat and delicately notched antlers, is the commonest buck in the Sabi game-preserves, and extends over most of the bush veld, as well as parts of Waterberg and a few farms in the south-east. The klipspringer is found on all the slopes of the great eastern range of mountains, and is very common on the Natal side of the Drakensberg. He is a beautiful and difficult quarry, having a chamois-like love of inaccessible places, and being able to cover the most appalling ground at racing speed. The vaal rhebok and the rooi rhebok are found in small numbers in the same localities, and the latter is also fairly common in the wooded hills around Zeerust. Both the bush-pig and the wart-hog are plentiful in the bush veld, and on the slopes of the eastern mountains. Finally, the bush-buck, one of the most beautiful, and, for his size, the fiercest of all buck, is widely distributed among the woods of Cape Colony and Natal, and in the belts of virgin forest which extend with breaks from Swaziland to Zoutpansberg. Living in the dense undergrowth, he has been pretty well out of the way of the hunter who killed for the pot. He is an awkward fellow to meet at close quarters in a bad country, for, when wounded, he will charge, and his powerful horns are not pleasant to encounter. There have been several cases of natives, and even of white men, who have died of wounds from his assaults. His elder brother, the inyala, does not, so far as I know, appear south of the Limpopo.

The favourite South African method of shooting such game as the springbok is by driving him with an army of native beaters down wind against the guns. In an open country buck can be stalked on horseback or ridden down in the Dutch fashion of "brandt." Elsewhere stalking on foot is the only way, a difficult matter unless the hunter knows the habits and haunts of the game. South African shooting seems hard at first to the new-comer, partly from the difficulty of judging distances in the novel clearness of the air, partly from the shyness of game, which often makes it necessary to take shots at a range which seems ridiculous to one familiar only with Scots deer-stalking, and partly from the extraordinary tenacity of life which those wild animals show,[13] limiting the choice of marks to a very few parts of the body. But experience can do much, and in time any man with a clear eye and good nerve may look for reasonable success. As has been noted in a former chapter, the best shots in the country, with a few exceptions, are to be found among English immigrants and Colonists of English blood. It is a kind of shooting which seems incredible at first sight to the ordinary man from home. I have known such a hunter to put a bullet at over 100 yards through the head of a korhaan, a bird scarcely larger than a blackcock: a feat which might be set down to accident were it not that the same man was accustomed to shoot small buck running at 200 yards with remarkable success. I should be very sorry to wage war against a corps of sharpshooters drawn from old African hunters.

There remain the numerous game-birds of the country. The finest is, of course, the greater paauw, but he is not very common in the Transvaal itself, though frequent enough in Bechuanaland, Rhodesia, and some parts of the northern bush veld. But of the bustard family, to which the comprehensive name of korhaan is applied, there are at least four varieties, two of which are very common. The bustard is an easy bird, save that he carries a good deal of shot, and has a knack of keeping out of range unless properly stalked or driven. The Dutch word "patrys," again, covers at least eight varieties of the true partridge, and if we include the sand-grouse (called the Namaqua partridge), of two or three more. None of the South African partridge tribe are equal to their English brothers; but there is no reason why the English bird should not be introduced, and thrive well, and indeed experiments in this direction are being made. There are three birds which the Dutch call "pheasant," two of them francolins and one the curious dikkop—birds which have few of the qualities of the English pheasant, but which are strong on the wing, offer fair shots, and make excellent eating. Quail are found at certain seasons of the year in vast quantities, and give good sport with dogs; but to my mind the finest South African bird, excepting of course the greater paauw, is the guinea-fowl, which the Dutch call by the quaint and beautiful name of *tarentaal*. There are two varieties, fairly well distributed—the ordinary crested (*Numida coronata*) and the blue-headed (*Numida Edouardi*). In parts of the bush veld they may be seen roosting at night on trees so thickly that the branches are bent with their weight. When pursued in broken country, what with dodging among stones and trees and his short unexpected flight, the guinea-fowl offers some excellent shooting, and as a table-bird he is not easy to beat. Wildfowl are an uncertain quantity on the uplands, though very common nearer the coast. They do not come to the rivers, but, on the other hand, they frequent in great numbers farm dams and the pans and lakes of Standerton and Ermelo. What the Dutch call specifically the "wilde gans" is the Egyptian goose; but several other varieties, including the spur-winged, are to be found. There are some ten kinds of duck, but it would be difficult to say which is the commonest, as they vary in different districts. The Dutch call a bird "teel" which is not the true teal, but the variety known as the Cape teal (*Nettion capense*), though there is more than one kind of proper teal to be met with. There is a black duck, a variety of pochard, a variety of shoveller, and a kind of shell-duck which is known as the mountain duck (*bergeend*). Wild pigeons exist in endless quantities; and I must not omit the pretty spur-winged plover, which cries all day long on the western veld, or that most cosmopolitan of birds, the snipe. Along the reed-beds of the Limpopo, in the bulrushes which fringe the pans in Ermelo, by every spruit and dam, you may put up precisely the same fellow that you shoot in Hebridean peat-mosses or on Swedish lakes, or along the canals of Lower Egypt. The little brown long-billed bird has annihilated time and space and taken the whole world for his home.

There is need of some little care lest we drive the wild birds altogether away from the neighbourhood of the towns. They are still plentiful, but, if over-shot, they change their quarters; and people complain that whereas five years ago they could get excellent shooting within three miles of their door, they have now to content themselves with a few stragglers. It is for the owners of land to see that its denizens are properly protected, for the disappearance of big game is an awful warning not to presume on present abundance. Some day we may hope to see the country farmer as eager to preserve his game as he is now to destroy it. There needs but the pinch of scarcity and the growth of a market value for shooting to turn the present free-and-easy ways into a perhaps too rigorous protective system.

There remain two sports which are still in their infancy in the country and deserve serious development—the keeping of harriers and angling. I say harriers advisedly, for though it would be better to stick to drafts from foxhound packs because of the greater strength and hardiness of the hounds, yet the sport can never fairly be dignified by the name of fox-hunting. The quarries will be the hare, the small buck, and in certain districts the jackal. The veld in parts is a fine natural hunting-ground, and the hazards, which will be wanting in the shape of hedges and banks, will exist very really in ant-bear holes and dongas. As the fencing laws take effect there will be wire to go over for those who have Australian nerves. The Afrikander pony is an animal born for the work, and once harrier packs were established there is every reason to believe that the Dutch farmers would join in the sport. The only two reasons I have ever heard urged against the proposal are—first, that hounds when brought out to South Africa lose their noses; and, second, that it would be hard to get a good scent in the dry air of the veld. The first is true in a sense, but only because a draft brought out from home is usually set to work at once and not acclimatised gradually to the change of air. There is no inherent impossibility in keeping a dog's nose good, as is shown by the many excellent setters and pointers that have been imported. In any case, if the master of harriers breeds carefully he ought in a few years to get together a thoroughly acclimatised pack. As for the matter of scent, there is no denying that it would not lie on the ordinary hot dry day, but this only means that it will not be possible to hunt all the year round. I can imagine no better weather than the cool moist days which are common on the high veld in autumn and early spring, and even in summer the mornings up to ten o'clock are cool enough for the purpose. South African hunts must follow the Indian fashion, and when they cannot get whole days for their sport make the best of the early hours.

Fishing, I am afraid, has been in the past a neglected sport. The Boer left it to the Kaffir, and the uitlander had better things to think about. Had the land possessed any native fish of the type of the American brook-trout or the land-locked salmon, perhaps it would have been different; but in the high-veld streams the only notable fish are two species of carp, known as yellow-fish and white-fish, which run from 2 lb. to 6 lb., and the barbel, which may weigh anything up to 30 lb.[14] There are also eels, which may be disregarded. I do not think these South African fish are to be despised, for though they may be dead-hearted compared with a trout or a salmon, they give better sport than English coarse fish, and the barbel is quite as good as a pike. The ordinary bait is mealie-meal paste, a locust or any kind of small animal, a phantom minnow, and even a piece of bright rag. I have known both kinds of carp take a brightly coloured sea-trout fly, and give the angler a very good run for his pains. But the great South African fish is the tiger-fish, confined, unhappily, to sub-tropical rivers and malarial country. He is not unlike a trout in appearance, save for his fierce head, which suggests the *Salmo ferox*. In any of the eastern rivers—Limpopo, Letaba, Olifants, Sabi, Crocodile, Komati, Usutu, Umpilusi—he is the chief— indeed, so far as I could judge, the only—fish, and he is one of the most spirited of his tribe. He will readily take an artificial minnow, and also, I am told, a large salmon fly, but the tackle must be at least as strong as for pike, for his formidable teeth will shear through any ordinary casting line. His average weight is perhaps about 10 lb., though he has been caught up to 30 lb., but it is not his size so much as his extraordinary fierceness and dash which makes him attractive. When hooked he leaps from the water like a clean salmon, and for an hour or more he may lead the perspiring fisherman as pretty a dance as he could desire. If any one is inclined to think angling a tame sport, I can recommend this experiment. Let him go out on some river like the Komati on a stifling December day, when the sky is brass above and not a breath of air breaks the stillness, in one of the leaky and crazy cobles of those parts. Let him hook and land a tiger-fish of 20 lb., at the imminent risk of capsizing and joining the company of the engaging crocodiles, or, when he has grassed the fish, of having a finger bitten off by his iron teeth, and then, I think, he will admit, so far as his scanty breath will allow him, that an hour's fishing may afford all the excitement which an average man can support.

So much for the fish of the country. But Central South Africa affords a magnificent field for the introduction and acclimatisation of the greatest of sporting fish. Ceylon and New Zealand have already shown what can be done with the trout in new waters, and in Cape Colony and Natal the same experiment has been made with much success. The high veld is only less good than New Zealand as a home for trout. To be sure, there is no snow-water, but there is the next best thing in water whose temperature varies very little all the year round. The ordinary sluggish spruits are of course unsuitable, but the mountain burns in the east and north are perfect natural trout-streams, with clear cold water, abundant fall, gravel bottoms, and all the feeding which the most gluttonous of fish could desire. The Transvaal Trout Acclimatisation Society, founded in Johannesburg in 1902, has established a hatchery on the Mooi River above Potchefstroom, and is making the most praiseworthy efforts, by the creation of local committees, to excite a general interest in the work throughout the country. It will still be some years before any trout-stream can be stocked and thrown open to anglers; but there is no reason why in time there should not be one in most districts. The Mooi and the Klip rivers near Johannesburg, the Magalies and the Hex rivers in Rustenburg, the Upper Malmani in Lichtenburg, every stream in Magatoland and the Wood Bush, the torrents which fall from Lydenburg into the flats, and all the many mountain streams which run into Swaziland from the high veld, may yet be as good trout-waters as any in Lochaber. The rainbow and the Lochleven trout will be the staple importation; but in some of the larger streams experiments might be made with the American ouananiche and the Danubian huchen. It is difficult to exaggerate the service which might thus be rendered to the country. If in the dams and streams within easy distance of the towns a sound form of sport can be provided at reasonable cost, the first and greatest of the amenities of life will have been introduced. At present on the Rand there are no proper modes of relaxation: most men work till they drop, and then take their jaded holiday in Europe. Yet how many, if they had the chance, would go off from Saturday to Monday with their rods, and find by the stream-side the old healing quiet of nature?

There is a future for South African sport if South Africa is alive to her opportunity. It is a country of sportsmen, and sport with the better sort of man is a sound basis of friendship. Game Preservation Societies are being started in many districts, and when we find the two races united in a common purpose, which touches not politics or dogma but the primitive instincts of humankind, something will have been done towards unity. The matter is equally important from the standpoint of game protection. The private landowner can do more than the land company, and the land company can do more than the Government, towards ensuring the future of sport. Many Dutch farmers have preserved in the past, and a general extension of this spirit would work wonders in a few years. Vanishing species would be saved, banished game would return, and our conscience would be clear of one of the most heinous sins of civilisation. As an instance of what can be done by private effort, there is a farm not sixty miles from a capital city where at this moment there are impala, rooi hartebeest, koodoo, and wild ostrich.

There are few countries in the world where sport can be enjoyed in more delectable surroundings. The cold fresh mornings, when the mist is creeping from the grey hills and the vigour of dawn is in the blood; the warm sun-steeped spaces at noonday; the purple dusk, when the veld becomes a kind of Land East of the Sun and West of the Moon, full of fairy lights and mysterious shadows; the bitter night, when the southern constellations blaze in the profound sky,—he who has once seen them must carry the memory for ever. It is such things, and not hunger and thirst and weariness, which remain in a man's mind. For the lover of nature and wild things (which is to say the true sportsman) it is little wonder if, after these, home and ambition and a comfortable life seem degrees of the infinitely small. And the others, who are only brief visitors, will carry away unforgettable pictures to tantalise them at work and put them out of all patience with an indoor world—the bivouac under the stars on the high veld, or some secret glen of the Wood Bush, or the long lines of hill which huddle behind Lydenburg into the sunset.

[12] In other parts of British Africa the policy of reserves has received full recognition. In East Africa there are two large reserves, one along the Uganda Railway and the other near Lake Rudolf. In the Soudan there is a vast reserve between the Blue and the White Niles, and most

of the best shooting-ground throughout the country is strictly protected.

[13] The eland is the one conspicuous exception.

[14] A Transvaal friend informs me that my classification, though the one commonly in use, is quite inaccurate. The yellow-fish and the white-fish are not carp but species of barbel, and what I have called barbel is another variant of the same family, called by the Dutch "kalverskop," or "calf's-head," from its shape. There is no true carp, though the Dutch give the name of "kurper" to a very curious little fish about four inches long which is common in streams flowing into the Vaal. The other chief varieties are the coarse mud-fish and the cat-fish, which latter is often mixed up with the barbel. It is to be hoped that some local ichthyologist will give his attention to the native fishes—a very interesting subject, and one at present in the most unscientific confusion.

PART III.

THE POLITICAL PROBLEM

CHAPTER XII.

THE ECONOMIC FACTOR.

After a three years' war, and at the cost of over 200 millions, Britain has secured for her own children the indisputable possession of the new colonies. In earlier chapters an attempt has been made to sketch roughly the historical influences which may help to shape the future and to describe the actual features of the land which charm and perplex the beholder. We have now to face the direct problems into which the situation can be resolved, and in particular that question of material wellbeing which is the most insistent, because the most easily realised, for both statesman and people. The economic factor in the politics of a country is always a difficult matter to discuss, for it is made up of infinite details, some of them purely speculative, all of them hard to disentangle. If a business man were to do what he never does, and sit down to analyse calmly his position, he would have to go far beyond balance-sheets and statements of profit and loss. He would be compelled to look into the social and economic conditions under which he lived; he would have to estimate rival activities and forecast their development; the money market, rates of exchange, the nature of the labour supply, the effect of political and social movements, even such matters as his own bodily and mental health, and his standing among his fellows, would properly make part of the inquiry. With the private individual the analysis would be ridiculous, because the component parts are too minute to realise; but with a nation, where the lines are broader, some stock-taking of this kind is periodically desirable. But in spite of, or because of, the complexity of the inquiry, the human mind is apt to complicate it needlessly by running after side-issues and losing sight of the main features of the problem. The economic position of a country embraces in a sense almost every detail of human life; but there is no reason why the mass of detail should be allowed to get out of focus and obscure the synthesis of the survey. Provided we remember that the economic factor is not correctly estimated by looking only at revenue and expenditure, imports and exports, and fiscal provisions, we may safely devote our energies to steering clear of the labyrinth of secondary detail in which the ordinary statistician would seek to involve us.

In the following pages it is proposed to confine the survey to what appear to be the main features of a complex question. It would be vain to embark on speculations as to the payable ore in the ground, market forecasts, suggestions for new industries, and the many hints towards a reformed fiscal system with which local and European papers have been crowded. It is sufficient to note the existence of such questions; the materials for a true understanding of the South African economy are not to be found in them. In particular it is proposed to avoid needless statistics, which, apart from the fact that they are often inaccurate and partisan, are the buttress of that particularist logic which is the foe of true reason. Two questions may be taken as the general heads of our inquiry: first, Wherein consists the wealth of the land, actual and potential? and, secondly, How best may that wealth be maintained and developed for the national good?

I.

The cardinal economic fact is the existence of gold—gold as it is found in no other country, not in casual pockets and reefs, but in quantities which can for the most part be accurately mapped out and valued months and years before it is worked; gold which is mined not as an adventure, but as an organised and stable industry. The Main Reef formation extends for sixty-two miles, from Randfontein to Holfontein,[15] but three-fourths of the gold mined has been produced in the central section, which is only some twelve miles long. In 1886 the district was proclaimed a public gold-field, and since that day ore worth nearly 100 millions sterling has been extracted. The development took place in spite of difficulties which vastly increased the working costs. The dynamite and railway monopolies, the heavy expense of the transit of machinery from the coast, the absence of subsidiary local industries to feed the gold industry, forced the work into the hands of a small circle of rich firms who could provide the large capital and face the heavy risks of a new enterprise. It is clear, therefore, that mining on the Rand, while a notable enterprise, has necessarily been a slow one, since the two natural factors, the amount of gold in the soil and the labour of working it, have been complicated by many artificial hindrances. The past is not the true basis for estimating the future of the industry; the proper premises for a forecast are the two natural factors—the quantity of gold in the earth and the normal cost of winning it. It is the first that concerns us at present.

All estimates must be merely conjectural, and can be used only with the greatest caution. But in the multitude of conjectures there may be such a consensus of opinion as to ensure us a fair certainty that this or that is the view of those who are best fitted to judge. Mr Bleloch, in a calculation based on the report of the most eminent engineers, values the amount of gold still in the Rand at 2871 millions sterling, showing a profit to the companies concerned of over 975 millions. If we put the life of the Rand at one hundred years, which is a mean between conflicting estimates, we shall have an average, allowing for reserve funds, of 8 millions to be paid yearly in dividends to shareholders. In 1898 twenty-six companies paid dividends amounting to over 4 millions: therefore, on Mr Bleloch's figures, we can promise at least one hundred years to the Rand of twice the prosperity of 1898. These figures include the deep levels, but do not take into account any of the Rand extensions, in which the Main Reef has been traced for over 300 miles. It is certain that in the direction of Heidelberg and Greylingstad gold in payable quantities exists for not less than seventy miles, and it is at least probable that a similar extension exists in the Potchefstroom and Klerksdorp districts in the west. So much for the peculiar "banket" formation of the Rand, which must remain the type of stable gold-mining,—stable, because the element of uncertainty over any group of properties is reduced to a minimum, and the high organisation necessary and the large initial outlay produce a community less of rivals than of fellow-workers. Quartz reefs and alluvial deposits are found in many parts of the country. In Lydenburg and Barberton, where the earliest gold mines were sunk, several producing companies are at work; and this type of mining will develop equally with the Rand under a system which abolishes monopolies and assists instead of discouraging enterprise. In the northern districts, around the Wood Bush and the Zoutpansberg ranges, there are quartz and alluvial mining, and indications of "banket" formation, and in the all but unknown region adjoining Portuguese territory, if tales be true, there may be gold in quantities still undreamed of.

No figures are reliable, all estimates are disputed, but from the very contradictions one fact emerges—that there is gold enough to give employment to a greatly increased mining population for at least fifty years, and to decentralise the industry and create large industrial belts instead of one industrial city. Nor is gold the only mineral. From Pretoria to Piet Retief run coal-beds, many of them of great richness and good quality, covering an area of more than 10,000 square miles. It has been calculated that 60,000 million tons are available. The quality of the coal in the undeveloped beds lying to the south of Middelburg is, in the opinion of experts, equal to the best British product. Iron-ore is abundant in many parts, particularly in the coal-bearing regions of the east. Lead has been worked near Zeerust, and there are good grounds for believing that copper in large quantities exists in Waterberg and in the tract between Pietersburg and the Limpopo. Diamond pipes are found in several places in the region due east of Pretoria, where the new Premier Mine seems to promise a richness not equalled by Kimberley; and it is probable that places like the Springbok Flats and the western parts of Christiana are highly diamondiferous. Sapphires have been found in the west, and diamonds and spinels are reported from the northern mountains. Few countries have a soil more amply mineralised; but the sparse population, mainly absorbed in the quest of one mineral, has done little to exploit its wealth. Mining, save for gold and coal, is still in the Transvaal a thing of the future. The agricultural and pastoral wealth is dealt with in another chapter. But we may note an asset, which is wholly undeveloped, in the cultivation and protection of the natural wood of the north and east, and the planting of imported trees. Timber in an inland mining country is a valuable product, and on the soil of the high veld new plantations spring up like mushrooms. Ten feet a-year is the common rate of growth for gums, and in the warmer tracts it is nearer twenty. Many indigenous South African trees, which a few years ago, under an unwise system of timber concessions, were disappearing from most places save a few sequestered glens in the north, might under proper care become a lucrative branch of forestry. Current estimates, rough and inaccurate as they must be, are the fruit of a very general conviction, which on the broadest basis is amply supported by facts. There is sufficient natural wealth—mineral, pastoral, and agricultural—to provide a sound industrial foundation for the new States. It is only on the details of its exploitation that experts differ.

In any calculation of natural wealth there is another factor to be noted which controls production and dictates its method. Whatever the natural riches of a country may be, climate and situation must be weighed in their practical estimate. A diamond pipe at the South Pole and acres of rich soil in Tibet are practically as valueless as a fine anchorage on the Sahara coast or a bracing climate in Tierra del Fuego. In the new colonies we have throughout three-fourths of their area a climate where white men can labour out of doors all the year round. The remaining fourth is less pestilential than many places in Ceylon, Burma, and the Malay Peninsula, where Europeans live and work. There are certain very real climatic disadvantages—frequent thunderstorms, hailstorms in summer when fruits and crops are ripening, rains concentrated over a few months, a long, dusty, waterless winter. But these are difficulties which can be surmounted for the most part by human ingenuity, and at the worst they place no absolute bar on enterprise. From the standpoint of health the climate is nearly perfect, inducing a vigour and alertness of body and mind which in the more feverish life of cities may ruin the nerves and prematurely age a man, but in all wholesome forms of labour enable work to be done at a maximum pressure and with the minimum discomfort. In valuing, therefore, the natural assets of the new colonies, we need write off nothing for climatic hindrances. The situation is a more doubtful matter. They pay for their freedom from the low heats of the coast by the absence of private outlets for trade and the consequent difficulties which all people must meet who have to hire others to do their shipping and carrying. It is not the difficulty of Missouri or Ohio or other inland states in one territory, but of separate peoples, with interests often conflicting, who have to submit to weary customs and railway arrangements before their outlet can exist. This is one, perhaps the only, genuine natural limitation which all schemes of economic development must take account of.

The country is not new, and therefore in sketching its natural wealth we do not exhaust the preliminaries of the question. There are ready-made industrial conditions to be considered which may modify our estimate of the initial equipment. Such are the commercial structures already built up in the great commercial centre, which for this purpose represents the new colonies; the nature and future of the labour supply; the existing markets; the already prepared means of transit. The gold industry, as was to be expected from its nature, has fallen into the hands of a few houses. Eight great financial groups control the wealth of the Rand: the Eckstein group alone has interests which might be capitalised at 70 millions; the Consolidated Gold-fields at about 30 millions. The reason for this state of affairs is obvious. Gold-mining in the Rand fashion is a costly business, and altogether beyond the reach of the small man: claims were bought up by the financiers who were first in possession, and, since they were able to hold and develop, the entry of other financial houses has been blocked. But the great mining firms do not confine their activity to gold. They own millions of acres of land throughout the country, and many valuable building sites in the towns. Originally, doubtless, land was bought purely as a mining speculation, but they are not slow, in the absence of minerals, to make out of it what they can. These Rand houses are the bugbear of a certain class of politician. The Rand is closed to the small man, so runs the cry; a system of trusts is being created; in a little while the country will be under the iron heel of a financial ring. It is assumed that the mining firms will turn their attention to ordinary commerce, and oust the independent trader and cultivator and the small manufacturer. Certain trading experiments by some of the chief houses, and an attempt to grow food-supplies for their own employees, give a certain support to the forecast.

If the Trust system in its American form were ever to become a reality in South Africa, the obvious and infallible checks against too wide an expansion would arise there as elsewhere. A trust can only exist in full strength under its originators. There can be no apostolic succession in trust management; the second or the third generation must be on a lower scale, and the great fabric will crumble. A huge combination can only be maintained by perpetual energy and ceaseless labour, and, like the empire of Charlemagne, it will dwindle under a successor. A trust can be created but not perpetuated. No group of directors, no paid manager, can maintain the nicety of judgment and the sleepless care which alone can preserve from decay an artificial structure imposed upon an unwilling society. But in the case of the new colonies there are special reasons which make this development highly improbable. A trust flourishes only on highly protected soil, and Free Trade must long be predominant in the Transvaal. Again, while there can never be a trust in gold, the market being unlimited and beyond any possibility of control, gold-mining must remain the chief interest for any group of firms who desired to establish a trust in other commodities. Now gold-mining is one-third an industry and two-thirds a scientific inquiry. An ordinary trust is concerned less with production than with the control of the markets and the methods of distribution. But all progress in Rand mining depends on nice and speculative scientific calculation. To reduce the working costs by improved appliances, so that ore of a low grade may become payable, is so vital a matter with every great firm which is concerned in gold-mining, that the commercial or trust side, which must be concerned not with gold but with other forms of production, is not likely to be given undue prominence. Human capacity is limited, and no man or body of men can meet these two very different classes of problems at the same time. The experiments of mining firms in other trades have been due far more to the immense cost of imports and the absence of subsidiary industries than to a Napoleonic desire for consolidation. There is room, abundant room, in the Transvaal for ironworks and factories, for the private trader and the independent farmer; and the bogey of the great houses resolves itself in practice into little more than a stimulating example in progressive business methods.

The foregoing remarks do not, however, touch the question whether or not the gold industry is to remain a preserve of a few groups. If it is, there can be little real objection. The market for gold can never be controlled like the diamond-market, and there is small fear of a gold-mining De Beers dictating to the world. Moreover, the great groups are not static but mobile, constantly dividing and subdividing, throwing off subsidiary companies and adding new ones, no more monopolists than the cotton-spinners of Manchester or the shipbuilders of Glasgow. The fact remains that they own most of the mining rights in the country, and all development must lie very much in their hands. The owner of the minerals on a farm in Potchefstroom is at liberty to form a company and work them himself. But the case will be uncommon, since the bulk of the mineral rights are already absorbed, and, on the Rand system of mining, an unknown adventurer would have difficulty in raising the large initial capital. It is only in this sense that there is any meaning in the charge of monopoly. A more real grievance is that a great house will often buy up claims throughout the country and leave them unworked till it suits its pleasure, thereby hindering industrial development. This, in a sense, is true, but the reason is to be found mainly in the difficulty of development under recent conditions,—conditions which, for the matter of that, would have pressed far more hardly on the small man than on the rich firms. So far as the gold industry is concerned, the plaint of the humble citizen on this score is a little ridiculous. He asks an impossibility, and in his heart admits the folly of the request.

It is time that the anti-capitalist parrot-cry were recognised in its true meaning. On the Rand it is not the wail of a downtrodden proletariat or of the industrious small merchant whose occupation is gone. It is the dishonest agitation of a speculating class who find their activity limited by the strenuous and rational policy of the great houses. I would suggest as a fair parallel the outcry of small and disreputable publicans in a rising town where it has been found profitable to open good restaurants and decent hotels. Without capital the Transvaal is a piece of bare veld; with capital wrongly applied it is a hunting-ground for the adventurer and the bogus-promoter. The gold industry depends on capital, because only capital combined with intelligence and patience could have raised it from a speculation to an industry. But facts are the most eloquent form of apologetics. At the moment over 30 millions have been spent on development by producing companies, leaving out of account the large administrative and office expenses. How much has been spent in the same way on mines which have not reached the producing stage it is impossible to say, but the figure must be very large. To start an ordinary deep-level mine costs nearly a million before any profits are made. Surely it is right to see in an organisation which is prepared to face such an outlay some qualities of courage and patience. It is possible that the great houses may find themselves in conflict with the best public opinion on certain matters before the day is done; but it is well to recognise that the very existence of an industrial population is due to capital wisely and patiently used by the strong men who were the makers of the country.

Last in our calculation of assets comes the existing or accessible machinery of exploitation and production— the labour supply, the means of transit, the available markets. The first is a complicated matter on which it is hard to dogmatise. For some months it has been the most strenuously canvassed of South African problems. On its solution depends without doubt not only the future prosperity but the immediate insolvency of the country. And at the same time, being bound up more than other economic questions with far-reaching political interests, its solution has become less a commercial adjustment than a piece of national policy. As was to be expected in this kind of discussion, the true issues have been habitually obscured. The antithesis is not between labour and no labour, but in one aspect between the cheap, unskilled native and the dear, more highly skilled white; and in another between a limited supply, which means the curtailment of enterprise, and an unlimited supply, even of a lower quality, which would allow full development. Again, the antithesis is not absolute, as has been often assumed: the true solution may lie in a compromise, a delicate cutting of the coat to suit the particular cloths employed in its making.

It is almost entirely a mining question. In most other industries the work can be done by white men with the assistance of a few natives. In agriculture, as things stand at present, sufficient native labour can be procured, and under an improved system of taxation the supply might be largely increased, within limits. The demand in agriculture should diminish rather than increase, save in the tropical and sub-tropical regions, where native labour is always plentiful. On the high veld a single farmer, if he ploughs with oxen, wants a boy as a voorlooper and another to use the whip; but this and similar work may well be performed in time by his own sons or by white servants. Railway construction will draw heavily on the supply, but its requirements are, after all, limited and small in comparison with the immense needs of the mines. For in the latter a very large number of employees is necessary, the bulk of the work is unskilled, and the conditions under which it must be performed are frequently such as to deter the ordinary European. The case is not quite that of labour in the West Indian plantations with which it has been compared, but there are many points of resemblance. The labour, on the current view, must be cheap; it must exist in large quantities; and the work is bound in certain respects to be hard and unpleasant—not perhaps harder than coal-mining in England, but, taking into account the superior average of comfort in the new colonies, indubitably more unattractive to the local workman.

Before the war some 90,000 natives were employed in the Witwatersrand mines. The average cost was from

1s. 6d. to 2s. a-day, food and lodging being provided; but the expense of acquiring the labour considerably raised the actual price per man. The old method was by a system of touts, who were paid as much as £5 a-head for their importation. The system led to great abuses, chicanery, needless competition false promises, which often cut off the supply in a whole territory. To meet the difficulty the Witwatersrand Native Labour Association was formed, whose duties were to recruit native labour and distribute it equitably to the mines within the association. Its agents were paid by salaries instead of by results, and the various native locations in the Transvaal, Swaziland, and Portuguese territory were exploited by them. But with all its efforts the mines were inadequately supplied. The 90,000 natives barely sufficed to maintain the *status quo*, and there was no margin for new development. The war scattered the accumulated supply. The local natives grew rich in military service, and declined to leave their kraals. Those imported from a distance returned to their homes, and the whole work of collection had to begin again. In October 1902, which may be taken as a fair date to estimate the condition of things after the war, only 31,000 natives were at work, one-third of the former staff. By May 1903, after herculean efforts, the supply had increased to a little over 41,000.

The problem is, therefore, a very serious one. To return to the old state of things the present supply must be doubled; to provide for any adequate progress it must at the lowest estimate be multiplied by ten. Any wholesale increase to the mining wealth of the country must come from the exploital of the deep level and the low-grade properties. The working costs per ton of ore run from 17s. 6d. to 30s.; on the Rand the average is about 27s.[16] But the ordinary low-grade mines produce ore worth little more than 18s. to 20s. a-ton. To make their development possible the working cost must be reduced to 15s.-17s. Improved machinery may do something, but the first necessity is cheap labour. But where are the natives to come from? The efforts of the Native Labour Associations have not succeeded in showing that the need can be met from any of the old supply grounds. New taxation and the spending of their war savings may drive some of the Transvaal natives to the mines; but as the total native population of the colony is only about three quarters of a million, the whole working male force, which may be taken at one in ten, would not meet the demand. In addition to this we have the fact that no taxation would reach more than one-half of the population, and that of this half three-quarters is probably unfit for mining work. The total native population south of the Zambesi is at the present moment a little over 6 millions. Supposing this field were worked to the uttermost, we should still scarcely meet the demands likely to arise within the next five years for the gold industry alone; and such exhaustive exploitation is beyond the wildest dream of any Chamber of Mines.

The case may be stated thus. With all assistance from local taxation and from the amended organisation of the Native Labour Association, Africa, south of the

Zambesi, will be unable to afford the unlimited supply of native labour which is the *sine quâ non* of mining progress. It would therefore appear that a new ground of supply must be sought. By those who admit this (and as will appear later, there are some who do not) three solutions have been advocated, none of which is unattended with difficulties. The first is to find a recruiting-ground in the vast district between the Zambesi and the White Nile, a region more densely populated by the aborigines than any other part of Africa. This scheme has been urged by Sir Harry Johnston with all the weight of his unrivalled experience. The advantages of the solution are numerous. Those natives live directly or indirectly under British sway. They are unsophisticated, and the old rate of wages would mean undreamed-of wealth to them. Moreover, the experiment would be of a certain assistance to Central Africa, for on their return home with their wages money would be put into circulation, the standard of living would rise, taxes would be easier to collect, and Government and governed would mutually profit. On the other hand, there are very many reasons against the proposal. Uganda and Nyassaland, to take the two chief instances, are in need of labour for their own development, and will strenuously resist its exportation. Their nascent civilisation will be dislocated if they are made the hunting-ground of labour agents. Nor is it clear that the Central African native is suited for mining purposes, since both in constitution and the food he lives on he differs from his southern kinsman, and, in the opinion of many good authorities, his transplantation to the high veld would mean a swollen death-rate. Overtures have also been made to Northern and Southern Nigeria, but the answer from those territories is still more hopeless. It is too early to pronounce on the future of the Central African scheme. A fair *prima facie* case can be made out for its success, and the result of the first experiments has not been wholly discouraging. But in any case it is certain that from this source no unlimited or permanent supply can come. A modicum, perhaps gradually increasing, may be secured, and in this day of small things we can be thankful for any increase in native African labour. But great care is necessary in its working. There must be no hint of coercion; the native must be vigilantly looked after from the day he leaves his kraal to the day he returns at the end of his twelvemonth's service,—for the districts must be nursed, and it is on the report of the first batches that the success of the enterprise depends. The transport will cost money, but it is doubtful if it will work out at more per head than the old premium for importation.

The second solution has roused a storm of opposition, and its adoption would mean the overthrow of the old economics of the mining industry. It is proposed to use Kaffirs only in the deepest levels and in work unsuited for white men (for which the present supply will suffice), and in all other tasks to employ white labour. The white workman on the Rand under present conditions will be more than four times as dear as the native, costing 8s. 6d. as against the Kaffir's 2s. a-day. Many arguments to justify the expense have been brought forward, of which the weakest is that the white man can do four times the Kaffir's work. In many branches of unskilled labour he can barely compete with him. The real argument is concerned with the more general aspects of the problem. In a highly organised industry there is bound to be a higher maximum efficiency and regularity from a staff of white employees, who are working intelligently to better themselves and have certain political and social interests at stake in their labour. On political grounds, again, it is most desirable, for apart from relieving the strain on congested home districts, it would provide a feeding-ground for South African development, a material wherewith to colonise the wilds of the north. The sons of the white men would go out to farm and mine for themselves; and in two generations, when the Rand has become a normal industrial centre, we should have that interchange of population between town and country which is one of the buttresses of civilisation.

The white labour movement has roused bitter opposition, partly from the mining houses, and to some extent from white workmen on the Rand, who wish to make a monopoly of their position. Many of the arguments against the scheme need not detain us. There is no objection to white and black labour working side by side, any more than there is an objection on a tropical fruit-farm to a white man digging an orchard and a Kaffir carting manure for it, or on board ship to a white mate and a black cook being part of the same crew. The white man will have the presence of his fellows, the chance of advancement, and a higher wage to support his self-respect, which must be a brittle article indeed if it requires further strengthening. Nor is there much justification for the fears of those who see in white labour the beginning of endless labour troubles, culminating in the tyranny of the working man. The situation would be the same as in any other industrial city—as in Manchester, Sheffield, or Glasgow, where the bulk of the population are industrial employees. Strikes and lockouts will come, but it is better to have in an English city a free and vigorous English population, than to bolster up the chief industry by an exotic labour system. Besides, there is always the Kaffir as a counterfoil, a very strong argument to inspire moderation in the labourer's demands. White labour remains the ideal, the proper aim of all right-thinking men; but for the present it is more or less an impossibility. It simply does not meet the economic difficulty. Unless the Mines are content to make the *gran rifiuto*, curtail production, and play a waiting game,—a decision, as we shall see, quite as ruinous to the country as to the shareholder,—cheap labour under present conditions is a sheer necessity. One argument on economic grounds has been brought forward for white labour, which runs somewhat as follows: Expansion and development depend upon an unlimited labour-supply; white labour gives such an unlimited supply,—therefore it would pay to give four times the present wage and secure expansion rather than keep to the old scale and stagnate. Supposing a mining group to have a capital of ten millions, of which four are sunk in working mines, three held in reserve, and three invested in good but undeveloped claims. The present state of things allows of a dividend of 40 per cent on the first four millions; white labour would reduce the dividend to 20 per cent. But if white labour allowed the exploital of the unworked claims, so that a dividend of 20 to 25 per cent could be paid on the other six millions, it would be good business for the firm. It would, but it is not the problem before us. The argument assumes that the new properties are of the same class as those at present paying dividends, whereas they are in the main of so low a grade or demand such an immense initial outlay that, so far from showing a profit with dear labour, they would be the ruin of their promoters.

The third proposal is to introduce Chinese[17] labour under short-time contracts and a rigorous supervision. Its supporters argue with much reason that the Chinaman has been found useful as a deep-level miner; that he is thrifty, intelligent, law-abiding, and tolerably clean; that, supposing 200,000 Chinamen were employed in the mines, it would still mean not less than 40,000 white workers, so that white labour would increase in a liberal ratio; that a proper compound system and a strict limit to the term of engagement would secure the country against the economic dangers which threaten Australia and the United States. It is not yet certain that this ample supply of Chinese labour can be obtained, the matter being in process of investigation; but there is this to be said for the proposal, that it is the only one which touches directly the needs of the situation. The others are counsels of perfection, ends of policy on which all are agreed; this alone offers an immediate satisfaction to a very pressing want. The only argument which can be brought against it is not economic[18] but political,—that its use would endanger the success of those very aims on which all are agreed. The Chinese are the born interlopers of the world. Whatever care we take there will be a leakage: a Chinese population, more feared, apparently, for its virtues than its vices, will grow up in the cities, the small trades will be shut to Europeans, the whole standard of life for the masses will be lowered, and the moral and social currency of the nation debased. The real case, therefore, of the opponent of Chinese labour, is that it is not possible to carry out the proposed plan; that we cannot import men on a fixed contract and deport them at the end of it; that we cannot build our compound walls so high as to prevent a leakage into the outer world; that, in short, the law is too weak to do its duty. There is no difference between any of the disputants on the danger of letting the labour loose in the country; but the one side maintains that with proper precaution this peril can be averted, the other that it is like the sea when it has found an entrance into a sea-wall, a little trickle which inevitably becomes a deluge. It is not a very convincing contention, though we can respect the honest political instincts which support it; indeed, there is a touch of that familiar fallacy, the "thin-end-of-the-wedge" argument, which opposes an undoubtedly beneficent reform because of its possible maleficent extension. The conflict is between an instant economic need and a potential political danger, and, with all desire to move cautiously, the wisest course would seem to be to meet the one, and trust to the good sense and courage of the people to avert the other. The problem of alien labour is indeed becoming a familiar one to many Crown Colonies. The Colonial Office has been asked to sanction the importation of Chinamen to Ashanti, and the Rhodesian Immigration Ordinance of 1901 made the enterprise legal for Southern Rhodesia.[19] In the Transvaal there is a unique field for an experiment on sane and politic lines, and for the creation of a sound administrative precedent for other colonies to follow. There is a result, too, which may reasonably be hoped for from the provision of cheap labour which would be of direct political value. It would enable some of the smaller properties throughout the country to be worked at a profit, and so might in time redeem the gold industry from the capitalist monopoly, which it must remain under present conditions, and create a class of small mine-owners, on the analogy of the small coal-owners in England.

There is one final argument against imported labour which demands a short notice, for it has been used by many serious men who are not given to captious objections. If we take the original capital of most mines we shall find that it has been extensively watered, and that even on the nominal capital there is a huge appreciation. A mine, to take an extreme instance, begins with a capital of £50,000 in £1 shares; subsequently the shareholders receive eleven £5 shares for every £1 share, making the present nominal capital £2,750,000. The quotation of those £5 shares is, say, £10⅞, making the total capital value £5,981,250. A gold output which, under present conditions, is not sufficient to pay a fair dividend upon this capitalisation, would be amply sufficient to pay a dividend on the nominal capital, and more than sufficient to pay 500 per cent on the original capital. The question, therefore, of dividend-paying is out of all relation to the actual margin of profit on the working of a mine. The deduction is that the companies have themselves to blame, and must face a depreciation in their shares; and the unfortunate investor who has bought £5 shares at £10, believing a return of 4 per cent on his capital certain, must console himself with the reflection that every man must pay for his folly. This argument is final against any *ad misericordiam* plea of the companies, but it does not touch the heart of the question. The working of the large over-capitalised properties is one thing, and the development of low-grade properties, on which large sums have been spent and for which no profits have yet been earned, is quite another. The old well-established mines can afford to fight their own battles, and for the matter of that, in spite of their heavy expenditure out of capital during the war, are mostly paying dividends even under present conditions: the new properties, on which the future of the country depends, are not, as a rule, over-capitalised, and, as we have seen, the margin of profit is so small on each ton of ore, that the question is reduced to its bare essentials—Is it possible to mine ore worth twenty shillings at a cost under a pound? But even as concerns the richer companies the argument is scarcely valid, for it leaves out of account that not inconsiderable factor, the credit of the country. It is so essential that new capital should be attracted for the twenty different needs of development, to which any Government loan can only be a trifling contribution, that anything which tends to shake the confidence of the world in the commercial structure of South Africa is the gravest danger. Is it certain, too, that that much-abused epithet of "*bonâ fide* investor" is not applicable to the men who bought high-priced securities, not as a speculation, but as a modest investment?

It is often said by opponents of imported labour that its introduction will scarcely have taken place before an agitation will be begun for its withdrawal. So far from being an argument against the experiment, this is precisely the strongest which could be urged in its favour. If the desire of the country is for white labour, then the Chinaman can be tried with little danger. The mine-owners will find in time that work on a time contract by alien labourers is far from satisfactory, and when other circumstances permit they will no doubt readily adopt that system of free competitive labour which only a white industrial class can create. Had there been any chance of the experiment being tried with complete popular approval, then the danger would have been considerable, for the Chinaman might easily have spread from mining to all industries and trades; but since it will be made in spite of an influential opposition, and will be jealously watched by unfriendly eyes, it seems inevitable that when it has played its part it will be willingly dispensed with. By refusing to accept the experiment we are doing our best to frustrate all hopes of a white population by cramping the development of the country at its most critical time and making a livelihood impossible for many of the existing white working men. When mines are shut down because of a lack of underground labourers, what becomes of the Englishmen who work above ground? It is a significant fact that many white miners, who were formerly the most bitter opponents of imported labour, are now its strenuous advocates, since they and their class are beginning to feel the pinch.

But if the importation of Asiatics is undertaken, it should be on a very clear understanding and with a very distinct object in view. The thing is far too dangerous at the best to be made the domain of unconsidered experiments. The ideal of white labour in the long-run must be preserved; and we must take jealous care that by the creation of a foreign labouring class the way is not barred to that industrialisation of the native races on which the future of South Africa so largely depends. A maximum might be fixed by law—say 300,000 unskilled labourers, which could be increased if necessary by later enactments; and in so far as the maximum could not be attained by white and black labour, Chinese might be imported as a complement. The complement would, let us hope, rapidly decrease as new machinery lessened the amount of labour required, and the native districts of Africa were more fully exploited. All imported labour would be subject to rigorous conditions as to compounds, length of contract, and ultimate repatriation—conditions which any ordinary police could enforce without difficulty. At the same time, the Native Labour Association should be made a Government department. As a private organisation it is not more efficient, and it is certainly less respected, than a Government department would be. What is wanted in all proper recruiting is the prestige of the Crown. Natives, who have been often deceived by touts, and regard the offers of the Labour Association agents as so many idle words, would be ready enough to listen to proposals made under the guarantee of the paramount chief. It is a risky game for a Government to embark in private business; but the Native Labour Association is not a business, but a department, conducted on the lines of a Government department, but without its prestige. Under the Crown its organisation would remain intact, but its status would be raised and its efficiency centupled.

The railway system, immature as it is, has worked wonders for the country. With few lines, and those single and narrow gauge, with exorbitant rates of transit and a frequently ineffective organisation, it has still above all other factors made development possible. In former days, when heavy mining machinery had to be brought by waggons from Kimberley or Natal or Delagoa Bay, a mine required to be rich indeed before it could be worked at a profit, enterprise was costly and perilous, and the result was the stagnation of all activities save that one where enterprise was a primal necessity. Under the late Governments one line ran through the two States, from Norval's Pont to Pietersburg, with small branch lines in the Orange Free State to Winburg and Heilbron, and in the Transvaal to Springs and Klerksdorp. The Natal line was continued from Charlestown to join the trunk line at Elandsfontein, and the Delagoa Bay line from Komati Poort to Pretoria, with a little branch to Barberton and the beginnings of a branch to the Selati gold-fields. The Transvaal had thus three direct outlets to the coast; the Orange Free State two, for a branch ran from the Natal line at Ladysmith to the little eastern town of Harrismith. Two broad necessities of railway policy therefore awaited the new Government. The existing system must be perfected and interconnected, new routes to the coast created to relieve the present strain, the railways of adjoining colonies brought into touch with each other, so as to make one general and consistent South African system. But more important than the perfecting of existing arrangements must be the tapping of the rich and remote districts. Occasionally both needs may be exemplified in one line, but, roughly speaking, they are separate branches of railway policy, undertaken on different grounds and in many cases organised and financed on different methods. The experience of the United States, where railways were regarded as the cause and not the consequence of development, and pushed boldly into desert places which in a few years, through their agency, became centres of industry and population, is a safe guide, within limits, for South Africa, provided that the wealth to be exploited is really there, and railway extension does not cripple other works of equal necessity.

Of the first class we have three chief examples. One—from Machadodorp to Ermelo—is already partially constructed. The second will run from Springs east to some point on this line, and so provide a direct route for the Johannesburg traffic from Delagoa Bay and avoid the awkward circuit by Pretoria. A further extension is projected by which the Springs-Ermelo line will be continued through Swaziland to Delagoa Bay and a complete alternative through route created. The third is the extension of the present Klerksdorp branch to Fourteen Streams, which would provide a shorter route from the Transvaal to the Cape, an infinitely shorter route from the Transvaal to Rhodesia, and would at the same time bring the coal districts of the country within reach of the diamond industry of Kimberley. In the second class there is no limit to the number of possible and desirable railways. The most important is, perhaps, the grain line, from Bloemfontein to Johannesburg by Ficksburg, Bethlehem, and Wilge River, which would bring the great wheat-producing tracts of the Conquered Territory within easy reach of the chief market. Next comes the now completed Rand coal line from Vereeniging to Johannesburg. Another coal line is projected from Witbank on the Delagoa Bay line to Springs, which would bring the produce of the chief Transvaal collieries directly to the Rand and relieve the congested line between Elandsfontein and Pretoria. Of equal importance in the long-run is a line from Krugersdorp by Rustenburg to some point, such as Lobatsi, on the Rhodesian railway, which would open up a district famous for its fruits and tobacco, and give the pastoralists of Bechuanaland, as well as of the more distant Rhodesia, a straight line to Johannesburg. Other lines of the same class are those from Belfast or Machadodorp to Lydenburg, from Nelspruit to Pilgrims' Rest, and from Basutoland to Bloemfontein. Lastly, and lastly only because of its greater difficulty, the line should be continued north from Pietersburg along the Sand River, brought east between the Spelonken and the Magatoland mountains, past the little township of Louis Trichard, and then turned south across the basin of the Klein and the Groot Letaba to Leydsdorp, where it could join the completed Selati railway from Komati Poort.

The Railway Extension Conference held at Johannesburg in March 1903 sanctioned the immediate construction of most of the lines mentioned above, and recommended the others as objects to aim at when sufficient funds were at the disposal of the Government. As the share of the Guaranteed Loan allocated for railway extension is only some five millions, and as the proportion of any railway surplus which can be devoted to the purpose is, as we shall see later, strictly limited, it is highly desirable to make use of private enterprise so far as possible in new constructions, providing always for an efficient State oversight and an ultimate expropriation. The Klerksdorp-Fourteen Streams and the Krugersdorp-Lobatsi railways have already been arranged for on this principle, and it is probable that the experiment will be adopted in many of the smaller development lines. It is reasonable that a rich company, owning lands or mines, or requiring for its own purposes some special railway connection, should, if it desires a new line, undertake the financing of it. But at the same time the principle of the ultimate State ownership of all railways should be strictly adhered to, for the very good reason that in the railways we have the chief security for development loans, and the most productive of all the State assets. In few countries in the world is the expenditure on construction and maintenance so small, so that under present conditions they yield a handsome return on capital outlay. The Netherlands and the Pretoria-Pietersburg railways have been acquired from their former owners, and the incomplete Selati and Machadodorp-Ermelo lines will shortly follow. If we take the price paid, with the addition in the latter case of the outlay necessary for completion, as the capital value, we shall find that the net receipts, even after the large reductions in rates which have been made and must be maintained, show a generous percentage of profit.[20] It will be explained later what part this important asset is called upon to play in the finance of the new colonies. So much for the main lines; but a system of light railways, constructed at small expense, is vital to the mineral and agricultural exploitation of such districts as Bethel, Lichtenburg, Wolmaranstad, and Waterberg, in the Transvaal and the southern part of the Orange River Colony. In a flat upland country, where animal transport for some years to come will be precarious and expensive, where the roads are still unsuitable for steam haulage, and where coal is cheap, perfect conditions exist for an extensive light-railway development.

Railway extension, then, is one of the first demands of the country: it is comparatively easy to achieve, and most of the necessary capital has already been found for it. But the omnipresent labour difficulty appears here as elsewhere, not indeed with the magnitude of the mining problem, but with an equal insistence. To carry out the programme sketched above in any reasonable time, say three years, some 40,000 natives will be required. At the present moment the number employed is scarcely 5000, and 10,000 is the limit which the railways may recruit in South Africa by an agreement with the Chamber of Mines. Many natives, such as the Basutos, will work on railways when they will not go underground; and the agreed limit is fair enough to both parties. But the balance cannot be secured without seriously trespassing upon the supply grounds of the mines. The Uganda railway was built with imported labour, and it seems inevitable that the Central South African railways must follow suit. The limited funds at their disposal, and the difficulties in the way of the country's absorbing at the moment large numbers of unskilled workmen, make the employment of white navvies alone impossible. The railways, indeed, furnish a fine experimenting-ground for the importation of indentured foreign labour under a short-time contract and a condition of repatriation. The number they require is small: 10,000 will tide them over all immediate needs; the nature of the work enables a complete supervision to be exercised; and while it is still doubtful whether alien labour can be secured for the mines, experience has shown that for surface railway work the supply is certain. In the congested districts of

India and China the small cultivator, to whom land is the object of his life, will gladly leave his home for one or two years if he can return with the money to buy a plot of ground; and when the return home is the cause of the setting out there will be no trouble in repatriation.

The premier market, now and for many years, must be the Rand. Its great industrial population and the higher scale of living make it the natural market for all native agricultural and pastoral products. So much so that the farmers in the eastern province of Cape Colony, in spite of heavy railway rates, found it profitable to send the bulk of their produce thither. This is at once the advantage and misfortune of the country: advantage, in having an accessible market which it will take years to glut; misfortune, in that the merits of the market to the country producer mean costly living to the industrial inhabitants. The difficulty will no doubt adjust itself; for if, as all believe, the new colonies take many steps towards feeding themselves, and in consequence the prices of necessaries fall, new and nearer markets will arise in different parts of the country, and a genuinely self-supporting provincial society will be organised. New mining centres in the north and east, possibly, too, in the west, may bring new townships into being; old and semi-decayed dorps will revive; and that novelty in the new colonies, towns like Brighton or Cheltenham, which exist purely for residence, may yet be found at Warm Baths for winter, or on the shores of Lake Chrissie for the summer heats. The Rand, again, will be the chief market for the subsidiary industries which must arise,—for coal and iron, for manufactured articles and dressed produce. It is too early in the day to talk in any serious sense of exports. The Transvaal, at any rate, will be for long a consumer rather than a producer among the nations of the world.

The tremendous cost of living is the subject of the chief complaints among new-comers to South Africa. Before the discovery of gold the Transvaal was a cheap country to dwell in. A bullock which now costs £20 could be bought for £5; and a native, who now draws £3 or £4 per month in wages, was then very well content with 5s. Now there is hardly anything which is not scarcer and dearer in South Africa than in almost any other part of the globe. The causes of this high cost are partly natural and partly artificial; but all, I think, are terminable. The demands of the gold industry, the long distance from ports, the sparse rural population, are obvious natural causes, all of which tend to modification and mutual adjustment. The artificial causes are three: the cost of ocean freightage, the high railway rates, and the monopoly in the hands of a small mercantile class. The first can never be reduced below a fairly high figure, and in the loud complaint of "shipping rings," which is in the mouth of most traders, there is a little unfairness. It is too often the cloak which they use to cover their own extortions. But reductions will certainly be made, and in any case the chief force of the grievance, so far as necessaries are concerned, will decline with the growth of local production. Railway rates have already suffered a substantial decrease, and will be further reduced down to a certain point, which for the present is determined by the fiscal needs of the country. For railway rates are a form of taxation: the railways are the chief revenue producer, and to lower the rates too far would be merely robbing Peter to pay Paul—a form of relief which would need to be balanced by some new form of taxation. The chief efficient cause of the expense of living is undoubtedly the exorbitant monopoly of local merchants. It is no exaggeration to say that anything sold at 100 per cent profit is to the ordinary trader a form of charity: legitimate business begins for him at 120, or thereabouts. No class is so clamorous about its interests, so ready to identify its profits with national wellbeing, and claim a monopoly of the purer civic emotions. But no part of the economic situation is so radically unsound. The Polish Jew and the coolie make a profitable living throughout the country, not because the white population have no prejudice against them, but because they are driven to their stores by the comparative reasonableness of their prices. This cause, as I have said, is artificial and terminable. The influx of a large population will increase the area of competition, and reduce profits to a normal basis. And this, again, depends on the prosperity of the mines; so that we are brought round to the starting-point of all South African economics. Once this result were achieved its benefits would react on the mines, for with the decrease of the cost of living wages would go down, and what is at present an ideal—an increase in the area over which white labour can be employed—would come within the sphere of practical politics.

The economic situation of the two colonies is therefore composed of a number of perplexing oppositions. The one certain fact is the great hidden wealth. But to make those riches actual there must be labour, and, over and above any question of imported and indentured workmen, to secure labour there must be reasonable cheapness in the necessaries of life and work. Customs tariffs, railway rates, general taxation, must all be calculated on a modest scale. But, on the other hand, if the country is to advance to that civilisation which is its due, money must be spent freely by the State on productive and unproductive enterprises; and in addition to such services, which are the basis of the Guaranteed Loan, there is the War Debt, 30 millions of dead-weight round the neck of a struggling people. To pay the interest on debts and to provide money for day-to-day needs there must be revenue, and so there comes a point where direct and indirect charges, whatever the demands of the situation, simply cannot be reduced further if the mechanism of Government is to continue in action. Heroic persons advocate heroic remedies, such as the cessation of all enterprise in favour of mining progress, or the renunciation of certain charges in favour of cheap living. In one sense all politics are a gamble; but there are limits beyond which statesmanship cannot go in the way of staking everything on a chance, and yet hope to justify itself in the eyes of the world in the event of failure. The real problem for the statesman is not how to plunge wildly—it requires little skill to do that—but how to adjust with nice discrimination. To preserve an adequate revenue, while at the same time giving ample play to the forces of production, is, in a word, the only policy which contains the rudiments of ultimate success.

[15] The latest information available on the subject of the Transvaal gold mines will be found in the exhaustive report prepared for Mr Chamberlain by the mining engineers, and published at Johannesburg in 1903.

[16] The following are some of the working costs of the mines. Low costs: Geldenhuis Deep, 22s.; Geldenhuis Select, 17s. 6d.; Geldenhuis Main Reef, 17s. 4d.; Meyer and Charlton, 18s. 2d.; Simmer and Jack, 20s. 7d. High costs: City and Suburban, 29s. 1d.; Bonanza, 27s. 6d.; Robinson Deep, 30s. 2d. The Robinson-Randfontein group have ore of a gold value of 34s. 9d. per ton, and a profit of 2s. over the working cost. The Bonanza has ore worth £5 a-ton.

[17] Imported labour reduces itself in practice to Chinese or Japanese. Even supposing that the Indian Government consented to the strict form of indenture necessary for mining purposes, the political danger of introducing coolie labour into a country which already contains a considerable coolie population would be very great.

[18] An argument often used in this connection is that the employment of Asiatic labourers, repatriated at the end of their contract, would mean that a very large sum of money annually left the country. But the same

thing will happen if native African labour is brought from Central or Western Africa or Somaliland. It is happening at present with the natives from Portuguese territory, who form 90 per cent of the existing labour-supply.

[19] I have said elsewhere that there are few South African problems which are not long-descended. The first proposal to introduce Chinese labour was made by Jan van Riebeck, the first Governor of Cape Colony, about the year 1653. He urged the scheme with great persistence, but home opinion proved too strong for him.

[20] The cost of the acquisition of the present railway systems was roughly 14 millions. This does not, of course, represent an accurate statement of capital outlay, as in the Orange Free State considerable sums were spent out of State revenue. But even if we put the figure at the outside limit of 20 millions, the net profits are still more than 10 per cent of the capital value.

II.

The foregoing is a rough survey of the assets with which the new colonies start on their career. As in all beginnings, a multitude of questions protrude themselves. Every politician has his own nostrum, every interest its own pressing demands. But the main questions are simple, at least in their outlines, and it is permissible to disentangle from the web the chief threads of economic policy. Three postulates there must be before a solvent and progressive nation can be founded. In the first place, life must be made possible,—life on the various scales which a civilised society demands. In the second place, industries—the gold industry and the host of subsidiaries which must follow—should be given free scope for development by enlightened legislation, and the removal of burdens from the raw material of progress. Finally, a sufficient revenue must be secured to meet the vast reproductive expenditure which the country demands. To reconcile these three needs, which in practice often appear contradictory, is the task of the new Government.

Taking the three axioms as our guide, we have to consider the two questions in all administration—the raising of revenue and the apportionment of expenditure. Our inquiry into revenue must be chiefly concerned with the Transvaal. The Orange River Colony is for the present prosperous, and its future solvency seems assured. With a certain income of half a million, and an expenditure of a little less, its fiscal problem is simplicity itself. But the Transvaal presents the case of a country with great potential wealth, which must borrow heavily to elicit its prosperity. Certain revenue-producing charges must be cut down to make life on a proper scale possible, but revenue must also be raised to make this life possible. It is the old story of Egypt—taking out of one pocket to put into the other, with somewhere behind the transaction an economic Providence to enhance values in the exchange. Such a policy is based upon a faith in the land, which by its productive power provides a natural sinking fund to wipe off encumbrances. Loans can be raised at 4 per cent, because the country repays a hundredfold.

The main items, exclusive of railways, which in the financial year 1902-3 made up the revenue of the Transvaal, were customs revenue at upwards of two millions, mining revenue at half a million, stamp and transfer duties at £720,000, taxes on trades and professions and post and telegraphs at a quarter of a million each, and native revenue at a little over £300,000. The total revenue was about £4,700,000. The estimated revenue for 1903-4 has been put at £4,500,000, made up of customs at £1,800,000, mining revenue at £750,000, post and telegraphs at £360,000, taxes on trades and professions at £200,000, native revenue at £500,000, stamp and transfer duties at £700,000, and £200,000 for miscellaneous items. Since the object of the present inquiry is to estimate the financial position of the country, it is necessary in the first place to take the various sources of revenue one by one, and estimate their value and their defects. Several may at once be omitted. Post and telegraphs barely pay for their working expenses, and cannot be counted upon as a source of revenue. Stamp and transfer duties, stand licences and rent, and the bulk of the miscellaneous items, are for the present static figures, or vary within narrow limits, and it is improbable that they will be altered so as to greatly increase their present revenue during the next few years. Revenue questions for the

Transvaal are concerned with two items which far excel all others in importance—mining revenue and customs. There is a third, and the largest of the three, railway profits; but, as will be explained later, this item has been excluded from the separate budgets of the two colonies.

The old mining revenue was mainly indirect. A tax on profits was indeed imposed by the late Government in February 1899, but war broke out before there was time to organise its collection. The real burden lay in the dynamite monopoly, which at its worst increased the price of explosives by £2 the case, and at its best by about 30s. The mines required an annual supply of 300,000 cases, which meant an annual charge, beyond the cost of material, of £450,000. The average net profits on the annual production of gold may be put at £6,000,000, which, with a 5 per cent profit tax, would return £300,000 a-year. Had the Boer *régime* continued, the mining industry would have contributed in the form of imposts something between £600,000 and £750,000 per annum (for a reduction of 10s. in the dynamite charge had been promised on the eve of the war). From the standpoint of the mines the whole sum was an impost, but only the yield from the profit tax would have found its way into the Exchequer.

The present charges on the mining industry consist of the prospectors' and diggers' licences, the 10 per cent tax on profits, imposed by Proclamation No. 34 of 1902, and the cost of native passes, which was formerly paid by the native himself, but is now borne by the employer.

The mining industry will therefore on its present basis pay from half a million upwards in profit tax, about £120,000 for native passes, and about £50,000 in licences. It is difficult to see how this taxation could be fairly increased. To add, for example, a charge of 20s. per case to explosives would be to tax the means of production,—a fatal heresy,—to keep some of the smaller mines out of the profit-making class, and in the long-run to harm the Exchequer itself. The true policy is not to hamper the earning of profits by excessive charges, but to enlarge by judicious encouragement the area over which profits are made. It is of the first importance that European capital should be attracted to, and not scared away from, the country. Under the present system the Government receipts will advance *pari passu* with any increase in the prosperity of the mines, and to secure the ultimate gain one may well be satisfied to forego a larger immediate return.

There is a fourth source of revenue from mining enterprise which may be roughly described as windfalls. The Government has a moral right, which no one denies, to profit by new discoveries, and in any case, as a large landowner, it will be interested as an immediate participant. The provisions of the old Gold Law have been so often discussed in print that it is sufficient here to give the briefest sketch of them. Legislation by the late Government on precious minerals began as early as 1858, and continued in a long series of resolutions and counter-resolutions till the somewhat confused position of affairs was simplified and regulated by the famous law,

No. 15 of 1898. The basis of this law is to be found in the principle that to the owner belonged the ownership of minerals found under his land, but to the State the right of regulating their disposal. It attempted to give to both owner and State a fair share of the proceeds, while at the same time the prospector and discoverer received a moderate reward for their enterprise. There can be no question about the validity of the three rights; the only dispute is concerned with their relative proportions. Besides the matter of share, there is one other question of great importance—how far it is permissible for an owner to refuse to allow the exploital of minerals under his land.

I take the last question first. Under the old law the owner of private property could prospect without a licence on his own land, and could give authority to any licensed person. If minerals were found, the State President, subject to certain compensation, could throw open the land as a public diggings. State land could be prospected and proclaimed in exactly the same way. But if the owner of private land refused to prospect himself or allow others to prospect, the State could not interfere to compel the exploital of his minerals. Much has been said of the right of the public in the shape of the prospector to go anywhere in his search; but no such *right* has ever existed or can exist. The whole question is one of policy. It is clearly not the interest of the State to leave the chief source of its wealth unworked; nor in any real sense is it the interest of the private owner. But it would be an intolerable burden to a farmer to be subjected to constant trespass by any prospector who cared to take out a licence. We must, however, clearly distinguish between Crown and private land, so far as the steps towards the discovery of the minerals are concerned. Crown land, under strict conditions, should be free to any licensed prospector; but, as the settlement of Crown land by agricultural tenants is a vital part of Government policy, provision must be made for ample compensation to such a tenant for disturbance caused by prospecting. Such provision should refer not only to unproclaimed or hereafter to be proclaimed Crown land, but should be brought to cover areas such as Barberton, Lydenberg, and the Wood Bush, which have been long working gold-fields. If compensation and security is not provided, some of the most valuable agricultural and pastoral lands in the country will be incapable of white settlement, and their only occupants will be the Kaffir, the coolie, and the bywoner, who have no interest in creating permanent homes. It is undesirable to tie up minerals, but it is equally undesirable to tie up agricultural wealth. People have talked of proclamation as if it were an inviolable contract between the Crown and the public, to which no new conditions could be added. There is neither legal nor historical justification for this view. It is right for the Crown, having given permission to the public to go upon its lands for a particular purpose, to impose from time to time conditions under which the permission may be exercised. On private lands the case is different. No owner of a private farm who is in beneficial occupation of it (when he is not, the land should be treated for this purpose as

Crown land) should be compelled to allow prospecting unless he has already himself prospected or given authority to others. To enact otherwise would be to make a freehold title little more than a farce. But in order to prevent a reactionary or indolent owner from tying up valuable minerals for an indefinite time, when there are reasonable grounds for believing that such minerals exist, the Commissioner of Mines should have the power to give notice to the owner that he must prospect or allow others to do so, and, if he still refuses, to issue to the public a small number of prospecting licences on the property. When prospecting has taken place, and, after an investigation by the Government, minerals are found to exist in payable quantities, the area, subject to all rights of compensation, should be proclaimed a public digging.

Under the old law the discoverer, if his discovery were made at least six miles distant from a locality already worked, was entitled to mark off six claims which he could work without payment of licence-moneys. He had also the ordinary public right of pegging off not more than fifty claims in the proclaimed area, and fifty additional claims on payment of reduced licences. The only real reward to the prospector for his trouble and expense was the six free claims—hardly a sufficient inducement to undertake laborious, and often costly, enterprises. The Gold Law Commission recommended that the discoverer should receive one-thirtieth of the proclaimed area, provided that in no case such one-thirtieth exceeded thirty claims. This seems a reasonable but not extravagant honorarium to the pioneer. He would be entitled to the first selection, and would hold his claims free of licence-moneys till they reached the producing stage.

The owner, under the old law, was entitled to reserve a *mynpacht*, equal to one-tenth of the proclaimed area, for which he paid either 10s. per morgen per annum or 2½ per cent of his gross profits. He was also entitled to mark off a *werf* or homestead area, on which prospecting was forbidden; and on this, too, he could claim a *mynpacht* from the State. He was entitled to a certain number of owner's claims, which could not exceed ten. He was entitled, before proclamation, to grant to other persons a certain number of claims called *vergunnings*. Finally, he was entitled to share equally with the Government in all licence-moneys on claims, and to receive a share, varying from one-half to three-fourths, of all licence-moneys on stands. This system gave the owner about one-sixth of the whole proclaimed area,—an extravagant share, and one complicated by the curious rights into which it was divided. Such unmeaning complexity must be abolished, and one form of title — claim licences—substituted. *Werf* and *vergunning* claims should be done away with, and the owner, as the Commission recommended, be allowed to peg out one-seventh of the proclaimed area, which should take the place of *werf, mynpacht, vergunnings*, and owner's claims. The Commission has also recommended that, while the owner should retain half of the proceeds of licences, the Crown should have the right, without consulting him, to remit or reduce the licence-moneys in what appear to be deserving cases.

The State, under the old law, received all licence-moneys on claims and stands situated on State lands, and half the licence-moneys from claims and stands on private lands. It received also certain payments from the owners of *mynpachts*. This in itself should provide for a considerable revenue. But in addition the Crown should have the right of sale of claims in proved districts, where the ground has a certain value. The former method, in places where pegging was out of the question, such as along the Main Reef, was to hold a claims' lottery, a method which was neither rational nor lucrative. The sale by auction of claims in proved districts would bring in a large additional revenue and do no injustice to the prospector. But in all places yet unproved the public should be free to peg out claims and try their fortune. It is important, also, to revise the present system of licence-moneys, so as to make the licences small during the prospecting and non-producing period, and raise them when mining actually begins. Under the old law all licences were £1 per claim per month, a payment which bore heavily upon the poor prospector who was still labouring to prove his claim. Prospectors' licences were issued at 5s. per month on private land and 2s. 6d. on Government land. The Commission recommended the abolition of prospectors' licences, and the substitution of one general licence to search for minerals, on which a stamp duty of 2s. 6d. per month should be charged. When minerals are found and a public digging has been proclaimed, licence-moneys of 2s. 6d. per claim per month should be paid on Government land, and 5s. on private land till the producing stage is reached. After that date the old licence of £1 would come into force.

The Transvaal Legislature will shortly be called upon to consider a new Gold Law based on the report of the Commission, of which I have sketched the chief features. Of almost equal importance, in the light of recent discoveries, is the new Diamond Law, where substantially the same questions of principle are involved. Owner, discoverer, and State should have a fair share of profit—but especially the State. We are none too well off in the ordinary course of things to be able to afford to neglect our windfalls. A serious and permanent increase of revenue can come only from a gradual increase of producing activity; but, apart from permanent needs, many occasions will arise for capital expenditure in reproductive works which are vital to progress. A windfall is a development loan without guarantee or interest or sinking fund to burden the mind of the Exchequer.

The other direct taxes are so few and unimportant that they may safely be neglected. But it is necessary to face the question of adjustment and new taxation, for the time may come when it may be expedient to lower many of the existing duties and to revise thoroughly railway rates, and it is desirable to have alternative proposals to meet the decline of revenue which will follow. It may be desirable, for instance, to abolish wholly the present charge on dynamite, as it most certainly will be necessary to lower still further the cost of transit on the railways. But new taxation must be imposed with the greatest caution. The present population of the Transvaal pays in indirect taxes £10 a-head as against £2 at home; the field for direct taxation is therefore strictly circumscribed. To certain taxes the road is barred. A land tax, however light, would bear heavily upon the impoverished rural districts, and in any case is impossible under the Terms of Surrender. An income tax would make life unbearable if the limit of exemption were low, and if the limit were high the yield would be inconsiderable. A general profit tax on the earnings of both companies and individuals may become feasible in time, but we must first await the return of normal conditions of life. One way may be found in increased native taxation, a matter which, as it is bound up with other questions of native policy, is discussed in another chapter. But the object of all new taxation must be to strike at the untaxed and unproductive elements in society, for reasons quite as much political as economic. On this ground two taxes seem just and desirable, though there are certain obvious difficulties to be surmounted before they can be levied. The first is a tax upon unoccupied lands, a quite possible and equitable tax which would meet with little real opposition. Land companies in the Transvaal alone possess some 12 million acres, the bulk of which has been bought for supposed mineral values. Not 10 per cent of the land is occupied, and nearly 50 per cent is capable of occupation of some kind. Quite apart from revenue considerations, a tax which would compel settlement, or, failing that, would drive some of the more obstinate companies to put good land in the market, would be sound policy. What applies to the companies would apply to the private landowner who has his half-dozen farms, and lives in a corner of one of them. *Latifundia* bid fair to be among the curses of the land, unless proper measures are taken to check them in time; and if this is done, the land troubles of the Australian colonies and their confiscatory legislation will be saved to South Africa. The machinery would be simple. A permanent commission would have to be established (the judicial committee of the Central Land Board, provided for in the Settler's Ordinance, could do the work). Each owner of unoccupied land would be summoned before it to state his case. He might show that three-fourths of his land was at the moment incapable of occupation, in which case he would only be assessed on the remainder. The tax might be an *ad valorem* tax of 2 or 3 per cent. A day might be fixed, say eighteen months from assessment, when the tax would come into operation. In case owners proved refractory and preferred to pay the tax, it might be increased on a sliding scale till settlement became compulsory. There would be no hardship to company or individual, since only land for which a white occupier could be found would be assessable for the purpose. The second tax is of equal importance but far greater complexity. The most difficult person to reach in taxation is the holder for the rise, the speculator who is nothing else, the great class which toils and spins not and grows fat on the energy of others. The basis of his activity is the quotation of shares, and a tax to affect him must be in relation to such market values. You cannot introduce a too cumbrous machinery without acting in restraint of legitimate trade, quite apart from the fact that most of the business is done with bearer shares which pass through fifty hands before registration. But it might be possible—it is a problem for a revenue expert to decide—to affect this class indirectly and curtail its activity by a tax on the profits of companies based on the average quotation for the preceding year. At the best it would be only a half measure, for it would be limited to dividend-paying companies, and the energies of the middleman are chiefly exercised on companies whose profits are still wholly speculative. But with all deductions there seems to be a chance of revenue in such a tax, and a certain general economic value. The tax, again, would be limited to new issues, for in the case of old issues, even when the shares stand at 1000 per cent premium, a high dividend may represent a very moderate dividend on the capital of the investor who bought in when shares were high. If the dividend of a new issue justified a high quotation, the quotation would be high in spite of the tax, but the existence of the tax would tend to keep down the speculative quotation to some reasonable relation to former dividends. If dividends declined, and the quotation fell, the tax would go automatically out of existence. Such a tax, if possible, would not yield in normal years a great revenue, but it would have certain salutary and permanent effects. It would touch companies only in a high state of prosperity. It would indirectly touch the man who buys not for dividends but to realise by taking away in some part the basis of his speculations. It would exercise a steadying influence upon the market, and prevent, at least in one class of security, fictitious rises. But as a means of revenue its position would be really that of a windfall, for it would enable the Crown to profit largely out of any period of great financial excitement. A boom, so eagerly desired by all but in many of its results so maleficent, might be delayed by its agency; and if it came, as no doubt it would in spite of any ingenious taxation, and share values became blindly inflated irrespective of past or present dividends, the Government would perform that rarest of feats, and derive an honest profit from the vices of the multitude.

The Transvaal, till the other day, was the only important South African state not included in the Customs Union. Its customs law was No. 4 of 1894, amended by Ordinance 22 of 1902. The basis was an *ad valorem* tax of 7½ per cent on all goods brought across the border, with an addition of 20 per cent to the valuation price for the purpose of the tax in the case of goods directly imported from over-sea. The purpose of this provision is obvious, since to goods bought at the coast the cost of over-sea freightage and handling is added in reaching the price on which the tax is assessed. But to this general duty there were two important exceptions. There was a lengthy free list, which included, in addition to goods imported for Government use, all live stock, books, tree, flower, and vegetable seeds and plants, tools and effects of immigrant mechanics, fencing material, mining and agricultural machinery, cement, and unmanufactured woods. There was also a list on which, in addition to the general 7½ per cent, special duties were charged. Beer paid 3s. per gallon, dynamite 9d. per pound, gunpowder 6d. per pound, spirits from 14s. to £1 per imperial gallon, manufactured tobacco 3s. per pound, leaf-tobacco 2s. per pound (when brought from over-sea), wine from 4s. to 12s. 6d. per gallon. The tariff was therefore moderately protectionist. Most articles necessary for the great industries were free; articles of common use were subject only to the *ad valorem* duty; while articles of luxury, and especially all fermented liquors, were subject to a fair but not excessive special tax.

The difficulty was that the tariff was not a fair guide to the real taxation of imports. The Transvaal has no seacoast; all her imports have to be landed at the ports of other colonies or states, and carried to her borders by alien railways. Moreover, all the seaboard colonies, as well as the Orange River Colony, were banded together in a Customs Union, from which she was excluded. A tariff hostility was therefore smouldering on, which gave acute annoyance to the Transvaal importer. I will take two instances of purely predatory imposts. The coast colonies levied a so-called transit due of 3 per cent on dutiable articles for the Transvaal, a due which was the same in principle as the levies which the barons of the Rhine used to make from the harmless merchants passing through their borders. Again, in the case of the Orange River Colony, the only inland colony in the old Customs Union, the duties were collected at the coast ports, and a collecting charge was made, which was simply another form of the transit due. At one time the charge was as high as 25 per cent of the duties collected; but on the petition of the Orange River Colony it was afterwards reduced to 15 per cent. How far such a rate was from representing the real cost of collection is shown by the fact that the Transvaal duties were collected by the coast colonies from the occupation of Pretoria to the end of 1901 at a charge of only 2½ per cent.

The Transvaal had thus a tariff in itself reasonable, but she was embarrassed by her isolation. It was obviously desirable that she should enter into the Customs Union, which would then comprise the whole of South Africa, for if federation is ever to become a serious policy it is well to begin by throwing down economic barriers. But economics have an awkward way of overriding all other considerations, and the entrance of the Transvaal into the Union could only be a matter of hard business—give and take on both sides. The interest of the two parties was on this matter far apart. The coast colonies are agricultural and pastoral, and their ports are forwarding depots. They are frankly protectionist, and their customs have always been their chief source of revenue. The Transvaal is industrial, and for the present a free-trader; she must have cheap food, cheap raw material, cheap necessaries. While at the moment customs form the largest item in her revenue, it does not overshadow all others, and in time it is probable that it will sink to a second place. The question was, therefore, What of her present tariff would the Transvaal relinquish to meet the wishes of the Union, and what compensating advantages could she expect from her membership?

The Bloemfontein Conference of March 1903 prepared a Customs Convention, which has since been ratified by the several states, and the old Customs Union has been amended and extended to include the whole of British South Africa. How far has this act improved the economic position of the Transvaal? In the first place, there is one solid gain, the abolition of the transit dues, estimated at between £250,000 and £300,000 per annum. There is, too, a gain in the mere fact of union, and the freedom which it gives from the incessant bickerings of conflicting tariffs. Since her duties are collected by the coast colonies at the moderate charge of 5 per cent, a saving may also be effected by the reduction of the customs establishment on her borders. The benefit which she has conferred in return is the opening of her markets without restraint to the products of British South Africa, an opening which should amply repay the coast colonies for the reduction in the protective tariff from over-sea. The actual tariff charges are in the nature of an elaborate compromise. To take first the case of the simple food-stuffs. In 1898, under the old Transvaal tariff, imported flour paid in duty £26,955, and imported mealies £16,290. Under the old Union tariff they would have paid respectively £114,068 and £69,332—a difference of over 400 per cent. The old Union rate was 2s. per 100 lb. for grain and 4s. 6d. per 100 lb. for flour, while the old Transvaal rate was an *ad valorem* duty of about 9 per cent. It was impossible that either party could accept the other's rate, so the present solution of 1s. for grain and 2s. for flour may be taken as a satisfactory compromise, which an industrial country could support. It must be further remembered that all food-stuffs produced elsewhere in South Africa enter free, and that the cost of bread under the new system will be if anything reduced. Article XV. of the Convention gives the Transvaal a further power in times of scarcity to suspend the duty on food-stuffs altogether, and give a bonus to imports of the same class produced in the neighbouring colonies. The ordinary manufactured article, which in a non-manufacturing country plays as large a part in the cost of living as bread, is also reduced for the purchaser. It pays an *ad valorem* duty of 10 per cent, which at first sight seems higher than the old rate of 7½, which with other charges worked out in practice at about 9. But 2½ per cent must be deducted on account of the 25 per cent preferential rate for British goods, and with the abolition of the transit dues the actual duty will work out at between 7 and 8 per cent. Raw material and the necessaries of industry remain much where they were under the old tariff, which was highly favourable to them; but the charge on dynamite has been reduced from 9d. a-pound to 1½d., which is a reduction of over 30s. on the 50-lb. case.

A mere comparison of tariffs does not show the real cheapening of the necessaries of life; for to get at the practical effect, the abolition of the transit dues, the reduction of railway rates, amounting to at least £300,000 per annum, and the preference rate on British goods, must all be considered. Under the old tariff and railway rates every 100 lb. of flour from Port Elizabeth to the Transvaal paid 9d. to the Transvaal in duty. The freight was 6s. 2d., so that it paid altogether in charges 6s. 11d. Under the Convention the same quantity of flour will pay 2s. in duty and 3s. 9d. in railway rates, so that, in spite of the higher duty, the charge is only 5s. 9d.,—a saving to the Transvaal consumer of 1s. 2d., and a gain to the Transvaal treasury of 1s. 3d. There are many instances of a similar kind. Ordinary groceries will be reduced by about 3 per cent, paraffin by 1s. 6d. a case, grease by 2s. 6d. per 100 lb., cement by 2s. 9d. a cask. Tea and coffee, on the other hand, show a slight increase. In one branch there is a very marked increase, and an exception to the inter-colonial free trade, which is the basis of the Convention. Each party to the Union is entitled to levy on the importation of spirits distilled in and from the produce of places within the Union a duty equal to any excise duty which it may levy on spirits made within its own borders. In the Transvaal there is no excise, for the manufacture of spirits is wholly forbidden. It is of the most urgent importance to keep fermented liquors out of reach of the native population, and to suppress all illicit traffic. The importation of Portuguese spirits has been stopped by treaty, and it was clearly impossible for the Transvaal to consent to the importation of spirits on easier terms from the other British colonies. The concluding paragraph of Article XVII., therefore, provides that "where a prohibition exists in any colony or territory of the Union against the manufacture of spirits for sale, it shall be lawful for such colony or territory to levy on spirits produced within the Union a custom duty not exceeding that levied on similar spirits produced outside the Union." The duty in force is therefore from 15s. to £1 per imperial gallon in addition to the 10 per cent *ad valorem* rate; which, it has been calculated, is an increase on the former cost of from 4s. to 6s. per case.

The new Union is therefore almost wholly in the favour of the new colonies. The cost to the consumer is lessened, but the revenue does not lose appreciably, since charges, formerly diverted by the coast colonies, now go to its coffers. The coast colonies, in an admirable spirit of statesmanship, have consented to surrender a part of their revenue in order that the chief industrial market of South Africa might be open to their people—an example of that policy of foregoing certain revenues on a narrow basis for the sake of a possible revenue in a wider field which is of the essence of good government. The preference given to British goods, while still further reducing rates in favour of a large class of imports, is also a step towards federation, which does not, as such experiments are apt to do, militate in any serious way against local commerce. The one person who might complain is the farmer of the Transvaal, who sees his markets thrown open to the old grain-lands of Cape Colony; but if the long railway journey which his rivals have to face is not a sufficient handicap to enable him to hold his own, then we need not lament his fall. Vital as agricultural progress is, it cannot hope for protection at the expense of industrial prosperity.

The normal expenditure of the Transvaal may be taken roughly at £3,600,000. This figure is exclusive of debt charges, or any capital outlay on development which may be met out of revenue. It represents merely the day-to-day cost of the administrative machine. As revenue is enlarged the expenditure will follow suit; but it is unlikely that the proportion of costs to receipts, which is roughly three to four, will ever increase. On the contrary, it might be considerably reduced by a more complete administrative decentralisation. At present there are a number of isolated departments—Native Affairs, Lands, Mines—with local representatives wholly independent of each other, and responsible only to the heads of their departments. The resident magistrate, who is really an administrative official, since the legal work is done by the assistant magistrate, and who as a rule is not a lawyer, has a very narrow control over a few subjects like local government and public health. The system is wasteful both of money and energy, for the isolated departments often overlap unconsciously; and since there is no local check, the tendency is for the head of a department to increase his local staff and to vie with other heads in securing large estimates. It also means that a constant inspection has to be kept up from headquarters, and each department supports a force of travelling officials. The Indian precedent might be followed with advantage, and real heads of districts established, who would have a control, direct or indirect, over all administrative work. They should be responsible for the efficient and economic working of their district, prepare their local estimates and reports, and answer for their work only to the Governor and Council. The great departments would exist as before, but their local staffs would be much reduced in number, so far as such staffs were administrative and not intrusted with expert work. Experts, such as inspectors of machinery, customs officers, and veterinary surgeons, would remain directly responsible to their own departments, though over these also the district administrator would exercise a general supervision. In this way a very considerable saving would be effected in salaries, the unnecessarily large force of travelling inspectors could be reduced, and the friction which inevitably attends the working of isolated and independent officials in any district would be saved by the establishment of responsible heads,—deputy administrators, whose business it would be to supervise all district Government work, and control all local expenditure.

III.

The natural assets of the country and the existing fiscal system have been roughly sketched in the foregoing pages. It remains to consider what burden these two factors in collaboration are called upon to bear. In view of the peculiar situation of the new colonies, the necessity of a loan for development is sufficiently obvious. The country was desolated by war. Large sums were necessary for compensation to loyalists and for the repatriation of the Dutch inhabitants. The backward system of our predecessors had left public works ill provided for in most places, particularly in the country districts. If the wealth of the provinces, mineral and agricultural, was to be exploited, and the existing industries granted reasonable facilities for progress, a heavy expenditure was imperative for railway extension. If the rural parts were to be developed and their population leavened with our own countrymen, considerable sums must be expended on settlement, and on such reproductive schemes as forestry and irrigation. Finally, certain heavy liabilities awaited the incoming Government. To buy out the existing railways and repay certain military debts and advances from the Imperial Treasury, fully 14 millions were required. The old debt of the Transvaal, amounting to 2½ millions, which carried 4 per cent interest, must be paid off, and the capital required for the repayment made part of a new loan at an easier rate. The liabilities and needs of the country stood therefore as follows: An advance by the Imperial Government to cover the estimated Transvaal deficit of 1901-2, £1,500,000; the old debt of the Transvaal, £2,500,000; compensation to loyalists in Cape Colony and Natal, £2,000,000; the acquisition of the railways and the repayment of the existing railway debt, £14,000,000; repatriation[21] and compensation in the new colonies, £5,000,000; railway extension, £5,000,000; land settlement, £3,000,000; various public works, £2,000,000,—a total of £35,000,000. This is the sum comprised in the famous Guaranteed Loan.

But this figure, large as it is, does not exhaust our burden. During the year 1901 and 1902 the question of the contribution of the new colonies to the imperial war debt was keenly discussed both in South Africa and in England. Some fixed the payment likely to be required at as much as £100,000,000; others argued that the new colonies were likely to have so many burdens of their own that they could not be called upon to contribute at all. Moderate men on both sides saw that some contribution was equitable, but asked that it should not be fixed so high as to cripple development. There were various proposals, such as the ear-marking of certain sources of revenue and all windfalls, or the allocating of a certain proportion of any annual surplus; but such schemes were liable to the objection from the side of the Imperial Government that there was no certainty in the contribution, and from the side of the new colonies that there was no finality in the liability. The settlement which Mr Chamberlain announced in his speech at Johannesburg in January 1903 was, perhaps, the best possible in the circumstances. The contribution was fixed at £30,000,000, to be raised in three years by contributions of £10,000,000 per annum. The first 10 millions at 4 per cent were underwritten without commission by the great financial houses of the Rand, and there is no reason to doubt that if they are called to make good their guarantee, it will prove a profitable investment. It is difficult to overestimate the merit of an arrangement which tends to bind the great houses to a closer interest in the general development of the country. The War Loan was secured wholly upon the Transvaal, but there is a contingent liability on the Orange River Colony to pay a further sum of £5,000,000 out of the

Government share of any discoveries of precious stones and metals.

We have, therefore, to face a total debt of £65,000,000, of which 35 millions at 3 per cent are a charge upon both colonies, and 30 millions at 4 per cent upon the Transvaal alone. It is a heavy responsibility for a white population of a few hundreds of thousands, face to face with a labour problem. That the world at large believes in the future of the country is shown by the way in which the Guaranteed Loan was taken up, the first 30 millions having been subscribed more than thirty times over. On this loan the interest charge, with 1 per cent sinking fund, will amount to an annual payment of £1,400,000: in three years time the War Loan, unless (which is probable) it can be issued at a lower rate than 4 per cent, will mean an annual charge of £1,200,000, with no sinking fund allowed. We have therefore in front of us a possible annual payment of £2,600,000, with a slight increase in the future when a sinking fund is provided. The payment, large in itself, was made more difficult by the circumstances of the two colonies. The larger loan is secured on both, but while the Orange River Colony had a fair claim to a considerable part of the proceeds, it was clearly impossible that she should pay a share of the charge proportionate to her receipts. If she shared in the loan only to the extent of the annual contribution which on her small revenue she could afford, many important public works both of land settlement and railway extension would have to be abandoned. Joined with this general administrative difficulty, there was a departmental one connected with the railways. The main line through the Orange River Colony had acquired, as one of the main feeders of the Transvaal, a purely fictitious value, and the Orange River Colony profited greatly by the receipts. But to have within one system two types of line, one a through line simply, the other connected directly with the great centres of production and consumption, and to have those two types of lines used as revenue-producing agents for two different administrations, was to make a consistent railway policy impossible. The country of the through line, whose fictitious value produced a very real revenue, would reclaim against reduction in rates for the benefit of the other.

Both difficulties have been met by a very ingenious scheme. The Inter-Colonial Council of the two colonies, created by Order in Council of 20th May 1903, is significant in many ways, notably as the first overt step towards federation; but for the present we may look upon it purely as a financial expedient. Two important departments, common to both colonies, were placed wholly under the administration of the Council—the Central South African Railways and the South African Constabulary; and a number of minor common services, such as surveys and education, were added, and power was given to the two legislatures to increase the number when they saw fit. A Railway Committee of Council forms the permanent controlling authority in all railway matters. All net profits of the railways in each year are assigned to Council to form its revenues. Out of these it has to meet the expenditure of the Constabulary and the minor common charges, as well as the annual charge and management costs of the Guaranteed Loan.[22]

The financial duties of the Council are therefore twofold. It has the entire administration of the Loan in its hands, it provides for its apportionment among the different services, and it undertakes the payment of its charges. It has also to meet the administrative expenditure of the common departments intrusted to it, and for this purpose it receives the net profits of the chief revenue-producing asset of the two Governments. The first duty is comparatively simple. A body composed of official and unofficial representatives of the two parties to the Loan can allocate speedily and equitably without the constant strife and jealousy which would attend the interference of two different publics. But the second duty, which is concerned with the annual inter-colonial budget, constitutes the index or barometer of the new colony finances. The Budget for 1903-4 shows the following figures: on the revenue side, £2,350,000 from the net railway receipts; on the expenditure side, £1,441,000 for the service of the Guaranteed Loan,[23] £1,520,000 for the Constabulary, and about £70,000 for minor common services. This leaves a deficit of about £680,000, which, according to the term of the Order in Council, will be met by contributions from the Transvaal and the Orange River Colony in proportion to their customs receipts—roughly, £600,000 from the first, and £80,000 from the second.

Let us take the revenue side of the Budget first. The position of the railways is anomalous. They are virtually a taxing-machine, and in this respect the most effective of Government properties. The normal position of a Government railway should be that of an institution worked for the public benefit, the receipts being little in excess of the working costs plus a moderate interest on the capital involved. In this railway system the net profits, as we have seen, are estimated for next year, allowing for the half-million decrease from the reduction of rates, at £2,300,000. No doubt it is economically unsound to levy a tax of such magnitude on what is virtually a necessity of life and a constituent of production. But bad economics may be sound statesmanship, if they are recognised as unsound—a temporary expedient to obviate a more serious difficulty. Railway profits are the buttress of inter-colonial finance: without them there is no satisfactory provision for the debt charges, and some form of direct taxation, which would interfere far more effectively with nascent industries, would be the only resort. The rates have been already reduced so as to provide, along with the new customs tariff, for a very real decrease in the cost of living. They will be still further reduced, always keeping a limit in view which is calculated on fiscal needs. To so adjust the rates that industrial and rural development will not be hindered, and at the same time to provide an adequate revenue, presents a very pretty problem in railway finance. It is the problem in the customs; it is the problem in direct taxation; it is the essence of the economic problem of the country. But with all reductions there is a good chance of railway revenue increasing. The 5 millions of the Loan which go to development will in a year or two bear fruit. It is difficult to see how the net profits can ever fall below £2,100,000, while it is not unreasonable to hope that in a few years they may rise to £2,500,000 or £3,000,000.

But while the revenue side is likely to increase, the expenditure side of the Budget will inevitably decline. When the full loan is raised the annual charge will be £1,408,000, a stationary figure till the loan is redeemed. The Council is a genuine *Caisse de la Dette*; its revenues are charged in the first instance with the loan charges, and the liability of the separate colonies to make up any deficiency distributes the weight of the debt equitably among the parties to it. The danger of a *Caisse*, that it tends to check general prosperity by a too arbitrary appropriation of revenue, is avoided by the very strict conditions of the Council's power and the nature of its constitution. The minor common services will not increase, and they may very probably decrease, as such branches as surveys and permits shrink to normal limits. The large item of 1½ million for the Constabulary will be lowered in future to about £1,200,000, which, on the present establishment, must be regarded as a final figure. We may, therefore, take £2,500,000 as the average expenditure in two years' time, which, if railway receipts increase to a like figure in the same time, would make the Inter-Colonial Budget balance.

In the meantime the Transvaal is able to pay any contribution which may be required from her. But in two years all or the greater part of the War Loan will have been raised, and she may have to face a maximum annual charge of £1,200,000, which contains no provision for any sinking fund. In these circumstances, on her present revenue she could pay nothing towards any inter-colonial deficit: she might even have to ask for a contribution. There is every probability that such help could be given, and an automatic system of adjustment might be framed by which any inter-colonial surplus could go to pay the charges or assist in the creation of a sinking fund for the War Loan. This is of course on the most unfavourable assumption,—that the War Loan has to be raised at 4 per cent, that the present industrial depression continues, and that the Transvaal gets no increase of revenue from that prosperity which she has a right to expect. It is far more probable that the Council will be free to devote any surplus it may show to the development of the common services, for which the Loan provision cannot in the long-run be found adequate.

[21] This figure does not cover the expense of repatriation. There was a free gift for the purpose of £5,000,000 by the Imperial Government.

[22] The Council is composed of the High Commissioner and Governor (President), the two Lieutenant-Governors, the Commissioner of Railways, the Inspector-General of the South African

Constabulary, two official members for each colony, nominated by the Lieutenant-Governors, two unofficial members for each colony, elected by the unofficial members of the two legislatures, and two members nominated by the Secretary of State.

[23] These figures require a word of explanation. Only 30 millions of the loan have been issued, so the charge for interest and management should only be £1,208,000; but as the loan year began in May and the financial year for the budget began in July, interest and management charges for fourteen months were included.

IV.

It is idle to deny that the present is a period of financial strain. The new colonies are solvent, but the margin is narrow. Like everything else in South Africa, their finances are on a needle-point, and require strenuous intelligence and constant economy. I have taken the railway profits and customs receipts as incapable of falling below their present level; but it is to be remembered that the past year is not a fair basis for prophecy, since the country has been in process of reconstruction, and the heavy importations for the purpose have swollen receipts in both departments. If industrial progress is still retarded, both figures will sink enormously, and the whole system of finance sketched in the preceding pages will require revision. If, on the other hand, progress is assured, both figures will increase largely, since, while this basis is high as compared with the present situation, it is low compared with any real prosperity. In this case the strain will be of short duration. *Ce n'est que le premier pas qui coûte.* Industrial development lies at the root of all things. The Transvaal can only hope for a large permanent increase of revenue from the licences and profit tax paid by the mining industry and from Customs receipts drawn from a wider basis of population. Unless this increase comes she may be unable to meet her own war debt, or to contribute anything to an inter-colonial deficit. Inter-colonial revenues, too, can only expand from the same cause, for mining prosperity is at the bottom of railway profits. The State finances depend upon mining development, and mining development depends on labour: this is the true statement of the problem, and all others are involved in a vicious circle. And this is as it should be. On the great industry of the country the chief burden must lie.

There is, of course, the possibility of windfalls. From the Crown share of gold and diamond properties very large sums of money may from time to time flow to the Exchequer. But it is the part of a prudent finance minister to base his forecasts on the normal only, and to accept windfalls as gifts of Providence, to be used for special purposes. It may be necessary to draw upon this source of income to meet the debt charges; but, should this misfortune be spared us, then we have in such windfalls the nucleus of a reserve fund for development. There is need, as we have seen, of a capital outlay on development far beyond that provided for in the Guaranteed Loan. Railway extension alone, before we have done with it, will need not 5 millions, but 10, and, in cases where new lines are built by private companies, we shall have to face sooner or later a considerable expenditure on expropriation. Public works, when all the loan moneys have been spent, will still be badly provided for. It may be necessary, too, to spend money in expropriating land for public parks, for game preserves, for public buildings, for new townships,—expenditure which in the first instance will fall upon the Government. So, too, with other schemes,—irrigation, the search for artesian water, the establishment of colleges and technical schools, and all the thousand activities of government in a new country, which will grow quickly and develop early a multitude of needs. Lastly, land settlement in the two colonies, if it is to serve the social and political purpose which is its chief justification, demands more than the 3 millions allotted to it. Such expenditure is in the fullest sense an investment, since the bulk of it will be returned in time to the Exchequer with a reasonable interest. It is proposed that, in so far as repayments of capital from settlers are concerned, such repayments should form a special fund, which can go out again in fresh advances and further purchases of land. In this way a permanent fund for settlement will be created, and the project will not be dependent upon a share of any annual surplus.

The economic problem of the new colonies finds a parallel in Egyptian reconstruction in more ways than the analogy of the *Caisse de la Dette*. There is the same undeveloped wealth in the country, the same heavy bondage of debt, the same demand for reproductive expenditure. To cut down the cost of living and the restraints on production, and at the same time to provide money for development and for the charges of an unproductive debt, is the threefold South African problem, as it was the Egyptian. Solvency here, as there, is to be found in an equipoise, and requires a nice and discriminating statesmanship rather than any heroic cutting of knots. In most respects the Egyptian difficulty was far the greater, for there the cast-iron debt regulations and the endless European surveillance frustrated at every turn the efforts of her statesmen. But one danger was absent. In Egypt patience and diplomacy, faith in the country and in the work of time, were so obviously the only cards to play, that, while there were many temptations to lose heart and abandon the struggle, there was no inducement to try short cuts and forsake the true path of policy for those showy and unconsidered measures which in the rare event of their success are called heroic. In South Africa the amateur financier is so abroad in the land that we may look to find many odd nostrums advocated to ensure prosperity. The kind of discussion which arose over the labour difficulty is a guide to what we may expect in the realm of high finance. But in both the one and the other the real problem is plain once the obscuration caused by conflicting interests is cleared away by a little common-sense.

The great questions of economics in relation to state growth are always simple. If high finance means anything it is the power of adding two and two together. Complicated financial adjustments belong to a lower plane: the great financier may have no aptitude in reducing results to a decimal. But there is this distinction, that whereas in the intricate calculations of secondary finance the figures are mere counters, the elaboration of accepted data, in the higher and simpler finance they are symbols. To the statesman they are the gauge of prosperity or decline, and behind them stand the millions of workers, the miles of crops, the floods and droughts and pestilences, the rise and fall of industries, the ore in the mine, the web in the factory, the cattle in the stockyard. The yield of a land tax is to him not a figure but a symbol, and in using it he has regard not only to its formal place in estimates and returns, but to its political meaning. It is, if you like, the quality which in other spheres constitutes the distinction between statesmen and high permanent officials, between economists and statisticians, between all leaders and all subordinates. In the finance of a country which is still in process of reconstruction, this power, so uncommon and so inestimable, of getting behind figures to facts, and keeping the hand on the pulse of national progress, is the only guarantee of ultimate success. In this light the prospects of the new colonies give good reason for hope. The budget of to-day, formally regarded, shows a delicate equipoise, in which a pessimist might find material for dark forebodings; but it is only the symbol of that stress of re-creation which must precede an ample prosperity.

CHAPTER XIII.

THE SETTLEMENT OF THE LAND.

I.

To the Boer the land was the beginning and end of all things: a town was only a necessary excrescence, an industry an uitlander whim. A land policy is therefore one of the first burdens which attend our heritage. Happily we are not seriously impeded by the wreckage of systems which have failed. The Boer Government had no land legislation, and the few laws, such as the Occupation Law of 1886, which touched on the question, were less statutory enactments than administrative resolutions. The Boer farmer, or his father, secured his land when the country was unoccupied, and he had merely to arrange the boundary question with friendly neighbours. He held it on freehold title, with no reservation of quit-rent to the Government. When the existing population had thus been settled, the balance of unoccupied country fell to the State; and this was further parcelled out by grants to poor burghers, doles for war service, establishment of native reserves, and in the wilder districts by the system of occupation tenure. But in spite of all grants a considerable portion remained State territory—over 44,000 square miles in the Transvaal, of which at least 19,000,000 acres are unsurveyed. In the Orange River Colony the State lands are smaller, not exceeding, with all recent purchases, 1,400,000 acres. The land question in the two colonies is therefore of the simplest: the best farms, including most of the rich pockets of alluvial land, are the freehold possession of a small number of Dutch farmers; the balance is the more or less encumbered perquisite of the State.

The condition of agriculture in the two colonies was primitive in the extreme, a truth quite independent of the question whether such elementary methods were not the only possible. The first comers were pastoralists and nothing more, coming as they did from the great pastoral regions in the north of Cape Colony. The average farm was laid out for stock, and was rarely less than 6000 acres. On the old estimate eight acres was required for each head of horned cattle and two for each sheep. The Boer was not an advanced stock-farmer in any sense of the word. He found certain diseases indigenous to the country which he did not seriously attempt to cope with. He rarely fenced his stock-routes and outspans or endeavoured to improve the carrying capacity of the land by paddocking. The high veld in winter is burned brown by sun and wind and nipped by frosts, so that it gives little sustenance to stock; but the rich vegetation in summer should have provided, by means of ensilage, ample feeding for the winter months. This simple device was never used, and when the grass failed the Boer trekked with his herds to his low-veld farm, whence he frequently brought back the seeds of disease in his animals. In the quality of his stock he was equally backward. In the Afrikander ox he had the makings of one of the hardiest and strongest draught animals in the world. In the Afrikander pony he had the basis of a wonderful breed of riding-horses, to whose merits the late war has sufficiently testified. He never seriously tried to improve one or the other. Stallions of wretched quality were allowed to run wild among his mares, and he had no system of culling to raise the quality of his herds. The market for his beef and mutton was small and uncritical, so that the amassing of animals became with him rather the sign visible of prosperity than a serious professional enterprise.

At first the Boer did little more than till a garden. On each farm there was a certain water-supply, and around the spruit or fountain a pocket of alluvial land. The ordinary soil, both in the Transvaal and the Orange River Colony, is, with some remarkable exceptions, poor and easily worked out; but those alluvial patches are so rich as to be practically inexhaustible. The Boer and the Kaffir shared one gift in common, an infallible eye for good country, though there was this difference between them that the Boer chose the heavy river-side lands, while the Kaffir, who was a shallow cultivator, preferred as a rule the lighter slopes where he could pick with ease. In 1885 the Boer farmer did little more than irrigate his garden; but the increase in the population of the towns, and the growth of a market for cereals, fruits, and vegetables, made him extend his irrigation farther, so that in a few years the whole of his alluvial pocket was under water. Formerly he had been a pure pastoralist; now he became also an agriculturist, and after his fashion a narrow-minded one, for irrigation, which was his first successful experiment, was at once exalted by him into an axiomatic law. The Kaffir, who in his way is a skilful farmer and an experimentalist on a far wider scale, believed in dry lands; but the Boer confined himself to his irrigation and his summer and winter crops. Two views have been promulgated on the Boer method. One is, that it is the true and only type possible in the country, discovered after long years of intelligent experience. The Boer, it is said, is unprogressive, because he knows the limitations under which he works, and all new-comers who have begun by trying new methods have sooner or later fallen into line with the old inhabitants. The supporters of this view point to the scarcity of English farmers in the land who have made a success of their farms on any other than the Boer methods. There seems to be no real justification for this opinion. The Boer has no settled principles of farming; he is an experimentalist in practice, whatever he may be in theory. We have seen that he began as a pastoralist, advanced to be also a gardener, and is now a cultivator of lands under irrigation. In some twenty years, had he been allowed to develop unchecked, he would doubtless have come round to the Kaffir view of the dry lands. Fifteen years ago the country store-keeper stocked only the old single-furrow wooden plough: to-day on Boer farms you may see double-furrow steel ploughs, disc ploughs, disc cultivators, not to speak of such elaborate farm machinery as aermotors, reapers and binders, steam chaff-cutters, and in some few cases steam-ploughs. The more progressive Boers have changed utterly their methods of orchard-management, and at the present moment they are reconsidering their methods of tobacco-growing. The point is important, because if the Boer has really found out long ago the limitations of the soil and the only principles of farming, then so far from deserving the name of unprogressive he has shown himself eminently wise. But the theory of Boer stability is a chimera. He changes every year in his attitude towards the soil,—changes unwillingly, it may be, but certainly; and though a few dogmas take a long time to alter, they alter in the end. It is equally incorrect to argue from the absence of successful immigrant farmers on progressive lines. They were few in number, because in a country where the rural population was mainly hostile, the new-comers who began by farming ended as a rule by drifting to the towns. But, to cite one case, mealies have been grown on dry lands on the American plan with great profit to the farmer; and the German tobacco-planters in the north have shown how profitable fruit and tobacco growing can become, if conducted on principles rather than on tradition.

But it is as great a mistake to regard the Boer farmer as utterly without capacity. He had no need to bestir himself. He lived simply and supplied his own modest needs. He saw his farm going up in price through the general appreciation of land values, and he sold a bit now and again and increased his herds; or he might receive a large sum for the option on the minerals under the soil. He was cheated by the country store-keeper, and he rarely attempted to reach distant markets. The old vicious system of allowing natives to farm on his land in return for a certain amount of compulsory labour—a system unchanged by that abortive piece of law-making, the Plakkerswet—made him unthrifty and improvident. He had no labour bill to cast up, no financial position which wanted investigation at each year's end. Hence the difficulty of framing any accurate forecast of the prospects of farming in the new colonies: there are no statistics to follow, no scale of values for land or produce. But the Boer had an empirical science of his own. He knew exactly the capacity of his irrigated land, though he never thought of formulating his knowledge. He had many rough and effective precautions against blight and disease, and he had a kind of gipsy veterinary skill. He was not industrious, but I think he must be allowed the credit of having done his best for the land on his own principles. He was a great buyer of new farm machinery, partly perhaps out of curiosity, and on this point at least his conservatism was not consistent. Some of his methods were based on common rural superstitions—for example, he always sowed, if possible, at the full moon. His habit, too, of seeking a theological explanation of all misfortunes was destructive of energy. When the locusts or the *galziekte* came he lit his pipe and said it was the will of God, a visitation which it would be impious to resist. Hardly, perhaps, the proper attitude for success in this modern world, but under his peculiar conditions he never felt its folly. It is impossible to believe that the Boer has done justice to the country, but we may readily grant him skill and good sense in the narrow world in which he dwelt.

The land problem in the new colonies is partly political and partly economic, and on the solution of the latter branch of the question the former largely depends. There are urgent reasons why an English population should grow up on the land; but unless this population can make a profitable living it would be folly to encourage its immigration. On this economic question it is impossible to dogmatise. Data, as I have said, are lacking and have never existed. At the best we can frame some sort of tentative answer—a hope rather than a promise; and we are justified in this course because those who attack the policy have no better argument to offer.

Before the war the ordinary farmer sold his stock and his produce at fair prices in his country town. The bulk of it, together with the produce which the more enterprising farmers sent direct, went to Johannesburg, where on the whole high prices were maintained. So good were the prices that the farmers of the eastern and western provinces of Cape Colony found it profitable, notwithstanding customs and heavy railway freights, to make Johannesburg their chief market. But in spite of all local production, Johannesburg was not fully supplied. Food-stuffs in large quantities had to be imported from abroad. In 1898 agricultural produce, raw and manufactured, to the value of nearly £2,500,000 was imported into the Transvaal. Arguing on these facts, many have predicted a rosy future for all branches of South African farming. What has been imported, they say, can be grown; the mining industry will advance, and agriculture will follow with equal steps. But such rudimentary hopes can scarcely be held to exhaust a very complicated and delicate problem, to which some answer must be suggested before any needs of policy can be thought of. There are two questions to be met: How far is the land capable of intensive and sustained production? and, granting the capacity, what guarantee is there of profitable markets?

The soil of the new colonies, as I have said, is sharply divided into alluvial pockets and dry lands,—the former highly cultivated, the latter, except for Kaffir locations, mainly neglected. But since for one alluvial acre there are a hundred dry morgen, the progress of the country may be said to depend upon the dry lands. It follows that pasturage must remain the staple form of farming. The bulk of the dry lands are light and thin in soil, and the natural humours of the ground have been much exhausted by the unthrifty habit of veld-burning. But in spite of all drawbacks it is a country of abundant summer grass, both sweet veld and sour veld, which is capable of great improvement by any proper system of paddocking and depasturing. Large quantities of veld grass might be cut for winter fodder, and roots and forage crops could be grown in summer for the same purpose. Farms, which at present carry an ox to every eight acres and a sheep to every two, might be made capable of supporting a vastly greater stock. But there are certain drawbacks to stock-farming peculiar to the country, the chief being the number of diseases indigenous and imported. At the present moment to bring in valuable stock to most districts of the new colonies is a dangerous experiment. Horses die of horse-sickness, sheep of scab and anthrax, cattle of rinderpest, red-water, and the immense variety of *ziektes* from *galziekte* to *gielziekte*. Before the new colonies can advance to the rank of great pastoral lands which is their right, vigorous methods must be taken to stamp out diseases wherever they appear, and to take precautions against their recurrence. The country must be fenced, stock-routes and outspans must be established and guarded, and a stringent Brands Act must be passed to give security to the stock-owner in a country where stock is notoriously prone to vanish.[24]

Given good laws, adequately administered, the Transvaal and the Orange River Colony may well become countries of large and prosperous stock-farms. Here, it has been argued, the matter ends. Agriculture must confine itself in most cases to the growth of domestic supplies and winter forage. I cannot, after a careful examination of most parts of the country, bring myself to accept this view. Much may be done by irrigation to increase the area of land under water. Sir W. Willcocks' Report[25] proposes to give to South Africa 3,000,000 acres of perennially irrigated land at a cost of about £30,000,000; but as he argues for the undertaking on the basis of certain doubtful land valuations, this large estimate may have to be considerably modified. Unirrigated land, he says, varies from 2s. 6d. to £3 per acre: irrigation costs from £7, 10s. to £15 per acre; and the price of good irrigated land runs from £20 to £100.

On this reasoning there is room for a handsome profit, but the argument is based rather on fictitious market values than on the intrinsic normal producing power of the soil. At the time when Sir W. Willcocks' Report was written—the last year of the war—land values were inflated, and the prices of produce grown under water were extremely high. In the average year for which we must provide little irrigated land will be worth to the farmer more than from £5 to £10 per acre, and certain irrigation schemes which, on Sir W. Willcocks' showing would return a profit, would in reality spell ruin to their promoters. Irrigation is necessary on a certain scale for a reason which we shall discuss later; and in many cases it could be effected at a moderate cost. But expensive irrigation works for agriculture alone are, I believe, of doubtful wisdom in almost every part of the country. What is of infinitely greater importance is the procuring of water in the dry tracts by tanks, wells, and, if possible, by artesian bores. Vast stock districts in Waterberg and Lichtenburg would have their value quadrupled if a permanent supply of water, even for stock purposes only, could be procured. The Australian method of tank-sinking has already been followed with success in the Springbok Flats, and it is at least possible that artesian water may be found. Everywhere the soil contains water at a low depth, which percolates through the porous rock, and is brought to a stand by dykes of harder stone. Hence has arisen the old African fiction of underground rivers, which is true to the extent that no man has far to dig before he finds water. It is rather with such tank- and well-sinking that a water expert should deal, and with the regulation of the present ridiculous apportionment of water rights. No serious work can be done in this department till the State assumes the right of distributing water, and has it in its power to prevent the riparian owner from following an obstructive course to the detriment of his neighbours. Irrigation in a few cases should be followed, and a greater portion of land brought under water in the interests of mixed farming; but it is in another direction that we must look for the sheet-anchor of South African agriculture.

The rainfall of the new colonies is generally well distributed. Copious rains fall from September to April, and then come the four dry and windy months of winter. On irrigated lands summer and winter crops are grown; on dry lands a summer crop only. But the Boer believed that the crops which he could grow on dry lands were very limited, and he habitually grew mealies, potatoes, lucerne, and tobacco under water. It is, of course, a great advantage to reap two crops a-year; but if a man can get two crops from 5 acres only and one crop from 500, this one crop, on ordinary principles of common-sense, should command his chief attention. Deducting the greater expense for labour, the one crop is still thirty or forty times as important as the other two. This is roughly the agricultural problem of the dry lands. They have never been really exploited. The Kaffir has picked at the edges; a few progressive farmers have made good profits by growing mealies and tobacco dry on the American plan. But it was much easier to potter about with a water-furrow than to attempt to plough the dry and unbroken flats. Dry-land farming is therefore pioneer farming, and pioneering with a good hope of success. Granted the markets, there is no reason why great tracts should not be ploughed from end to end, and a huge crop of cereals and roots raised yearly. Steam-ploughing and every labour-saving device will be necessary, for this is farming on the grand scale. The outlook is made brighter when we realise that those despised dry lands are some of the richest in the country. The famous Standerton black soil, the environs of Middelburg, part of the Bloemhof and Klerksdorp districts, and, above all, the Springbok Flats,[26] where there may be half a million acres of the richest black soil 12 feet deep, and another half million acres of excellent red soil—such are a few instances of lands which await an early development.

There is still another aspect of this problem which concerns a small group of semi-tropical products—fruits, tobacco, rubber, coffee, and, possibly, cocoa. There are tracts which have proved themselves to be as highly fitted for such crops as any in the world. They are crops, too, for which the acreage required is small, and whose value is so high in proportion to bulk that the freightage does not seriously detract from profits. Given, again, the market, and there is no reason why the present yield should not be centupled.

The market—that is the rock on which arguments divide. The rosy hopes of the market to be furnished by the Transvaal which some minds entertained during the war have given place with many to an equally fantastic pessimism. I do not propose to provide a tabulated statement of costs and prices. I have seen such statements arrive by the clearest reasoning at opposite conclusions. But it is worth while to consider soberly what are the market prospects in the future for the farmer of the new colonies. A comparison of imports gives little assistance. In the year 1902 the raw agricultural produce imported into the Transvaal, all of which might be locally produced, was worth over 2 millions sterling; and the imports of manufactured and partially manufactured produce, the bulk of which might be produced and manufactured locally, came close on another million. These figures may be taken as below normal, since supplies for the army of occupation are not included, and at the same time the number of inhabitants in the towns and natives in the mines were largely below the ordinary figures. On the other hand, little agriculture existed, and practically all supplies for the existing population, such as it was, had to be brought from the adjoining colonies or from over-seas. On this basis, therefore, there is a considerable and highly profitable market for the limited agriculture and pastoral enterprise of the country. But in framing any forecast two new factors must be taken into consideration. If the towns are to develop, the cost of living must be greatly reduced; which means in the first instance that all ordinary food-stuffs must be imported free of duty and at cheap railway rates. Again, when all the Boer farmers have been resettled on their lands and a multitude of new-comers occupy Crown farms, the local agricultural output will be very largely increased. The farmer, who at the moment can sell his garden stuff, his crops of potatoes, mealies, and forage, and his stock at a good profit, will find himself faced by over-sea produce, grown wholesale under the most favourable conditions, and sold at a price with which he cannot compete and live. This is, I think, a true forecast—for the small improvident farmer. The man who grows mealies on a large scale with labour-saving appliances, or who has a well-managed stock-ranch, will make a profit on wholesale dealings. In agriculture and pasturage, as in other activities, Providence is on the side of the bigger battalions, and the small man who grows on an expensive scale will be pushed out by the large man who grows economically. Prophecy is an intricate task, especially on land questions, but it seems clear that the only class who will not have to dread to some extent a change in present conditions, a cheapening of the means of life, and the influx of a large agricultural population, will be the wholesale farmers and pastoralists, who follow the methods of over-sea producers and enjoy the advantage of living at their customers' doors.

But this does not exhaust the question. Is, then, the small holder of 100 or 200 acres, or the owner of a mixed farm of 1000 acres, to become extinct in the land? It depends entirely on themselves. In districts such as Waterberg, Zoutpansberg, and Barberton, the holder of 50 acres under water will be able to put vegetables and fruit on the Rand market a fortnight before any other grower in the world. His price is assured beyond doubt; and if he may find little profit for six months in the year, he is in no worse case than many prosperous market-gardeners in Kent and Surrey. It is here that the value of irrigation appears. Such a small holder, again, may be able to make a profit from dairying all the year round, provided local creameries are established, and he goes the proper way about it. So, too, with mixed farming, of which the essence is that one product can be set off against another. If a farmer finds cereals unproductive, he can put part of his land into pasture; it is unlikely that the price of meat will fall below a paying point, granted the expected industrial development. In addition there are certain crops, such as tobacco, where the profits, even allowing for a large decline in present prices, are great, the freightage small, and the market worldwide. The aim of mixed farming is to provide an elaborate system of alternate schemes, which between them will preserve a fairly permanent average of profit.

The basis of all farming prosperity is the growth of the mining industry and the creation of new industries. Any attempt to protect farming by tolls or imposts is foredoomed to a miserable failure. Sink, if necessary, farming considerations altogether for the moment; look only to mining development, if need be; abolish the old market prices and ruin the old local producer: it is all good policy, and in the long-run the true agricultural interest. When the present fictitious basis is got rid of, the true and lasting agricultural prosperity may begin. There seems no reason to doubt that in the future there will be a sound local market for the large producer, for the favourably situated small holder, and for the judicious farmer of mixed land. Nor is there any reason why in time a considerable export trade should not be established. As the great produce-exporting countries of the world grow more populous, South Africa may yet play its part in feeding Europe. With improved internal communications, and thousands of miles of fine pasture land, there is no reason why, a fortnight nearer Europe than Australia, she should not take her share of the frozen-meat traffic of the world. In tobacco, again, to take only one instance, a very considerable export trade may arise. The soil is well suited; the rough leaf, grown on the most unscientific method, is as good as anything produced by Virginia and Borneo. The large tobacco-growers, or the small holders attached to a tobacco-factory, may very well find a profitable outlet for their wares abroad, and the English manufacturers discover a new producing ground in a British colony with which to resist the attacks of transatlantic combines.

The farming prospects in the new colonies, even if stripped of all fanciful stuff, are sound and hopeful. There may come bad times for all. The ordinary market-gardener will for a certainty find himself poorly off five years hence; and all classes may have their periods of stress and despair. Such visitations are part of the primeval curse upon tillers of the soil. The New Zealand and Australian pastoralists had sunk very low before the discovery of cold storage saved the situation. The Ceylon planters, after the coffee blight, seemed on the brink of ruin, when the introduction of tea-growing more than restored their former prosperity. An immunity from farming risks can no more be guaranteed in the new colonies than in other countries. The real question is, Can they offer the settler no greater risks than he has to face elsewhere, and at least a fair chance of greater prosperity? On a reasonable survey of the case, I think it will be found that they can.

With this clearing of the ground we can turn with an open mind to the political question. The secular antithesis of town and country is as marked here as elsewhere, and the political problem varies accordingly. In the country we have to create in a large measure from the foundation; we have to meet and nullify the prevailing apathy, and undertake as a Government many tasks which would elsewhere be left to private enterprise. There the wounds of war gape more widely, and have to be healed by more cunning simples. People have spoken as if the towns were the sole factor in the case. Make the towns prosperous and wholly British, it has been said, and the land is ours. The towns are the loyal units; as they advance in prosperity the rural districts will sink out of account; and rightly, for their wealth is small, their population hostile, and their future barren. "Twenty years hence," wrote in 1896 an observer as clear-sighted as he was hopeful, "the white population is likely to be composed in about equal proportions of urban and rural elements. The urban element will be mainly mining, gathered at one great centre on the Witwatersrand, and possibly at some smaller centres in other districts. The rural element, consisting of people who live in villages or solitary farmhouses, will remain comparatively backward, because little affected by the social forces which work swiftly and potently upon close-packed industrial communities, and it may find itself very different in tone, temper, and tendencies from its urban fellow-citizens."[27] So we find one class of mine-owners arguing that any attempt to settle the country districts is a work of supererogation, and urging the Government to concentrate all its efforts on the promotion of their own industry, declaring that from their prosperity every blessing will flow forth to the rural parts. It is impossible to contemplate with equanimity the result of merely letting things alone. No industrial development would ever compensate for it, for the unleavened Dutch rural districts would become centres to collect and focus and stereotype the old unfaltering dislike. A hard-and-fast division between town and country is always to be feared; but when the barrier is between white men, and is built up of race, wealth, and civilisation, it can only be a dire calamity. We cannot rear up for our children a race of helots, and by our very exclusiveness solidify for all time an irreconcilable race division. If we preserve such an enemy within our bounds, and just beyond our gates, the time may come when a few isolated townships will represent Britain in South Africa. To prevent this cleavage, urban and rural development should advance with equal steps. The two races will be joined not by any trivial sentimental devices, but by the partnership of Dutch and British farmers in the enlightened development of the land.

There is another and a profounder reason for this introduction of British blood. The day may come when the South African, splendid as has been his loyalty and many his sacrifices, may go the way of most colonists, and lose something of that close touch with the mother-country which is necessary in the interests of a federated empire. It is always the temptation of town-dwellers, with their busy life and their own engrossing interests, and the tremendous mixture of alien blood in the country may serve to hasten this result beyond the ordinary rate of colonial progress. But the country settler is a different person. He retains a longer and simpler affection for the country of his birth. An influx of such a class would consolidate South African sentiment, and, when self-government comes, protect imperial interests better than any constitutional guarantee. This is the class which has the true stake in the country, deriving its life from the nurture of the earth, striving with winds and weather, and slowly absorbing into the fibre of its being those influences which make for race and patriotism.

South African agriculture, as the shrewdest observers have long foreseen, could never be improved until there arose a political reason for its improvement. The reason for the experiment has arrived, and its basis is in existence. In the inheritance of Crown lands which remains from the mismanaged estate of the late Government, and in the long lists of ex-irregulars and others who sought land, there was the raw material of settlement. It is no case for flamboyant prophecies. The certain difficulties are as great as the probable advantages.

But to shrink from those difficulties is to have towns where British ideas of government, can be realised and outside vast rural districts, suspicious, unfriendly, potentially dangerous; to neglect a golden opportunity of increasing the British element in South Africa; and to turn the back upon farming, which must always be the most permanent asset of any nation. The determinant fact in the case is that the alternative is so black that all risks must be faced rather than accept it. With such considerations in mind, the Government put forth a scheme of settlement, with the examination of which the remainder of this chapter is concerned. It is not my business to write the history of the Crown Colony administration, and therefore no time need be given to the many difficulties which faced the scheme, the mistakes made, and the hopeful results attained in certain cases. It is the problem itself which demands attention, and the adequacy or inadequacy of the policy which has been framed to meet it. Land settlement is from its very nature a slow business, with tardy fruits: twenty years hence we may be in a position to judge by results. But in the meantime it is possible, when the data are known, to ascertain whether a policy is on *a priori* grounds adapted to meet them.

[24] A Fencing Act, a Stock-Route Act, and a Brands Act on the most progressive lines have been prepared for the Transvaal. An excellent Fencing Act, badly administered, has always existed in the Orange River Colony, and a Brands Act, inferior to the Transvaal measure, has been passed in that colony. But it is the

effective administration of the Acts which is of importance.

[25] Parliamentary Paper C.D. 1163.

[26] My friend, Colonel Owen Thomas, had some samples of Transvaal soil analysed, and the report was very discouraging. To set against this, a sample of Springbok Flats soil was pronounced by a distinguished English expert, to whom it was sent, to be one of the richest specimens of virgin soil he had seen.

[27] Bryce, Impressions of South Africa, 3rd edition, p. 451.

II.

The Crown lands of the Transvaal, as I have said, amount to upwards of 29 million acres, the Crown lands of the Orange River Colony to under 1½ million. So far as the latter colony is concerned, land settlement is rather in the nature of estate management. The lands are too small for any serious political purpose, nor would the most extended settlement make much impression upon the solid Dutch rural community. But in the Transvaal the Crown in several districts is by far the largest landowner, and in others it holds the key of the position. Take a Transvaal map coloured according to ownership, and red is easily the master colour. A solid block of it occupies the north-east corner; large islands of it appear in the western and eastern borders; and the centre is plentifully dotted. Save in the little known north-east those lands are generally pasture, and in too many cases dry and arid bush-veld. In the Standerton district, and in parts of Rustenburg, Potchefstroom, and Bloemhof, there are tracts of good irrigated or irrigable lands; while in Barberton, Lydenburg, Zoutpansberg, and Marico there are considerable districts well watered and well suited for tropical and sub-tropical products. Taken as a whole, however, only a small portion of the Crown holding is suitable for early settlement—say 2½ million acres within the next three years. But there is a wide hinterland for development, and in settlement, as in empire, a hinterland is a moral necessity. There must be an open country to which the sons of farmers, in whom the love of the life is born, can trek as pioneers, otherwise there is a futile division into smaller holdings, or a more futile exodus to the towns. Besides, there should be room for the townsman—the miner, the artisan, the trader—to feel that there is somewhere an open country where he can invest his savings if he has a mind for a simpler life. As railways spread out into new districts, land will become agricultural which is now pasture; and, as the pastoral industry develops and herds are formed and diseases are mastered, the ranchman will occupy large tracts of what is now the unused hunting-veld.

The Government scheme aims at making a beginning with this settlement—a beginning only, for no government has ever been able to reconstruct alone, and the bulk of the work must be done by private enterprise. If 2000 farmers from England and the colonies can be settled in the rural parts before the day of stress arrives, then the work has been fairly started. A nucleus will have been formed to which the years will add, an element which will both leaven the slow and suspicious rustic society and provide a make-weight against the parochialism of the great towns. A country party is wanted which can look beyond the dorp and the mine-head, and view South African interests broadly and soberly. Such a party must be common to both town and country, but it cannot be built up wholly from either. It must, in the first instance, be a British party; but if this British party is to become a South African party, it must stand for interests common to both races and to all classes. The formation of this leavening element cannot be left to time and chance, but must be aided by conscious effort. The land is largely unproved, and full of dangers to crops and stock. The new-comer must therefore be treated gently, and helped over the many stiles which confront him. He will usually be a man of small means, and his limited capital must be put to the best use, and eked out with judicious Government advances. He should have few payments to make during his early years, when payments will necessarily come out of capital. Above all, the acquirement of the full freehold in his land on reasonable terms, and within a reasonable time, should be kept constantly before him as an encouragement to thrift and industry, for the sense of freehold, as the voortrekkers used to say, "turns sand into gold." Much of the Crown lands will never be suitable for any but the largest stockholders. These it is easy to deal with as a mere matter of estate-management; but the political purport of the scheme is concerned with intensive settlement, with the small holder and the mixed farmer of moderate means, who can provide a solid colony of mutually supporting and progressive Englishmen.

The Transvaal "Settlers' Ordinance" of 1902 is based upon the mass of legislation which embodies the settlement schemes of the Australasian colonies. The usual method in such experiments has been to begin in desperate fear of the settler, tying him up with cast-iron rules, and ruining him in a very few years. Then the pendulum swings back, and settlement is made easy and profitable, the old safeguards are abolished, and the land becomes full of rich squatters and companies, who fatten on State munificence through the numerous dummy settlers in their pay. Finally, after long years a compromise is effected, and that shy creature, the *bonâ-fide* settler, is sought for far and near. By this time it is probable that the thing has got a bad name, and men whose fathers and grandfathers lost money under former schemes, are chary of trusting themselves again to the tender mercies of a land-owning State. This, or something like it, has been the experience of the Australasian colonies. Either land was given out indiscriminately and a valuable State asset cheaply parted with, or the conditions of tenure were such as to ruin the small holder and put everything in the hands of a few rich syndicates. The land laws of Australia and New Zealand form, therefore, a most valuable precedent. We have their experiments before our eyes, and can learn from their often disastrous experience.

Settlement in New South Wales, to take one instance, was begun partly as a Treasury expedient and partly as an election cry. Under the Act of 1867 a settler was allowed to peg off, as on a mining area, a claim not exceeding 320 acres, without any attempt at a previous valuation and survey. The result was a wild rush, where nobody benefited except the blackmailer, who seized the strategic points of the country, such as water-holes, and had to be bought out at a fancy price. It does not surprise one to learn that of settlers under this scheme not one in twenty remains to-day. By subsequent Acts the maximum acreage was increased; but in any case it was an arbitrary figure, and it was not till 1895 that it was left within the widest limits to the discretion of the Minister of Lands. Areas proved too small, since no provision could be made for the increase of stock and the necessary fall in prices which attended settlement. In valuation the extraordinary plan was adopted of giving a uniform capital value of £1 per acre to all land. The country being unproved, values were absolutely unknown, nor was any provision made for revaluation. The result was that the settler struggled along till he was ruined and his holding forfeited, when the holding lapsed to the State, which, being unable to find a new tenant, was compelled to let it remain vacant, having accomplished nothing but the needless ruin of the first man. The "Settlers' Ordinance" has endeavoured to avoid laying down any rules which experience has not tried and tested. The determination of the size of any holding is left to the land officials, without defining any area limits. A holding which proves too small may be increased on appeal, and the boundaries are at all times made capable of adjustment. Holdings are first surveyed and valued, then gazetted for application, and finally publicly allotted, after full inquiry into the case of each applicant, by a Central Board. The division and valuation of farms, in the absence of reliable data, is a work of great nicety and difficulty. The country contains within its limits many districts which differ widely in soil, vegetation, and climate. It is therefore impossible, in deciding on the size of holdings, to follow any arbitrary rule; and to restrict survey to a maximum and minimum acreage would be fatal. The only method is to ascertain from local evidence the carrying and producing capacity of similar land, and so frame the boundaries of a farm as to provide on such figures a reasonably good living for the class of settler for whom it is intended. The danger of putting too high a price on land is not less great. If the current market price is taken it will in most instances be overvalued, and in any case it is a method without any justification in reason. The best solution is probably the plan at present in use. Schedules have been prepared for the different types of holding, in which the profits are calculated, using as a guide the present price of stock and imported produce at the coast to ensure against the inevitable fall in prices. Taking such estimated profits as a basis, the valuation is so fixed as to give the settler, after all living expenses, annual payments to Government, probable loss of stock, and depreciation of plant have been written off, a clear profit of 12 per cent on his original capital. From this figure some further deductions may fall to be made for such disadvantages as unhealthiness of climate and excessive distance from the conveniences of civilised life. In the absence of more scientific data this seems to form as fair a basis in valuation as any man can expect.

But if early Australasian legislation erred in rigour, it also erred in laxity. The settler was often the nominee of a syndicate or a large run-holder, and before the 1895 Act a class of professional selectors existed. This system of *latifundia* brought its own punishment. The run-holder ruined the small selector. To pay the instalments on his many selections he had recourse to the banks, which speedily ruined him and took over his holdings. The banks in their turn ruined themselves, chiefly through being obliged to pay instalments on land valued at £1 per acre, of which the actual value for stock was less than 5s. Again, the settler was compelled to improve the land at the rate of so many shillings per acre within a given time. This led to cheap fictitious improvements by which the letter of the law was satisfied and the spirit evaded. The "Settlers' Ordinance" has certain stringent provisions to prevent such frustration of the true aims of settlement. Subletting or transfer of any sort, except with Government consent, is strictly forbidden till the tenant has acquired the freehold. Residence for at least eight months in the year, unless a special dispensation is granted, is required during the same period. The settler is compelled to build a satisfactory house and to fence his holding within a given time. He is compelled to occupy it solely for his own benefit, to cultivate according to the rules of good husbandry (whatever that may mean), and the decision of the local Land Commissioner is the test by which he is judged. He is encouraged to improve by the potent fact that the Government will advance pound for pound against his improvements. But there are certain elastic provisions to temper the rigour of such restrictions. The Commissioner of Lands is given a very wide dispensing power with regard to most conditions. Partnerships are allowed; settlers may reside together in a village community; and the residence conditions may be temporarily fulfilled by a wife or child, to allow a settler in hard times to make money by his labour elsewhere. Special relief is provided during periods of disease or drought by the cessation or diminution of the annual payments, and by advances in excess of the ordinary limits.

The Ordinance has been framed on experimental lines, leaving much to the discretion of local officials (subject to an appeal to the Central Board and thence to the High Court), and hesitating to dogmatise on details which are still unproved. But in spite of much which is empirical, one or two root principles are maintained. One is that a fair chance must be given to all to acquire the freehold, without which magic possibility the best men will not come forward. Another, and perhaps the most important of all, is that the payments to Government shall be so arranged as to be scarcely felt during the early years when they are paid out of capital, and to rise to any considerable sum only when the holding is producing a revenue. The two chief forms of tenure are leasehold and purchase by instalments over a period of thirty years. The common form of lease is for five years, with a possible extension for another two, and the rental may be at any rate (not exceeding 5 per cent) which the Commissioner of Lands thinks suitable. This method will enable back-country to be taken up, to start with, at a nominal rent; and it will also allow a settler on an unimproved stock-farm to devote the bulk of his capital to the necessary stocking and improvements. At the end of the lease, or without any preliminary lease, the settler can begin to purchase his holding on the instalments system. By a payment of £5, 15s. per cent per annum on the gazetted valuation, principal and interest (which is calculated at 4 per cent) will be wiped off in thirty years. But a settler is permitted any time after ten years from the date of his first occupation to pay up the balance and acquire the full freehold. In the case of preliminary leaseholders who take up a purchase licence, the licence, so far as the ten years' period is concerned, is made retrospective so as to date from the first day of the lease.

Such is a rough outline of the Government proposals. They aim only at making a beginning, and it is to the large private owner and the land company that we must look for the completion of the work. South African agriculture can never be a Golconda like the Canadian wheat-lands of the West. But it is of inestimable value to the country in providing a background to the immense temporary mining development—a permanent asset, which will remain to South Africa's credit when the gold-mines of the Rand are curiosities of history. In itself it is a sound investment, offering no glittering fortunes but a steady and reasonable livelihood. No people can afford to develop solely on industrial lines and remain a nation in the full sense of the word, for in every commonwealth there is need of the rural forces of persistence to counteract the urban forces of change. All settlement is necessarily a leap in the dark, but, so far as a proposal can be judged before it is put into practice, the present scheme offers good chances of success. There seems little doubt that it will receive full justice. The war spread the knowledge of the country to every cranny of the Empire. English and Scottish farmers' sons, Australian bushmen, Indian planters, farmers from New Zealand and Ontario, having fought for three years on the veld, have fallen in love with it and are willing to make it their home. No more splendid chances for settlement have ever offered; for when the wastrels have been eliminated there remain many thousands of good men, from whom a sturdy country stock could be created. There can be no indiscriminate gifts of land as in some colonies. The land is too valuable, the political purpose too delicate and urgent, the need of nice discrimination in selection and careful fostering thereafter too imperative, to allow farms to be shaken up in a lucky-bag and distributed to the first comers. The best men must be attracted, and assisted with advice and loans to the measure of success which is possible. It is the soundest form of political speculation, if done with sober and clear-sighted purpose. The young men from home and the colonies, to whom South Africa is a memory that can never die, turn naturally towards it in search of a freer life and a larger prospect. On the model farms which are being established in each district the proverbial "younger sons of younger sons" will be given a chance of learning the requirements of the land, and so starting work on their own account with intelligence and economy. Some day—and may we all live to see it!—there will be little white homesteads among trees, and country villages and moorland farms; cattle and sheep on a thousand hills where now only the wild birds cry; wayside inns where the thirsty traveller can find refreshment; and country shows where John Smith and Johannes Smuts will compete amicably for the King's premiums. And if any one thinks this an unfounded hope, let him turn to some such book as Ogilby's 'Itinerarium Angliæ,' where he will find that in the closing years of the seventeenth century the arable and pastoral land in England scarcely amounted to half the area of the kingdom, and the most fruitful orchards of Gloucestershire and Warwick were mere heath and swamp, and, as it seemed to an acute observer, doomed to remain so.

Settlement, indeed, is but one, though the most important, of the land problems. An enlightened agricultural department, working in conjunction with local societies, can do much to unite the two races by conferring benefits which are common to both. The introduction of pedigree stock to grade up the existing herds is a necessity which any Boer farmer will admit. So, too, are stringent regulations for the prevention of disease, experiments in new crops, field trials of new machinery, and a provision for some form of agricultural training. Central creameries and tobacco-factories would work wonders in increasing the prosperity of certain districts. Something of that tireless vigilance and alert intelligence which has made the Agricultural Bureau of the United States famous, a spirit which brings into agriculture the procedure and the exact calculation of a great business house, is necessary to meet the not insuperable difficulties which now deter the timid, and to give farming a chance of development commensurate with its political importance. It is only another case in which a South African question stands on a razor-edge, a narrow line separating ample success from a melancholy failure.

CHAPTER XIV.

THE SUBJECT RACES.

No question is more fraught with difficulties for the home philosopher than this, but there is none on which practical men have made up their mind with such bitter completeness. The root of the trouble is that England and South Africa talk, and will continue to talk, in different languages on the matter. The Englishman, using the speech of conventional politics, seems to the colonist to talk academic nonsense; while the South African, speaking the rough and ready words of the practical man, appears as the champion of brutality and coercion. The difficulties are so real that one cannot but regret that they are complicated by verbal misunderstandings. There is no real divergence of views on the native question: the distinction is rather between a seriously held opinion and a slipshod prejudice. "Exeter Hall" is less the name of a party than of an attitude, as common among the robust colonists as ever it was among the mild pietists of Clapham. It consists in a disinclination to look simply on facts, to reason soberly, and to speak accurately,—a tendency to lap a question in turgid emotion. The man who consigns all native races to perdition in round terms, and declares that the only solution of the difficulty is to clear out the Kaffir, is as truly a votary of Exeter Hall as the gentle old lady to whom the aborigine is a model of primeval innocence, whose only joy is the singing of missionary hymns.

Out of the confusion of interests and issues two main problems emerge which may form useful guides in our inquiry. One is economic. What part are the native races to play in the labour-supply and the production of South Africa? what is to be their tenure of land? what is to be their economic destiny in face of the competition of modern life and the industrial development of the country? The second is the moral question, of which the political is one aspect. A coloured race living side by side with a white people furnishes one of the gravest of moral cruces. The existence of a subject race on whatever terms is apt to lead to the deterioration in moral and mental vigour of its masters. Perpetual tutelage tends to this result; full social and civic rights, on the other hand, lead to political anomalies and, too often, to the lowest forms of political chicanery. A doctrinaire idealism is fraught with dire social evils; but an obstinate maintenance of the "practical man's" *status quo* is apt to bring about that very degeneration which justifies the doctrinaire. How to reconcile freedom of development for the native by means of spontaneous labour, education, and social rights with the degree of compulsion necessary to bring them into line with social and industrial needs, or, to put it shortly, how to keep the white man from deterioration without spoiling the Kaffir,—this is the kernel of the most insistent of South African problems.

The native races south of the Zambesi present a curious problem to the student of primitive societies. All, or nearly all, of kindred race, they are not autochthonous, and the date of their arrival in the country can in most cases be fixed within the last five centuries. Five centuries do not give a long title to a country, as savage titles go, but even this period must be cut down in most cases, since the wars of the great Zulu kings scattered the other races about as from a pepper-box, with the result that few tribes save the Zulus, some of the Cape Colony Kaffirs, the Swazis, and small peoples like the Barolongs, can claim an occupation title of more than a hundred years. This state of affairs, so rare in our dealings with savage peoples, has, politically, both merits and defects. The absence of the autochthonous hold of the soil and of long-settled immovable traditions of tribal life makes the native more malleable under the forces of civilisation. It is easier to break up the tribes and to acclimatise the Kaffir to new localities and new conditions. But this lack of a strong, settled, racial life makes it fatally easy for him to fall a victim to the vices of civilisation, and to come upon our hands as a derelict creature without faith or stamina, having lost his old taboos, and being as yet unable to understand the laws of the white man. This process of disintegration has been going on for a century, and the result is a clearly marked division. We have the tribal natives, who are still more or less strictly under the rule of a chief, and subject to tribal laws sanctioned and enforced by the Governments. The native population of the Transkeian territories in Cape Colony, such as the Pondos, the Amaxosas, and the Tembus; Bechuanaland, with the people of Khama, Bathoen, Sebele, and Linchwe; Basutoland; Zululand; the northern and eastern parts of the Transvaal under such chiefs as Magata, 'Mpefu, and Siwasa; Swaziland;

and the Matabele and Mashona tribes of the vast districts of Northern and Southern Rhodesia are the main instances of this first class. The aim of the different Governments has always been to keep the tribal organisation intact, and, after eliminating certain tribal laws and customs which are inconsistent with the ideas of white men, to give their sanction to the remainder. Basutoland is a Crown colony; the Transkeian territories are a native reserve; Bechuanaland is a native protectorate; in Rhodesia a number of native chiefs control large tracts of land under the Chartered Company's administration. Elsewhere the tribes live in Government reserves, or in certain cases in locations situated on private land. Between Pretoria and the Limpopo there are dozens of small chieftains and chieftainesses, with tribes varying in numbers from a hundred to several thousands. The second class, the detribalised natives, are to be found scattered over the whole country, notably in the western province of Cape Colony, and in the vicinity of all South African towns. They live as a rule in locations under municipal or Government supervision. In many cases such locations are far larger than those of a small chief; but their distinguishing feature is that they are governed solely by the law of the country or by municipal regulations framed for the purpose, and owe no allegiance to any chief or tribal system.

It is obvious that for purposes of policy this distinction cannot maintain its importance. The rule of the chief is being rapidly undermined by natural causes, and no taking thought can bolster it up for ever. Education, too, and the closer settlement of the country by white men, are rapidly breaking down tribal customs and beliefs, which, as a rule, have more vitality than the isolated sentiment of allegiance. For us the real distinction is between the natives who can be kept in large reserves or locations, whether tribal or otherwise, and the floating native population, which is every day growing in numbers. Sooner or later we must face the problem of the overcrowding of all reserves, and the consequent efflux of homeless and masterless men. The needs of progress, too, are daily tending to change the tribal native into the isolated native attached to some industry or other. Politically the question is, How far and on what lines the large reserves and locations can be best maintained, and what provision can be made for incorporating the overflow, which exists now and will soon exist in far greater numbers, on sane and rational lines in the body politic?

Such being the main requirements of the problem, it remains to consider the forms in which they present themselves to the ordinary man. For the working aspect of a question is generally very different from the form it takes in an academic analysis. The translation into the terms of everyday life is conditioned by many accidental causes, so that to one section of the community the labour problem is the sole one, to another the educational, to a third the social. It is important to realise that all are part of one question, and that no single one can be truly solved unless the whole is dealt with.

This incompleteness of view, more than any other cause, has complicated the native question, and produced spurious antagonisms, and policies which are apparently rival, but in reality are complementary.

The first is the grave difficulty which must always attend the existence of a subject race. Slavery is the extreme form of the situation, and in it we see the evils and dangers on a colossal scale. A subject population, to whom legal rights are denied, tends in the long-run to degrade the value of human life, and to depreciate the moral currency,—a result so deadly for true progress that the consensus of civilised races has utterly condemned it. The denial of social and political rights is almost equally dangerous, since, apart from the risks of perpetual tutelage in a progressive community, there follows necessarily a depreciation of those political truths upon which all free societies are based. Many honest men have clearly perceived this; but after the fashion of headstrong honesty, they have confused the issues by an inaccurate use of words. Legal rights must be granted, and since the law is the child of the fundamental principles of human justice, legal equality should follow. Social and political rights also must be given; but why social and political equality? The most embittered employer of native labour does not deny that the black man should share certain social privileges, and be made to feel his place in the political organism, but he rightly denies that rights mean equality of rights; while his doctrinaire opponent, arguing from exactly the same premises, claims a foolish equality on a misunderstanding of words. The essence of social and political equality must be a standard of education and moral and intellectual equipment, which can be roughly attributed to all members of the community concerned. But in this case there can be no such common standard. Between the most ignorant white man and the black man there is fixed for the present an impassable gulf, not of colour but of mind. The native is often quick of understanding, industrious, curiously logical, but he lives and moves in a mental world incredibly distant from ours. The medium of his thought, so to speak, is so unique that the results are out of all relation to ourselves. Mentally he is as crude and naïve as a child, with a child's curiosity and ingenuity, and a child's practical inconsequence. Morally he has none of the traditions of self-discipline and order, which are implicit, though often in a degraded form, in white people. In a word, he cannot be depended upon as an individual save under fairly vigilant restraint; and in the mass he forms an unknown quantity, compared with which a Paris mob is a Quaker meeting. With all his merits, this instability of character and intellectual childishness make him politically far more impossible than even the lowest class of Europeans. High property or educational qualifications for the franchise, or any other of the expedients of Europe, are logically out of place, though they were raised to the possession of a fortune and a university degree; for the mind is still there, unaltered, though it may be superficially ornamented. Give the native the full franchise, argues one class of observer, and he will in time show himself worthy of it, for in itself it is an education. On a strictly logical view it would be as reasonable to put a child on a steam-engine as driver, trusting that the responsibility of his position would be in itself an education and would teach him the necessary art.

Social and political equality will seem to most men familiar with the subject a chimera, but social and political rights the native must have, and in most cases has already obtained. But unless such rights are carefully adjusted the absolute cleavage remains. We have two races, physically different, socially incapable of amalgamation: if we make the gulf final, there is no possibility of a united state; if we bridge it carelessly, the possibility is still more distant. We may scruple to grant rights, such as the political franchise, which are based in the last resort on a common moral and intellectual standard; but we can grant rights which are substantive and educative and capable of judicious extension. The Glen Grey Act, as we shall see, made a valuable experiment in securing to the native the social status which attends individual tenure of land. Some form of representation might be devised, by which a chief might have a voice on a district council, or a representative elected by an industrial location assist in local government. Such measures, joined with a rational system of education, will leave the door open for the extension of rights till such time as the native has finally shown whether he is worthy of equality or condemned by nature to rank for ever as a subject race. There are men, able men with the courage of their opinions, who see no hope in the matter, and who would segregate the natives in a separate territory under British protection. The chief objection to this policy is that it is impossible. The native is in our midst, and we must face the facts. We have a chance to solve a burning question which no other nation has had, since, as in the United States, the matter has either been complicated by initial slavery, or, as also in the States, a thoughtless plunge has been made into European doctrines of liberty, equality, and fraternity. If we patiently and skilfully bring to bear upon the black man the solvent and formative influences of civilisation, one of two things must happen. Either the native will prove himself worthy of an equal share in the body politic; or, the experiment having been honestly tried, he will sink back to his old place and gradually go the way of the Red Indian and the Hottentot. For it is inevitable that civilisation, if wisely applied, must either raise him or choke him,—raise him to the rank of equal citizenship, or, by its hostility to his ineradicable qualities, prove a burden too heavy to support.

The second is the ever-recurring problem of labour. In an earlier chapter the economic aspect of the question has been discussed; for the present we have to face that aspect which is connected with a native policy. The Kaffir is fundamentally an agriculturist, and when his lands are well situated he reaps enough for his simple existence with a minimum of labour. If he is rich enough to have several wives, they do the necessary picking and hoeing, and their lord and master sits in the shade of his hut and eats the bread of idleness. This was well enough in the old hunting and fighting days, when the male folk lived a strenuous life in the pursuit of game and the slaughter of their neighbours. But with civilisation close to their gates, the old system means a degraded somnolent life for the man, and the continuance of a real, though not necessarily unpleasant, form of slavery for the woman. And this in a country which is crying aloud for labour and development! To be sure, the foregoing is not a complete picture of all Kaffir life, but it is true of the larger reserves and the wealthier kraals. To most men it is an offence that the native, who is saved by British power from insecurity of life and limb, should be allowed to remain, by the happy accident of nature, an idler dependent only on the kindness of mother earth, multiplying his kind at an alarming rate, and untouched by the industrial struggle where his sinews are so sorely needed. The Kaffir owes his existence to the white man; in return he should be compelled to labour for hire and take his proper place in a world which has no room for his vegetating habits. He holds his land by our favour, he is protected from extinction by our arms, he enjoys the benefits of our laws; and he must pay for it all, not only in taxes but by a particular tax, a certain quantity of labour. This mode of argument sounds so serenely reasonable that one is apt to miss the very dangerous political doctrine which underlies it. Stated shortly, it runs thus. Compulsory labour without payment is to be reprobated like all forms of *corvée*, but if we pay what we regard as a fair price and make the compulsion indirect, then we get rid of such an objection. This doctrine involves two principles which seem to me to be subversive of all social order, and in particular of that civilisation which they profess to support. The Kaffir would be placed outside the play of economic forces. His wages would be arbitrarily established on an artificial basis, unalterable save at the will of his white masters. In the second place, compulsion by high taxation is not indirect compulsion, but one of the most direct forms of coercion known to history. To constrain a man indirectly is to use unseen forces and half-understood conditions which, being unrealised, do not impair his consciousness of liberty; but this is not the method which is proposed. A white man, it is argued, suffers want if he does not work. Well and good,—so does the Kaffir; but the work which he does, unless he is rich enough to have it vicariously performed, is different in kind from the work which others want him to do, and hence the trouble arises. To force a man, black or white, to enter on labour for which he is disinclined, is to rank him with beasts of burden, and prevent him, as an industrial creature, from ever attaining the conscious freedom which labour bestows. The old truth, so often misapplied, that a man who does not work shall not eat, is a statement of economic conditions to which those who quote it in this connection would seek to do violence.

But such truisms do not exhaust the question. It is not the Kaffir who chiefly matters, for in his present stage of development he might be as well off one way as another; it is the white man's interests which must decide. If the whole of Kaffirdom were sunk in a state of feminine slavery and male indolence, violence might be done to political axioms with some show of reason; but the Kaffir is emerging from his savagery and has shown in more ways than one a capacity for industrial development. But, taking the Kaffir on the lowest plane, what is to be the effect on the white population of South Africa if forced labour is to stereotype for ever a lower race, to which the free selection of labour, the first requisite of progress, is denied? "The safety of the commonwealth," wrote John Mackenzie, "absolutely demands that no hatches be battened down over the heads of any part of the community." At the back of all the many excellent cases which have been made out for compulsory labour by high taxation, there lie the immediate needs of the great gold industry—needs which it is now clear can never be met in South Africa alone by any native legislation. An instant industrial demand is apt to blind many good men for the moment to those wider truths, which on other occasions they are ready enough to assent to. The case has been further prejudiced for most people by the bad arguments used on the native side, and the intolerable cant with which obvious truths have been sicklied over. We need not concern ourselves with the so-called degradation of Kaffir manhood implied in compulsory labour, for such self-conscious manhood does not exist; but we are very deeply concerned with the degradation of white manhood, which will inevitably follow any of the facile solutions which are cried in the market-place. If by violent methods economic laws are checked in their play, a subject race in a low state of civilisation is checked on the only side on which development can be reasonably looked for. The harder and lower forms of toil will fall into Kaffir hands for good; the white population will become an aristocracy based on a kind of slave labour; and with the abolition of an honest hierarchy of work, degeneration will set in with terrible swiftness. It is a pleasing dream this, of a community of cultivated white men above the needs of squalid or menial toil, but on such a dream no free nation was ever built. The old tribal system is crumbling, and in a hundred years or less we shall see the Kaffirs abroad in the land, closely knit to all industries and touching social and political life at countless points. If they are a portion, however small, of the civic organism, there is hope for the future; but if they are a thing apart, denied the commonest of all rights, and remaining in their present crude and stagnant condition, they will be a menace, political and moral, which no one can contemplate with equanimity. There are, indeed, only two entirely logical policies towards the native. Either remove him, bag and baggage, to some Central African reserve and leave him to fight his wars and live as he lived before the days of Tchaka, or bring him into close and organic relation with those forces of a high civilisation which must inevitably mend or end him.

There is a third chief aspect in which the native problem presents itself to the ordinary man. The Kaffir, south of the Zambesi, already outnumbers the white man by fully five to one, and he increases with at least twice the rapidity. Most native reserves and locations are overcrowded, the Kaffir is being driven on to private land as an unauthorised squatter, and the floating population in and around the towns is daily increasing. What is to be the end of this fecundity? Living on little, subject apparently to none of the natural or prudential checks on over-population, there seems a real danger of black ultimately swamping white by mere gross quantity. In any case there will soon be a grave economic crisis, for, unless prompt measures are adopted, a large loose vagabondage will grow up all over the land. It is to be noted that this danger is the converse of the two problems we have already discussed. They referred to the stereotyping of the Kaffir races as a settled agricultural people out of line with industrial progress; this concerns the inevitable break-up of the old agricultural condition by mere excess of population and the difficulty of dealing with the overflow. This complementary character which the problems assume is one of the most hopeful features of the case. Natural forces are bringing the Kaffir to our hands. The *débâcle* of his old life is turning him upon the world to be formed and constrained at our pleasure. The field is clear for experiment, and it behoves us to make up our minds clearly on the forms which the experiment must take.

To recapitulate the results of the preceding pages. The central problem is how to bring the native races under the play of civilising forces, so that they may either approve themselves as capable of incorporation in the body politic, or show themselves eternally incapable, in which case history would lead us to believe that they will gradually disappear. To effect this vital experiment, no rigid economic or social barrier should be placed between them and the white inhabitants. Since the old tribal organisation is breaking up, the ground is being rapidly prepared for the trial. It is our business, therefore, to consider how best the system of tribes and reserves can be maintained, so long as there is in it the stuff of life, and what new elements can be introduced which will make its fall more safe and gradual; and, in the second place, to devise ways and means for dealing with the rapidly increasing loose native population, for replacing the former tribal traditions with some rudiments of civilised law, and for leaving an open door for such development as may be within their capacity. It will be convenient to look at ways and means under three heads. There is, first, the general question of taxation, which is common to all. There is, secondly, the problem of the larger reserves, and the maintenance, so far as is desirable, of the old rural life, with the kindred questions of land tenure, of local government, of surplus population, and of labour. And, finally, there is the problem of the class which in the last resort is destined to be most numerous, the wholly non-tribal and unattached natives, whose mode of life must be created afresh and controlled by Government. This is the most difficult problem, since such natives are peculiarly exposed to the solvents of white civilisation, and everything depends upon the method in which the solvents are used.

The native is, for the most part, under special taxes. In certain parts of Cape Colony and Natal the fiscal system is in practice the same for black and white, but for the purposes of this inquiry the native who has adopted the white man's life may be disregarded. In Cape Colony the hut tax is 10s. per annum, whether the hut is situated on private or Crown lands, and on locations within municipalities a similar municipal tax is paid. In Natal the hut tax is 14s., in Basutoland £1, in Rhodesia 10s., and in the Transvaal and Orange River Colony 10s. under the old *régime*. In Natal, the Orange River Colony, the Transvaal, and Rhodesia, there was also a native pass law, under which certain sums were charged on travelling passes, varying from 6d. in the Orange River Colony to 2s. per month in the mining areas of the Transvaal. It is unnecessary to go into the numerous details of native taxation, which within narrow limits are constantly varied, but it is worth while to look at two instances which may be taken as the extreme types of such taxation, the Transvaal under the former Government and the districts of Cape Colony subject to the Glen Grey Act. In the Transvaal the natives for the most part are tribal, and the system of taxation was based on tribal considerations; but the bulk of the revenue under the Pass Law came from the large fluctuating population of natives at work on the mines. Under the old Government the ordinary native paid 10s. as hut tax, £2 as capitation fee, with sundry other charges for passes, &c., which brought the whole amount which might be levied up to fully £4. The tax was loosely collected, but on the whole the taxation per head was reasonably high. One of the first acts of the new administration was to consolidate all native taxes in one general poll tax of £2, with a further charge of £2 per wife for natives who had more than one. The pass fee was also charged upon the employer in districts where it fell to be levied. The net result, therefore, is that for a native, who is the husband of not more than one wife, the sum payable yearly is about £3, made up of the poll tax and the registration fee. A native may have to pay more than the old Government exacted, but if he pleases he can pay less. In the districts under the Glen Grey Act individual ownership of land is encouraged, and the native who has attained to such tenure is practically in the position of a white citizen—that is, he pays no hut tax or poll tax, and his contributions to revenue consist in the payment of such rates as his district council or the Transkeian General Council may levy. For the native who holds no land either on quit-rent or freehold title, there is a labour tax of 10s. per annum, which he can avoid by showing that he has been at work outside the district for a period of three months during the previous year, and from which he can gain complete exemption by showing that at some time he has worked for a total period of three years. Such a tax is not a compulsory labour tax, but should rather be regarded as a modification of the hut tax, which can be remitted as a bonus on outside labour.

The contrast between the two forms of taxation is obvious, the one being a special and peculiar type, the other a modification of the general fiscal system of the colony. It is to the latter type that all systems of native taxation must tend to approximate. There are certain obvious objections to the hut tax, of which the chief is that it leads to overcrowding and bad sanitation, and prevents young men from building huts of their own;

and perhaps it would be well if, following the new Transvaal precedent, all native taxes were consolidated into one comprehensive poll tax. But, speaking generally, natives are not heavily taxed[28] having regard to their wage-earning capacity, though hitherto the Customs have been unduly hard upon their simple commodities. In the Transvaal, for example, there is little doubt that the native population could bear for revenue purposes in most years a poll tax of £3 per head. This might be reduced in case of natives in industrial employment, in consideration of the fact that such natives contribute otherwise to revenue through the Pass Law. It is one of the ironies of this South African problem that increased and reasonable taxation for revenue purposes will continue to be identified in many minds with compulsory labour through high taxation. The two things are as wide apart as the poles. The native, in return for protection and good government, is required to pay a certain sum per annum calculated solely on fiscal needs and his earning capacity. That is the only basis of native taxation; but when the sum has been fixed, it may be expedient as a matter of policy to reduce the tax in the case of natives working under an employer, partly because such natives contribute to the Exchequer in another way, and partly as a bonus to encourage outside labour. But the general form of taxation might well be altered, slowly and cautiously, as the time ripened. The hut tax might be gradually transmuted into a form of rent which, as in the Glen Grey districts, could be lowered as a bonus on outside labour, and the extension of local government might provide for the rating of locations and reserves on some system common to all districts. Taxation may have an educative force, and to ask from the native a contribution for something of which the purpose is apparent and the justification obvious, is to bestow on him a kind of freedom. It is the first step to taxation with representation to provide that taxation should be accompanied by understanding.

The second question is that of existing reserves and the possibility and method of their maintenance. In the case of many the problem is still simple. Basutoland, the chief tribes of the Bechuanaland Protectorate and Southern Rhodesia, Swaziland, Zululand, the races of the north and north-eastern Transvaal, and a considerable part of the Transkeian territories, will find for many years protected tribal government suitable to their needs. Tribal customs and laws, in so far as they are not *contra bonos mores*, are recognised by the protecting Governments, and given effect to by any white courts which may have jurisdiction in the district. The old modes of land tenure, the succession to the chieftainship, the tribal religion, if any exists, should be given the sanction of the sovereign Power till such time as they crumble from their own baselessness. The disintegrating forces are many and potent. Taxation will compel the acquisition of wealth other than in kind, and will therefore strengthen existing trade, and, if gradually modified in character till it approach a rating system, will replace the tribe by the district as a local unit. The growth of population will compel a certain overflow, which must either be accommodated on new land under special conditions, or must go to swell the general industrial community. Education, the greatest of all disintegrators, is loosening slowly the old ties, and is increasing the wants of the native by enlarging his mental horizon. Outside labour, whether undertaken from love of novelty or from sheer economic pressure, leaves its indelible mark on the labourer. The Kaffir who has worked for two years in Kimberley or Johannesburg may seem to have returned completely to his old stagnant life, but there is a new element at work in him and his kindred, a new curiosity, a weakening of his regard for his traditional system. Agriculture itself, which has hitherto been the mainstay of his conservatism, is rapidly becoming a force of revolution. Formerly no self-respecting native would engage in cultivation, leaving such tasks to his women; but a native who would not touch pick or hoe is ready enough to work a plough, if he is so fortunate as to possess one. The growth of wealth and a spirit of enterprise among the tribes leads to improved tillage, and once the native is content to labour himself in the fields, his old scheme of society is already crumbling.

But, in addition to natural solvents, there is one which we might well apply in our own interest against the time when the tribal system shall have finally disappeared. Any form of political franchise, however safeguarded, is in my opinion illogical and dangerous. It is inequitable to create barriers which are themselves artificial, but it is both inequitable and impolitic to disregard natural barriers when the basis of our politics is a presumed natural equality. But it may be possible to admit the Kaffir to a share in self-government without giving any adherence to the doctrine involved in a grant of a national franchise. Local government is still in its infancy all over South Africa, but the common type is some form of urban or district council. The questions which such councils discuss do not involve high considerations of statescraft, but simple practical matters, such as roads and bridges, sanitary restrictions, precautions against stock diseases, and market rules. Supposing that in any district there exists a tribe or a location sufficiently progressive and orderly, I see no real difficulty in bringing the chief or induna sooner or later directly or indirectly into the local council. It is a matter on which it is idle to dogmatise, being one of the many questions on which South Africa must say the last word, and being further dependent on the status of the natives in each district; but on a nominated or elective council a native, or a white member with natives in his constituency, might do valuable work in assisting with matters in which natives were largely concerned. A native who cannot reasonably be asked to decide on questions such as fiscal reform or military organisation, may be very well fitted to advise, as a large stock-holder, on precautionary measures against rinderpest. If such a step is ever taken—and the present exclusive attitude of South Africa is rather a sign of the growing solidarity of the community than an index of a permanent conviction—an advance of enormous import will have been made in that branch of native education in which we are almost powerless to move directly, namely, his training as a responsible citizen.

As the tribal system breaks down from whatever cause, the tribesmen must do one of three things—either settle on the land on new conditions, or live permanently in the service of employers, or swell the loose population of town and country. The second course does not concern us, being a matter for the private law of master and servant. But in each of the other courses the State is profoundly interested. For the sake of the future it is necessary to have the existing reserves thoroughly examined, for, since the fluctuations of native populations are very great, many are too small for their present occupants and a few are too spacious. Majajie's location in Zoutpansberg, and one or two of the reserves on the western border of the Transvaal, may be quoted as instances of tribes which have shrunk from the original number on which the grant of land was based. In such cases the land might reasonably be curtailed, since it is still Crown land held in trust for the natives' use, and not private land purchased by the chiefs themselves. But it is more usual to find locations far too narrow, and the result in many parts is that a certain number of natives who have been compelled to leave their old reserves are farming private lands on precarious and burdensome terms, or are squatting on Crown lands with no legal tenure at all. A law of the late Transvaal Government (No. 21 of 1895) made it illegal to have more than five native households on one private farm; but this law, like many others which conflicted with the interests of the governing class, was quietly allowed to become a dead letter. There are men to-day who have a hundred and more native families on a farm, paying often exorbitant rents either in money or in forced labour, and liable to be turned adrift at a moment's notice. The old Boer system was to allow natives to squat on land in return for six months' labour; but this mode of payment is never satisfactory with a Kaffir, who soon forgets the tenure on which he holds his land, regards it as his own, and makes every attempt to evade his tenant's service. The whole position is unsatisfactory, the master being cumbered with unwilling and often worthless labour, the tenant subject to a capricious rent and a permanent possibility of eviction. In the interests of both white and black it is desirable to end this anomaly. Some form of the Squatters' Law might be re-enacted and enforced, a farmer being allowed a reasonable number of native families, who give work for wages and pay a fair rent for their land. The balance might well be accommodated as tenants on such portions of Crown land as are suitable for Kaffirs and incapable of successful white settlement. Such lands exist in the parts where the native population is densest, as in the northern and eastern districts of the Transvaal. The situation affords an opportunity for the Government policy towards outside labour. If the rent per holding were fixed at some figure like £10 (which is less than many natives pay to private owners) it might be reduced to £5, if a certain proportion of the males of a household went out to labour for a part of the year in the towns or in some rural employment other than farming. Such a policy would give immediate relief to the really serious congestion in many districts, would establish a better system of native tenure, and would pave the way for a closer connection between the industrial native and the country kraal.

The wholly detribalised native is a more important problem, because he represents the type of what the Kaffir will in some remote future become—a man who has forgotten his race traditions, and has become an unpopular attaché of the white community. Towards other natives our policy must be only to maintain an amended *status quo*, but for him we must make an effort at construction. It is no business of mine to frame policies, but only to sketch, roughly and imperfectly, the conditions of the problem which the constructive statesman (and South Africa will long have need of constructive statesmen) must face. Individual tenure of land—and by this is not necessarily meant freehold, even under the Glen Grey restrictions as to alienation, for a long lease may be more politic and equally attractive[29]—and the spread of education and commerce will work to the same effect in the rural districts as industrial employment in the towns. But for the present the towns furnish the gravest problem—how to make adequate provision for the increasing native population, which is neither living permanently in the households of white masters nor working in the mines under a time contract. It is desirable to have locations for natives, as it is fitting to provide bazaars for Asiatics, since the native should be concentrated both for administrative and educational purposes. Those municipal locations, which already exist in many towns, will have to be taken vigorously in hand. Something must replace the biscuit-tin shanties where the native, ignorant of sanitation, lives, under more wretched conditions, what is practically the life of a country kraal, and with the reform of their habitations a new attraction to industry will exist for the better class of Kaffir. It is a common mistake to class all natives together, a mistake which a little knowledge of South African ethnology and history would prevent. Many have highly developed instincts of cleanliness, and much race pride, and will not endure to be huddled in squalid locations with the refuse of inferior tribes. Given decent dwelling-places, education on rational lines, and after a time, perhaps, a share in municipal government, might lay the foundation of a civic life and an industrial usefulness far more lasting than can be expected from casual labourers brought from distant homes for a few months' work, and carried back again.

South Africa has in her day possessed one man who desired to look at things as they are, a murky and distorted genius at times, but at his best inspired with something of a prophet's insight. The fruit of Mr Rhodes' native administration was the Glen Grey Act, which still remains the only attempt at a constructive native policy. It is hard enough to govern, but sometimes, looking to the iron necessities in the womb of time, it is wise to essay a harder task, and build. We must keep open our communications with the future, and begin by recognising the fundamental truths, which are apt to get a little dimmed by the dust of the political arena. The first is that the native is psychologically a child, and must be treated as such; that is, he is in need of a stricter discipline and a more paternal government than the white man. South Africa has already recognised this by the remarkable consensus of opinion which she has shown in the prohibition of the sale of intoxicants to coloured people. He is as incapable of complete liberty as he is undeserving of an unintelligent censure. The second is that he is with us, a permanent factor which must be reckoned with, in spite of the advocates of a crude Bismarckian policy; and because his fortunes are irrevocably linked to ours, it is only provident to take care that the partnership does not tend to our moral and political disadvantage. For there is always in the distance a grim alternative of over-population resulting in pauperism and anarchy, or a hard despotism producing the moral effects which the conscience of the world has long ago in slave systems diagnosed and condemned. There are three forces already at work which, if judiciously fostered, will achieve the experiment which South Africa is bound to make, and either raise the Kaffir to some form of decent citizenship, or prove to all time that he is incapable of true progress. Since we are destroying the old life, with its moral and social codes and its checks upon economic disaster, we are bound to provide an honest substitute. The forces referred to are those of a modified self-government, of labour, and of an enlightened education. The first is an experiment which must be undertaken very carefully, unless our case is to be prejudiced from the outset. I have given reasons for the view that a political franchise for the native is logically unjustifiable; but on district councils and within municipal areas the native, wherever he is living under conditions of tolerable decency and comfort, might well play a part in his own control. It may be doomed to failure or it may be the beginning of political education, but it is an experiment we can scarcely fail to make. In labour, short of a crude compulsion, every means must be used to bring the Kaffir within the industrial circle. We shall be assisted in our task by many secret forces, but it should be our business so to frame our future native legislation as to place a bonus on labour outside the kraal. The matter is so intimately bound up with the wellbeing of the whole population that there is less fear of neglect than of undue and capricious haste.

A word remains to be said on native education. In this province there is much need of effective Government control, since in the past the energies of educationalists have tended to flow in mistaken channels or be dissipated over too wide an area. The native is apt to learn in a kind of parrot fashion, and this aptitude has misled many who have devoted their lives to his interests. But in the present state of his culture what we are used to call the "humanities" have little educational importance. At the best the result is to turn out native pastors and schoolmasters in undue numbers, unfortunate men who have no proper professional field and no footing in the society to which their education might entitle them. It is a truth which the wiser sort of missionaries all over the world are now recognising in connection with the propagation of Christianity—that the ground must be slowly prepared before the materialist savage mind can be familiarised with the truths of a spiritual religion. Otherwise the result is a glib confession of faith which ends in scandal. The case is the same with what we call "secondary education." The teaching of natives, if it is to produce any practical good, should, to begin with, be confined to the elements and to technical instruction. The native mind is very ready to learn anything which can be taught by concrete instances, and most forms of manual dexterity, even some of the more highly skilled, come as easily to him as to the white man. When the boys are taught everywhere carpentry and ironwork and the rudiments of trade, and the girls sewing and basket-making and domestic employments, a far more potent influence will have been introduced than the Latin grammar or the primer of history. The wisest missionary I have ever met had a station which was a kind of ideal city for order and industry, with carpenters' and blacksmiths' shops, a model farm, basket-making, orchards, and dairies. "By these means," he said, "I am teaching my children the elements of religion, which are honesty, cleanliness, and discipline." "And dogma?" I asked. "Ah," he said, "as to dogma, I think we must be content for the present with a few stories and hymns."

[28] It is proposed to assimilate native taxation in Southern Rhodesia to the system now in vogue in the Transvaal, and impose a poll tax of £2, with a tax of 10s. for each extra wife. In the Orange River Colony it is proposed to raise the hut tax to £1.

[29] The question of native ownership of land in the new colonies is not very clear. In the Transvaal land was generally held in trust for natives by the Native Commissioners; but apparently half-castes could own land, and Asiatics under certain restrictions. In the Orange River Colony ownership by Asiatics is forbidden; but certain native tribes, such as the Barolongs in Maroka, and the Oppermans at Jacobsdaal, as well as half-castes and the people known as the Bastards, were allowed freehold titles, subject to certain restrictions on alienation.

CHAPTER XV.

JOHANNESBURG.

It is a delicate matter to indulge in platitudes about a city. For a city is an organism more self-conscious than a state, and a personality less robust than an individual. Comments which, if made on a nation, would be ignored, and on an individual would be tolerated, awaken angry reprisals when directed to a municipal area. The business is still more delicate when the city concerned is not yet quite sure of herself. Johannesburg is a city, though she has no cathedral to support the conventional definition, or royal warrant to give her dignitaries precedence; but she is a city still on trial, sensitive, ambitious, profoundly ignorant of her own mind. Her past has been short and checkered. She has done many things badly and many things well; she has been the target for universal abuse, and still with one political party fills the honourable post of whipping-boy in chief to the Empire. Small wonder if her people are a little dazed—proud of themselves, hopeful of her future, but far from clear what this future is to be.

At first sight she has nothing to commend her. The traveller who drags his stiff limbs from the Cape mail sees before him a dusty road, some tin-roofed shanties, with a few large new jerry buildings humped above them: a number of straggling dusty pines and gums, a bit of bare hillside in the distance, and a few attenuated mine chimneys. Everything is new, raw, and fortuitous, as uncivilised and certainly as ugly as the desert ridge on which an old Bezuidenhout planted his homestead. The chief streets do not efface the first impression. Some buildings are good, but the general effect is mean. The place looks as if it had sprung up, like some Western township, in a night, and as if the original builders had been in such a desperate hurry to get done with it that they could not stop to see that one house kept line with its neighbours. It is a common South African defect, but there is here no *mise-en-scène* to relieve the ugliness. Looking at Pretoria from the hills one sees a forest of trees, with white towers and walls rising above the green. The walls may be lath and plaster, but the general effect is as pretty as the eye could wish. For Johannesburg there is no such salvation. Looked at from one of her many hills, the meanness and irregularity are painfully clear. She has far more trees than Pretoria, but she is so long and sprawling that the bare ribs have pushed aside their covering. An extended brickfield is the first impression: a prosperous powder-factory is the last.

Yet in her way she has many singular beauties. Doubtless in time to come she will be so great that she will contain more cities than one in her precincts, and there may well be a residential quarter as fine as any in Europe. The Rand is a long shallow basin with hilly rims, within which lie the mines and the working city. The southern rim shelves away into featureless veld, but the northern sinks sharply on a plain, across forty miles of which rise the gaunt lines of the Magaliesberg. What fashionable suburb has a vista of forty miles of wild country, with a mountain wall on the horizon? Below on the flats there are many miles of pine woods, valleys and streams and homesteads, and the Pretoria road making a bold trail over a hill. In winter the horizon is lit with veld-fires; in summer and spring there are the wild sunsets of the veld and soft mulberry gloamings. The slope behind shuts out the town and the mine chimneys, and yet the whole place is not three miles from Market Square. Whatever happens, nothing can harm the lucky dwellers on the ridge. Though the city creep ten miles into the plain beneath, there is still ample prospect; and not all the fumes from all the industries on earth can spoil the sharp vigour of the winds blowing clean from the wilds.

But the place has not yet found itself. The city proper is still for the future; for the present we have a people. What the real conception, current in England, of this people may be it is not easy to tell, the whole matter having been transferred to party politics, and presented, plain or coloured, to partisan spectators. So we are given every possible picture, from that of Semitic adventurers nourishing the fires of life on champagne, to that of a respectable and thoroughly domesticated people, morbidly awake to every sentiment of Empire. "Judasburg," "the New Jerusalem," "the Golden City," and a variety of other pet names, show that to the ordinary man, both in and out of parties, there is something bizarre and exotic about the place. And yet no conception could be more radically false. Johannesburg is first and foremost a colonial city, an ordinary colonial city save for certain qualities to be specified later. You will see more Jews in it than in Montreal or Aberdeen, but not more than in Paris; and any smart London restaurant will show as large a Semitic proportion as a Johannesburg club. For a "Golden City" it is not even conspicuously vulgar. For one fellow in large checks, diamonds, and a pink satin tie, you will meet fifty quietly dressed, well-mannered gentlemen. A man may still be a beggar to-day and rich to-morrow, but less commonly and in a different sense. The old mining-camp, California-cum-Ballarat character of the gold industry on the Rand has utterly passed away. Gold-mining has ceased to be a speculation, and has become a vast and complicated industry, employing at high salaries the first engineering talent of the world. The prominent mine-owner is frequently a man of education, almost invariably a man of high ability. In few places can you find men of such mental vigour, so eagerly receptive of new ideas, so keenly awake to every change of the financial and political worlds of Europe. The blackguard alien exists, to be sure, but he is rarely felt, and the hand of the law is heavy upon him. That Johannesburg is made up wholly of adventurers and Whitechapel Jews is the first piece of cant to clear the mind of.

The second is the old slander that the people think of nothing but the market, are cowardly and selfish, indifferent to patriotism and honour. It says little for Englishmen that they could believe this falsehood of a place where the greater part of the inhabitants are English. The war meant dismal sufferings for the artisan class, who had to live in expensive coast lodgings or comfortless camps; and it is to the credit of Johannesburg that she stood nobly by her refugees. The old Reform movement was not a fortunate enterprise, but there was no lack of courage in it; and even those who may grudge the attribute can scarcely deny it to the same men at Elandslaagte and Ladysmith. There have been various sorts of irregular regiments—many good, some bad, one or two the very scum of the earth; but no irregular soldiers showed, from first to last, a more cool and persistent courage than the men who for years had sought to achieve by persuasion an end which required a more summary argument. The truth is that the Johannesburger has suffered by being contrasted, as the typical townsman, with the Boer, as the typical countryman. Dislike the particular countryman as we may, we have at the back of our minds a feeling that somehow, in George Eliot's phrase, an unintelligible dialect is a guarantee for ingenuousness, and that slouching shoulders indicate an upright disposition. It is Johannesburg's misfortune that this anomalous contrast should be forced on us. It is as if a sixteenth-century peasant, without enterprise, without culture, wholly un-modern and un-political, believing stoutly in a sombre God, were living side by side with a race of *intellectuels*, scientists, and successful merchants. Whatever reason or, as in this case, patriotism may say, most men have a sneaking fondness for the peasant.

In every community which is worth consideration we find two forces present in some degree—the force of social persistence and the force of social movement. Critics of Johannesburg would have us believe that the second only is to be found, and in its crudest form: the truth is that, considering the history of the place and its novelty, the first is remarkably strong. The point is worth labouring at the risk of tediousness. It must be some little while before a mining city shakes off the character of a mining camp. Men will long choose to live uncomfortably in hotels and boarding-houses, looking for their reward on their home-coming, discomfort none the less unpleasant because it is tempered with unmeaning luxury. To its inhabitants the place is no continuing city,—only a camp for the adventurer, who, when he has made the most of it, returns to enjoy the fruits of his labour in his own place. And then, after many years, there suddenly comes a day when a man here and a man there realise that they have lost the desire to return: they like the place, settle down, and found a home. Whenever there is any fair proportion of this class in a mining city, then we have a force of social persistence. The tendency is found in every class of society. At one time the miner from Wales or Cornwall saved his earnings and returned home; now he has his wife out and settles for good. There is also a large commercial class, traders and small manufacturers, who belong as thoroughly to the place as the South African born. And with the more educated classes the same thing is true. The price of building sites in the suburbs and the many pretty houses which have arisen show that even for this class, which was most nomadic in its habits, domesticity has become a fact.

This, then, is the cardinal achievement of Johannesburg, an unparalleled achievement in so short a career. She has in a few years changed herself from a camp to a city, acquired a middle class and a decent artisan class,—both slow and difficult growths,—and shown a knack of absorbing any species of alien immigrant and putting them on the way to respectable citizenship. She has but to point to this solid achievement as a final answer to the foolish calumnies of her enemies. The mines are her staple industry, but the mines, so far as she is concerned, are an industry and not a speculation; and she is creating a dozen other industries of quite a different character, and may well create a hundred more. She has become a municipality, with all the traits, good and bad, of a nourishing municipality at home. She has become colonial, too,—as colonial, though in a different way, as Melbourne or Wellington. Formerly she was a mixture of every European capital plus a little of the Dutch dorp: now she is English in essence, the most English of all South African towns.

The future of the chief municipality of South Africa cannot be without interest, for most problems will concern her first, and receive from her their colour and character, and, possibly, their answer. She must continue to represent one of the two foremost interests, and though it is idle to distinguish political interests by their importance when both are vital, yet we can admit that Johannesburg has for the moment more obvious difficulties in her problems, and that her answer will be more stormily contested. So far her development has been continuous. The difficulties which she met with from the Kruger *régime* were a blessing in disguise, being of the kind to put her on her mettle. But the present stage in her history is more critical. Formerly the question was whether she was to remain a foreign cesspool or rise to the status of an English city. Now it is whether she will go the way of many colonial cities, and become vigorous, dogmatic, proud, remotely English in sentiment, consistently material in her outlook, and narrow with the intense narrowness of those to whom politics mean local interests spiced with rhetoric; or, as she is already richer, more enlightened, and more famous than her older sisters, will advance on a higher plane, and become in the true sense an imperial city, with a closer kinship and a more liberal culture. The question is a subtle and delicate one, as all questions of spiritual development must be. A year ago much depended on the attitude of England. Johannesburg had suffered heavily in the war. Time and patience were needed to repair the breaches in her fortunes, and to permit her to advance, as she must advance, if the Transvaal is to become a nation. She was rightly jealous of her reputation and future prosperity. If taxation was to be crudely imposed, if her just complaints were to be met with the old nonsense about a capitalists' war, if she was to be penalised for her most creditable industry, then there was a good prospect of a serious estrangement. There was no issue on the facts. She never denied her liability, and she was willing to pay cheerfully if a little common tact were shown in the handling. A man who may have his hand in his pocket to repay a debt will withdraw it if his creditor tries to collect the money with a bludgeon. Happily the crisis has passed. A scheme of war contribution was arranged which, while still bearing heavily, almost too heavily, on the country in its present transition stage, is yet a small sum if contrasted with the lowest estimate of her assets. But much still depends on the attitude of England. A little sympathy, a little friendliness, a modest diminution of newspaper taunts, some indication that the home country sees and appreciates the difficulties of its daughter, and is content to trust her judgment: it is not much to ask, but its refusal will never be forgotten or forgiven. For Johannesburg in this connection represents the country on its most sensitive side, and acts as a barometer of national feeling.

In this imperfect world there can be no development without attendant disorders. A dead body is never troublesome, but a growing child is prone to exasperate. A young city which is perfectly reasonable and docile deserves to be regarded with deep mistrust, for it is likely to continue in a kind of youthful sensibility till it disappears. Ferment is a sign of life, and the very crudeness of the ideals which cause the ferment is a hopeful proof of vigour. Municipalities since the beginning of time have been the home of aspirations after self-government, however ill-suited they may have been to rule themselves. At this moment the Transvaal is a Crown colony, which is to say that a mode of government devised for subject races is being applied for a time to a free and restless British population. The justification is complete, but we need not be shocked when we find Johannesburg chafing at her fetters. The less so when we reflect that in one aspect she is a colonial city, full of the exaggerated independence of the self-made. The fastidiousness which comes from culture and tradition, the humour which springs from unshaken confidence, must necessarily be absent in a municipality which is still diffident, still largely uneducated. Politics must begin with the *schwärmerisch* and the vapid,—"that vague barren pathos, that useless effervescence of enthusiasm, which plunges with the spirit of a martyr into an ocean of generalities." Embryo cities are drunk with words, with half-formed aspirations and vague ideals; wherefore the result must be sound and fury and little meaning till by painful stages they find themselves and see things as they are. So far this unrest has taken two forms—a continuous and somewhat unintelligent criticism of the Administration, and an attempt by means of numerous associations to give voice to popular demands in the absence of representative institutions; and the beginnings of a labour party. The first is as natural as day and night. Many grave matters, chiefly financial, are being decided above Johannesburg's head, and it is reasonable that she should wish to state her own case. This is her strong point: the weakness of her position is that it is also a criticism of a reconstruction which is still in process, still in that stage when the facts are far more clearly perceived by the man on the watch-tower than by the crowd in the streets below. A pawn in a game is not the best authority on the moves which lead to success. Patience may be a distasteful counsel, but why should she disquiet herself when all things in the end must be in her hands? "The people," to paraphrase a saying of Heine, "have time enough, they are immortal; administrators only must pass away." But we cannot complain of this critical activity, however misplaced. It is a sign of life, and is itself the beginnings of political education. The second form of agitation is less reasonable and more dangerous, though perhaps less dangerous here than anywhere else in the world. There must exist on the Rand, in mines, railways, and subsidiary industries, a large white industrial population; and the imported agitator will endeavour to organise it in accordance with his interests. There is little theoretical justification for the movement. There are no castes and tyrannies to fight against in a country which is so new and self-created. The great financial houses will not develop into Trusts on the American model; and even if they did, the result would have small effect on the working man, either as labourer or consumer. There are dozens of false pretexts. The working man of the Rand may try, as he has tried in Australia, to stereotype his monopoly and prevent the influx of new labour; or he may use the necessary discomforts of a transition stage as a lever to raise his wages; or the idle and incompetent may grumble vaguely against a capitalism which has been built up by their abler brothers. The pretexts are light as air. He lives in a free society, and within limits can secure his comfort and independence beyond a chance of encroachment. But unhappily it does not require a justification in reason to bring the labour agitator into being. That type, so well known in Australia, has already appeared, the unreasoning obstructionist, who, armed with a few platitudes and an entire absence of foresight, preaches his crude gospel to a class which is already vaguely unsettled by the intricacies of the economic problem. There is almost certain to be an attempt to organise labour on Australian lines, and to create a party like the Sand Lot agitators in San Francisco, in order to do violence to the true economic interests of the land on behalf of a prejudice or a theory. Yet I cannot think that there is more in the prospect than a temporary inconvenience. No labour party can be really formidable unless it is based on profound discontents and radical grievances; and the annoyances of the Johannesburg proletariat are, as compared with those of Europe, like crumpled rose-leaves to thorns. There is too strong a force of social persistence in the city to suffer it ever to become the prey of a well-organised gang of revolutionaries; and if such a force exists, the experience of Victoria in its great railway strike of 1903 would seem to show that in the long-run no labour war can succeed which tends to a wholesale disorganisation of social and industrial life.

But if Johannesburg shows a certain unrest, she also reveals a curious solidarity—the strength of narrowness and exclusion, which is partly natural and due to the struggle for self-conscious existence, and partly accidental and based on a profound disappointment. Her citizens believed that the end of the war would begin a golden age of unprecedented prosperity. Money was to flow into her coffers, her population to grow by many thousands each year, and she herself was to stand out before an envious world as a type of virtue rewarded. She miscalculated the future, and the facts left her aghast. Conservative estimates, a few years back, put the value of the gold output in 1902 at between 20 and 30 millions: the actual figures during the first year of peace show little over 10 millions—a reduction on the output of 1898. Hence the almost hysterical concentration of interest on the one great industry. Men who in other matters are remarkable for their breadth of view, are to be found declaring that everything must be made subordinate to mining development,—not in the sense in which the saying is true, that the prosperity of the country depends in the first instance on the mines, but in the quite indefensible sense that any consideration of other things, even when there is no conflict between them and the mining interest, is a misapplication of energy which should go to the greater problem. It is fair to argue against a programme of public works which might draw native labour from the mines, because, unless we cherish the goose, there will be no golden eggs to pay for our programmes. But to condemn schemes of settlement which are no more a hindrance to the gold industry than to the planetary system, is to show a nervous blindness to graver questions, which is the ugliest product of the present strain and confusion. This trait, however, cannot be permanent; and we may look to see the gold industry in time, when its own crisis is past, become that enlightened force in politics which the ability of its leaders and the weight of its organisation entitle it to be. For the other form of narrowness, which consists in the limitation of citizenship, there is ample justification in present circumstances. A new city must begin by drawing in her skirts and showing herself, perhaps unwarrantably, jealous and sensitive. More especially a city which has hitherto been rather a fortuitous gathering of races than a compact community, is right in straining after such compactness, even at the cost of a little injustice. The only danger lies in the perpetuation of this attitude when its justification has gone.

The fault of Johannesburg, to sum up, lies for the moment in a certain narrow hardness of view: her hope is in the possession of rich elements unknown in most new cities; while her greatest danger lies in the fact that she cannot yet honestly claim those elements as her own. She is apt to judge a question from a lower point of view than the question demands—to take up a parochial standpoint in municipal affairs, a municipal standpoint in national affairs, a national standpoint in imperial questions. In spite of her many splendid loyalties, she will find it hard to avoid the assertive *contra mundum* attitude which seems inseparable from flourishing colonial cities—a dogmatism natural, but unfortunate. On the other hand, her history and her present status give her a chance beyond other new cities. She starts on her civic career already rich, enterprising, the magnet for the first scientific talent of the world. A fortunate development might give her a cultivated class, true political instincts, and the self-restraint which springs from a high civilisation, without at the same time impairing that energy which she owes to her colonial parentage. The danger is that her ablest element may continue alien, treating the city as a caravanserai, and returning to Europe as soon as its ambition is satisfied. So far the intellect has not been with the men who have made the place their home, but, subject to a few remarkable exceptions, with the men who have never concealed their impatience to get away. If she fails to make this class her citizens, then, whatever her prosperity, as a city she will remain mediocre. Nothing can deprive her of her position as the foremost market; but if she is to be also the real capital of South Africa, she must absorb the men who are now her resident aliens. There are signs, indeed, that the process has begun in all seriousness. As she becomes a more pleasant dwelling-place, many who find in the future of the country the main interest of their lives will find in Johannesburg the best field of labour for the end they desire. And the growth of such a leisured class, who take part in public life for its own sake and for no commercial interests, will not only import into municipal politics a broader view and a healthier spirit, but will do much to secure that community of interest between town and country by which alone a united South Africa can be created.

CHAPTER XVI.

CONSTITUTIONAL QUESTIONS.

The constitutional requirements of a country are never determined solely by its political needs. Some account must be taken of its prior history, for theories of government are apt to sink deep into the mind of a people and to become unconsciously a part of its political outlook. No form of education is less conscious or more abiding in its effects. It may even happen that the fabric which such theories created has been deliberately overthrown with the popular consent, but none the less the theories are still there in some form or other to obtrude themselves in future experiments. It is always worth while, therefore, in any reconstruction to look at the ideas of government which held sway before, whether in the shape of a professed creed or in the practical form of institutions. The constitutional history of South Africa is not long, and it is not complex. In Natal and Cape Colony we possess two specimens of ordinary self-governing colonies. Natal, which began life as a Crown colony, subject to the Governor of the Cape, was granted substantive independence by charter in 1856, and in 1893 was given representative government. It possesses a nominated legislative council of nine members, and an elective legislative assembly of thirty-nine members, elected on an easy franchise. Cape Colony also began as a Crown colony, and followed nearly the same path. Her legislative council was created in 1850, and by an ordinance of this legislature in 1872, ratified by an Act of the Imperial Parliament, she obtained full representative institutions. Her council and her house of assembly are each elected and on the same franchise. In these two colonies we have, therefore, types of colonial autonomy—that is to say, an unfettered executive and freedom to legislate subject to the consent of the Governor and the Crown in Council, a limitation which is daily becoming more of a pious fiction. In Southern Rhodesia we have a specimen of that very modern experiment, government by a commercial company. It is a provisional form, and has been made to approximate as far as is reasonably possible to a Crown colony. The executive power is in the hands of the company's officials, subject to an indirect control by the Imperial Resident Commissioner, the High Commissioner, and ultimately by the Crown. There is a legislative council, partly nominated by the company and partly elected, and all legislation is contingent upon the sanction of the imperial authorities. Lastly, there are the native states, the Crown colony of Basutoland, and the protectorates of Bechuanaland, North-West Rhodesia, and Swaziland, all of which are directly or indirectly under the authority of the High Commissioner. So far there is no constitutional novelty—Crown colonies advancing to an ordinary type of self-government, or remaining, provisionally or permanently, under full imperial control.

There remain the late Governments of the Republics, which to the student of constitutional forms show certain interesting peculiarities.[30] These constitutions were framed by men who had no tradition[31] to fall back upon, if we exclude the Mosaic law, and no theories to give effect to—men who would have preferred to do without government, had it been possible, but who, once the need became apparent, brought to the work much shrewdness and good sense. The Natal emigrants in 1838 had established a Volksraad, but the chief feature in their scheme was the submission of all important matters to a primary public assembly, a Homeric gathering of warriors. By the time the Sand River and Bloemfontein Conventions were signed and the two republics became independent, the people were scattered over a wide expanse of country, and some form of representation was inevitable. At the same time, it had become necessary to provide for a military organisation coextensive with the civil. In the Transvaal transient republics had arisen and departed, like the changes in a kaleidoscope. Around both states there was a native population, actively hostile and potentially dangerous. Some central military and civil authority was needed to keep the country from anarchy. But if the farmers were without political theories, they had a very vigorous sense of personal independence; so the doctrinal basis of the new constitution lay in the axiom that one burgher in the State is as good as another, and that the people are the final repository of power. In this at least they were democratic, though from other traits of democracy they have ever held aloof.

The *Constitutie* of the Orange Free State was rigid—that is, it could be altered only by methods different from those of ordinary legislation: in the Transvaal *Grondwet*, on the other hand, there was no provision for change at all, and reforms, when necessary, were made in the ordinary legislative manner. The *Constitutie* created one supreme legislature, the Volksraad, elected by the qualified white population. The President was elected by the whole people, though the Volksraad, like the Roman consuls, reserved the power to make nominations, which were generally accepted. The Volksraad had not only supreme legislative power, but, while formally independent of the President and the executive, it could reverse any executive Act, except the exercise of the President's right of pardon and the declaration of martial law. It was limited only by its own charter, which forbade it to restrict the right of public meeting and petition (one of the few Bill of Rights elements in this constitution), and bound it to promote and support the Dutch Reformed Church. The Transvaal *Grondwet* began by making the Dutch Reformed Church an established national Church (a provision repealed later), and declaring that "the people will not tolerate any equality between coloured and white inhabitants in Church or State." No man was eligible for a seat in the Volksraad unless he was a member of a Protestant Church.[32] In the Transvaal, as in the Orange Free State, the Volksraad was the supreme legislative authority, but when any law was proposed the people were given the opportunity of expressing their opinion in a mild form of the referendum. The President was elected by the whole people and acted as chief of the executive, though responsible to the Volksraad, which could dismiss him or cancel his appointments. He could sit and speak in the Volksraad, but had no vote. The chief military authority was the Commandant General, who was elected by all the burghers, and under him there was a long hierarchy of district commandants and field-cornets. The local administrative officer for civil matters was the landdrost or district magistrate. It is unnecessary to consider the Second Volksraad, which was an ineffective advisory body elected on a wider franchise, a mere sop to the Cerberus whose hundred tongues were clamouring for representation. But there was one curious development of considerable historic interest. In cases of urgency the Volksraad could pass laws without reference to the people at large, but such an enactment was called a resolution (*besluit*) as contrasted with a law (*wet*), and was supposed to have only a provisional force. But the habit grew of calling most matters "specially urgent," and allowing the old popular referendum to fall into desuetude.

The common feature of both constitutions was the immense nominal powers of the legislatures. Nominally they had the right to make all appointments, to veto the President's action, and to say the last word in all questions of revenue and expenditure. But certain facts wrought against this legislative supremacy. The members came from districts widely apart, and there was no serious attempt to form groups or parties; the President could sit and speak in the Volksraad, and he might be elected as often as he could persuade the people to elect him. The way was paved for the tyranny of a strong man. In the Orange Free State, that country of mild prosperity and simple problems, the system worked admirably; but in the Transvaal, when burning questions arose, the republican methods for all serious purposes broke down, and were replaced by a dictatorship. There remain, however, certain doctrines from the old *régime* which will have to be reckoned with under the new. The supremacy of the legislature is not one, for no Boer cared much for the dogma, and Mr Kruger ruled on the simple maxim, "L'état c'est moi." But the democratic principle of equality among citizens is one cherished belief, and another is the absolute disqualification of all coloured races.[33] The Boer is not a parliamentarian in the ordinary sense, and he did not grieve when his Volksraad was slighted and made impotent; but he likes his representative to go to Pretoria, as a sort of tribute to his importance, and, if he is to vote, he demands to vote on an equal basis with all. He was attached to his local administration with its landdrost system, and any change which bore no relation to the old plan might begin by confusing and end by souring him.

We have therefore to face two existing constitutional traditions—among the British from the Cape or Natal or over-seas, the old love of colonial self-government; among the Boers, at least in the Transvaal, a kind of ingenuous republican independence, quite consistent with a patient tolerance of absolutism, but not so easy to adapt to the gradations of our representative system.

Hence in many ways the Boer is far more likely to remain patient for years under a Crown colony Government than the English or colonial new-comer. He does not particularly want to vote or interfere in administration, so long as he has no personal grievance; but it might annoy him to see the franchise denied to him and given to his cousin who was a little richer or better educated, when he remembered the old *Grondwet* doctrines of equality, and it would certainly exasperate him to learn that any native had been granted a civic status beyond him.

Such being the constitutional history, we may turn to the present. The term Crown colony is used so loosely that very few of its many critics could define the peculiar features of this form of government. "One of the greatest of all evils," wrote Lord Durham in the famous Report which has become the charter of colonial policy, "arising from this system of irresponsible government, was the mystery in which the motives and actual purposes of their rulers were hid from the colonists themselves. The most important business of government was carried on, not in open discussions or public acts, but in a secret correspondence between the Governor and the Secretary of State." This feature, more than any other, tends to dissatisfaction. The Crown colony system is necessarily a secret one. The newspapers, till blue-books are issued, are informed only as much or as little as the authorities may think good for them; and the natural critics of all administration have the somewhat barren pleasure of finding fault with a policy after it has become a fact.

There is no safety-valve for the escape of grievances, no official channel even for sound local advice. It is not to be wondered at, therefore, if it seems an intolerable burden to men full of anxiety about the methods by which they are governed.

The Crown colony system is not new to Africa. It existed for years in the Cape and Natal; it still exists in its most rigid form over native states, and at its worst it does not spurn public opinion in the fashion of the Kruger *régime*—it simply neglects it. The name is really a misnomer, for it is no part of the English colonial system. The American Revolution is sometimes described as the revolt of an English people from Crown colony government, but in those days the thing was not in existence. It is fundamentally the method invented to govern a race which is incapable of free representative institutions, or to tide over a temporary difficulty. The Governor is absolute, subject to the conditions of his appointment and the instructions accompanying his letters-patent. He may be assisted by a council, but it is his privilege, on reasons shown, to override his council. He is the sole local fountain of executive and legislative power. But if he is absolute in one sense, he is strictly tied in another. The methods of his administration are subject to certain regulations issued by the Colonial Office. The Secretary of State must approve his appointments, and all important administrative acts, as well as all legislation. Further, in serious questions the Home Government exercises a general oversight of policy before the event, and the Governor in such matters is merely the mouthpiece of the Cabinet. It is in itself a rational system, and works well under certain conditions. In a serious crisis, when large imperial issues are involved, and when local policy is but a branch of a wider policy, it is highly important that this day-to-day supervision should exist; and in a case where speed is essential, Crown colony methods, though slow enough in all conscience, are rapidity itself compared with the cumbrous machinery of representative government.

The necessity of treating the Transvaal and the Orange River Colony temporarily as Crown colonies was beyond argument. Reconstruction began in the midst of war, when the material of self-government was wanting. It goes on amidst unsettled and dimly understood conditions, where certain facts of policy stand out in a strong light and all else is shadow. It involves many financial transactions in which the Home Government is deeply interested; and it is natural that a close administrative connection should be thought desirable. It comes at the end of a costly war, and it is right that England should have a direct say in securing herself against its repetition. The racial problem is still too delicate to submit to the arbitrament of popular bodies; and if it were settled out of hand there might remain an abiding cause of discontent. The time is not ripe for self-government, the country has not yet found herself, having but barely awakened from the torpor of war and begun to set her house in order. Again, there are factors to be borne in mind in re-creating the new colonies which extend far beyond their borders. It is impossible to imagine that due consideration could be given to them by the ablest elective body in the world, called together in the present ferment. Above all, what is to be done must be done quickly. The wants of the hour are too urgent for delays. There must be some authority, trusted by the British Cabinet, capable of determining the needs of the situation, and giving summary effect to his decision.

On this all thinking men in the new colonies are agreed. I do not suppose that any of the more serious critics of the expedient would be prepared to propose and defend an alternative. But irritation remains when reason has done its best, and it is not hard to see the causes. One is the natural disinclination of Englishmen to be ruled from above, a repulsion which they feel even when arguing in its favour. Another is the secrecy of Crown colony government, to which I have already referred. It is painful to find matters of vital importance to yourself decided without your knowledge, even when you have the fullest confidence in the deciding power. There is also, perhaps, a little distrust still left in South Africa of the British Government,—not of particular Ministers, but of the vague entity behind them—a distrust which has had in the past such ample justification that it is hard to blame it. The colonial mind, too, is averse to English officialdom, even when represented by the several highly competent men who have shared in the present administration. Red-tape, which in its place is most necessary and desirable, seems to lurk in the offices of men who are in reality trying hard to deal with facts in the simplest way. A certain amount of formal officialdom is necessary in all government. There must be people to keep an office in order, to make a fetich of etiquette, to insist on a stereotyped procedure, and to see the world dimly through a mist of "previous papers." It is a useful, but not very valuable, type of man, and we cannot wonder that a South African, who imagines that such a one has, what he rarely has, an influence in grave decisions, should view with distrust the form of government which permits him. It is a mistake, but one based on an honest instinct.

Self-government is the goal to which all things hasten, and critics of the present administration check their complaints at the thought of that beneficent day. Meanwhile it is our business to set things in order so that the chosen of the people, when they enter into their inheritance, may find it swept and garnished. Representative institutions should not spring full grown from an Order in Council, like Athene from the brain of Zeus: if they do, there is apt to be a painful crudeness about their early history. The way should be prepared by gentle means, for, after all, it is a country in which the bulk of the residents have had no experience of governing themselves. The experiment has so far been tried in two ways. The municipalities represent the highest level of intelligence and political training; in municipal affairs, therefore, it is safe to begin at once with representation. The first town councils were for all practical purposes Government departments, nominated by Government and assisted on their difficult career by

Government supervision. But a nominated town council is an anomaly even within a Crown colony, since a town council is not concerned with high politics but only with the administration of the area in which its citizens choose to dwell, and any owner of property has a right to a voice in determining the ways in which his property shall be safeguarded. The basis of any municipal franchise is the payment of rates, which imply the ownership of property; and questions of race, loyalty, even of education, have no logical place in what is simply a practical union for the protection of proprietary interests and the care of the amenities of civilised life. The question of elective municipalities is therefore a simple one, and as soon as a municipal law could be put together, the system was inaugurated. This is not the place to examine the type of municipal franchise adopted in the Transvaal, which is a skilful compendium of various colonial precedents. But on one matter, the coloured and alien vote, there was manifested a vigorous tendency to conservatism and exclusion. As I have said, this is a province where racial distinctions have no logical place. If a black man is a ratepayer he has the citizen's right to vote. Nor can we on purely rational grounds confine this franchise to British subjects. But the country thought differently. As the municipal was her only form of representation, political considerations crept in unawares, and the result, while logically indefensible, has a certain practical justification. For in a time of reconstruction a community is apt rather to narrow than enlarge its boundaries, feeling above all things the need of a compact front against the unknown. In time, no doubt, the true theory of municipal franchise will reassert itself, and if, when the time comes, a constructive policy towards the subject races has also come into being, the delay will have been not in vain.

A more important step towards self-government was the creation of nominated legislative councils for both colonies, which held their first meetings in the early part of 1903. In the Transvaal there were sixteen official members representing the different Government departments, and fourteen non-official members selected from representative Englishmen and Boers in the country. In the Orange River Colony there were six official members and four non-official. Some of the new measures which concerned more deeply the people of the colonies were kept back on purpose for the opinion of the new councils. Such were the new gold and diamond laws, the municipal franchise law, and the ordinances governing the disposal of town lands. So far the expedient has promised well; an outlet has been created for public opinion, though for the present such opinion cannot carry with it practical force; and the procedure of Government has ceased to be a state secret, and is patent to any one who has the curiosity or the patience to attend the council's debates. It is interesting to observe how the unofficial members already appear in a quasi-representative capacity, and are beginning to attach themselves to particular districts, for which, so far as airing grievances and obtaining information go, they perform most of the duties of an elected member. There is no reason why such members should not be elected instead of nominated, and in this way provide a trial for the form of franchise on which autonomy is to be based. There are many obvious difficulties in any franchise for the new colonies, and it would be well for such difficulties to be realised and faced while the whole matter is still mainly academic, and errors are not yet attended with practical disaster.

The franchise for the new colonies is the constitutional problem which is of the most immediate importance. It will not be wise to delay the era of self-government long, for between the most elastic Crown colony and the narrowest free colony there is an inseparable gulf, and though it may be said justly that with an elective legislature the colonies have something very like freedom, the one thing needful will still be lacking. It is not enough to put the oars into their hands; we must cut the painter before they are truly free. There is one postulate in all franchise discussions which is likely to be vigorously attacked. The franchise must be based in the first instance upon the principle of giving adequate representation to all districts and every interest; but, once this has been recognised, the second principle appears—of providing for the supremacy of the British population. That saying of Dogberry's, "An two men ride of a horse, one must ride behind," is a primary law not only of equitation but of politics in the treatment of a conquered country. For conquered it is, and there is little use disguising it: we have not been fighting for the love of it or for fine sentiment, but to conquer the land and give our people the mastery. The last word in all matters must rest with us—that is, with the people of British blood and British sympathies. Both men must be on the horse, or, apart from parable, each race must have fair and ample representation. To deny this would be to sin against sound policy. But not to take measures to see that our own race has the casting vote is to be guilty of the commonest folly. "An two men ride of a horse, one must ride behind."

Whoever denies this principle may spare himself the trouble of reading further, for it is proposed to treat it as axiomatic. The first type of franchise need not be permanent: a day may come when it will be needless to consider the distinction of Dutch and British. But as it was right and politic on the conclusion of war to disarm our opponents, so it is right and politic in the first franchise to put no weapon of offence into their hands. The primary adjustment of the franchise and the primary distribution of seats must be made with this clear end in view—to secure a working majority for the British people. It is obvious that the words "British population" are vague, and include many odd forms of nationality, but the thing itself is simple, the class whose interests and sentiment are on the British side, who seek progress on British lines. It does not follow that the majority of the Dutch will go into opposition, but it is ordinary prudence to keep on the safe side. Such a policy involves no distrust of the Dutch population, but is the common duty of those who for a certain period must, as conquerors, take the initiative in administration, and, as bearing the responsibility, preserve an adequate means of control.

The terms of the franchise are a more difficult matter. In Cape Colony citizenship and a low property qualification are the chief conditions. In Southern Rhodesia, whose franchise law is an especially clear and sensible code, an oath of loyalty is accepted in lieu of technical citizenship, and an easy educational test is demanded—the ability of a voter to sign his name and write his address and occupation. In Natal there is a sharp distinction drawn between Europeans and all others. To them the only tests are citizenship, and the ownership or occupation of property of a certain value, or the receipt of a certain amount of income. The native is practically disqualified by a law denying the franchise to any person subject to special courts or special laws, and though a means of escape is provided, the conditions are too complex even for more intelligent minds than the native. It is an ingenious but not wholly satisfactory device. Asiatics are excluded by the law which denies votes to natives, or descendants in the male line of natives, of any country which does not enjoy the blessings of representative government; and though in their case also there is a way of escape, it is almost equally difficult. The root distinction between types of franchise lies in the method employed to exclude an undesirable class, whether a direct one, by disqualifying in so many words, or an indirect, by setting one standard of qualification for all, to which, as a matter of fact, the undesirable class cannot attain. The balance of argument is, on the whole, on the side of the second method, which has been adopted in Cape Colony and Rhodesia, though, perhaps, with too low a standard. But the first method, if followed more frankly than in Natal, has something to be said for it. There is no reason why the better class of Indians should not vote, if their race is considered fit to mix on equal terms with English society elsewhere; but to my mind there is a very good reason why the native should not vote—at least, not for the present. The easy way of securing this result is the old method of the Transvaal *Grondwet*, which said shortly, "There shall be no equality between black and white." It is the way, too, which, under the Conditions of Surrender, would have to be adopted in any trial franchise put into force before self-government. I am not sure whether it is not the most philosophic as well as the simplest way, for it denies the native the franchise not for a lack of property or educational qualification, but for radical mental dissimilarity. In any case it is a matter which must be left for the people of the colony to settle for themselves. But for all others, while the property basis of the franchise should be low, there are grounds for thinking that a reasonably high educational test should be added. The lower type of European and the back-veld Dutchman have in their present state no equitable right to the decision, which the franchise gives, on matters which they are unable to come within a measurable distance of understanding. The fact that the fool may have a vote at home is no reason for exalting him to the same level in a country which is not handicapped by a constitutional history. Some form of British citizenship, obtainable by a short and simple method, must also be demanded if the land is to remain a British colony.

Once the franchise has been determined there remains the division of constituencies. The axiom has already been explained which appears to govern this question. But in the absence of anything approaching correct census returns it is difficult to suggest, even tentatively, a distribution of seats. The fairest way to secure the representation of all interests seems to be to divide constituencies into three types. First, there are the large towns, which for the present, to take the Transvaal, may be limited to Johannesburg and Pretoria. These would be given members according to their population. Second, come groups of country burghs, such groups as the Northern Burghs, with Nylstroom, Warm Baths, Piet Potgieter's Rust, and Pietersburg; and the Eastern Burghs, with Middelburg and Belfast, Lydenburg and Barberton. Here, too, members would be allotted according to population, though the number of voters required to form a constituency should be fewer. Lastly, there would be the country districts, substantially the present fourteen magisterial divisions, and there the numbers of a constituency would be still smaller. That it is fair to differentiate in favour of the counties against the burghs, and in favour of the burghs against the large towns, will appear on a brief consideration. The interests of the different constituencies in a city, at least in a new city, are practically identical. In the country burghs the interests vary, but still within narrow limits. In the counties, on the other hand, there is often a very wide variation. The dwellers in Barberton have wholly different problems and grievances from the dwellers in Bloemhof or Standerton. But while this principle is right, the former axiom must be kept in mind, that, provided fair representation is granted to all, the constituencies must be so arranged as to ensure British predominance. Certain counties will, I believe, be on the whole British in time—Bloemhof, Marico, Zoutpansberg, possibly Waterberg, possibly Lydenburg, undoubtedly Barberton. The burghs, too, will yield on the whole a British voting population. In all likelihood, therefore, our purpose will be secured by the division of constituencies which I have suggested, even allowing for a differentiation in favour of the rural districts. Figures are still impossible in the absence of a census, but on the roughest estimate there may be in the Transvaal at the present moment a Boer population of 100,000, with a voting proportion of 30,000, and a British population of perhaps 150,000, with a voting proportion of 50,000 or upwards. In the Orange River Colony before the war the voters' roll showed just over 17,000, and if we put the vote on an enlarged franchise at 20,000, we may be near the mark. The position of the latter colony will not change greatly in the next decade, but the Transvaal may easily in a few years show a million inhabitants and more. With a population thus constantly increasing and liable to great local fluctuations, redistribution may soon become a vexed question and a source of political chicanery. It would be well if the endless friction which attends redistribution courts and commissions could be saved by some automatic system under which sudden local inequalities could be speedily and finally adjusted.

The greatest constitutional calamity which could befall South Africa would be for the Dutch in the new colonies to go as a race into opposition. I have said that they are not born parliamentarians, and that, to begin with at least, they will be a little strange to the forms and methods of English representative government. But they are a strong and serious people, and if they desire, as a race, to form an opposition, they will learn the tactics of a parliament as readily as their kinsmen have done in the Cape. It will be difficult to form out of so practical and stable a folk such an opposition as the Nationalist party in Ireland; but if they have real grievances to fight for, it is conceivable that the Dutch people might be organised into as solid a voting machine as the Irish peasantry under the control of the Land League and the Church. Attempts will doubtless be made to bring this about. Certain institutions will spare no pains to secure so promising a recruit in their policy of emphasising every feature in the South African situation which tends to disunion. On the other hand, certain of the natural leaders of the Dutch people, who have acquired the spurious race-hatred which intriguers and adventurers have built up during the past twenty years, in a desperately discreet and orthodox manner may work to the same end. But fortunately there are signs that the party division, when it comes, will be lateral and not vertical. It is a phenomenon often observed in a long war, that a day of apathy sets in, differences arise in a party, and one section begins to dislike the other far more than it hates the common enemy. This phenomenon, which in war spells disaster, is salutary enough in civil politics. In both races there are signs of divisions, and on each side there is a party unconsciously drawing nearer to their old opponents. The majority of the Dutch have little rancour, except against each other; to many the Bond is as much an object of suspicion as, let us say, Mr Chamberlain. The old nebulous Pan-Afrikander dreams were in no way popular with the Transvaal Boer, who would have been nearly as much annoyed at being harassed with an Afrikander federation as at being annexed to Natal. Besides, he is not a good party man, being too sincere an individualist. Intrigue of the carpet-bag and secret-league variety he will never shine in, and he does not desire to, though apt enough at a kind of rustic diplomacy. There is, further, a party ready made for him. He is frankly anti-Johannesburg, a pure agrarian. Already the anomalous labour party of the Rand are making overtures to him, and with loud declamations on his merits strive to attract his sympathies. On certain matters he may join them, but it will be an odd union, and not a long one. Town and country will never long remain in conjunction, and there are few items, indeed, of a labour programme to which he would subscribe.

It is difficult to draw with any confidence the political horoscope of the new colonies. Certain eternal antitheses will exist,—Capital and Labour, Rand and Veld, Progress and the staunchest of staunch

Conservatisms,—but none of them seem likely to coalesce so as to form any permanent division of parties. It is as easy to imagine Rand capitalists and country Dutch united on certain questions as Boer and Labour. Possibly the old distinction of Liberal and Tory in some form or other will appear in the end. It is said that the colonies are aggressively Liberal; but these are different from other colonies, and the groundwork of Conservatism already exists. We have a plutocracy and a landed aristocracy. We have also in the legal element a class, in its South African form, peculiarly tenacious of the letter of the law. We have an established kirk in all but name, and a racial tradition of resistance to novelty. With the growth of a rich and leisured population, and of social grades and conventions, there will come a time when politics may well be divided between those who are satisfied with things as they are, and those who hunger for things as they cannot be—with, of course, a sprinkling of plain men who do their work without theories. We shall have the doctrinaire idealist, doubtless, to experiment on the labour and native questions; and in place of having politics based on interests, we may have them based in name and reality on creeds and dogmas, which is what English constitutionalism desires. All such developments are just and normal, and in any one the land may find political stability.

There is one contingency alone which must be regarded with the greatest dread—the growth of a South African party, which is South African because anti-British. The war raised colonial loyalty to a height; but such loyalty is like a rocket, which may speedily expire in the void in a blaze of brightness, or may kindle a steady flame if the material be there. We must remember that we have in the Dutch a large population to which the British tie means nothing; a large and important class, in the cosmopolitan financiers, who may be covertly hostile to British interests; and even in some of the most sterling and public-spirited citizens men who, if the Dutch Government had allowed them, would have surrendered their nationality and become citizens of the republics. South African loyalty, splendid as it is, is rather fidelity to British traditions than to that overt link which constitutes empire. You will, indeed, hear the true theory of colonial policy well stated and strongly defended; but it must not be forgotten that in South Africa it is still somewhat of an exotic plant, and wants careful tending before it can come to maturity. Unadvised action on our part may nip the growth, and give a chance for a party which might declare, to adopt the words of the old loyalists of Lower Canada, that it was determined to be South African even at the cost of ceasing to be British. A too long or too straitly ordered tutelage might do it, or a harsh dictation on some local question of vital interest, or the continuance of the old calumnies about the Rand, the old vulgar sneer at the colonial-born. It is well to remember that while the land is a Crown colony it is one only in name, and that all the tact and discretion which we use in dealing with self-governing colonies should be used in this case also.

Such a party may arise, but there is no reason in the nature of things for its existence. South African and British are not opposites. As I understand the theory of colonial government, England stands towards her colonies as a parent who starts his sons in the world, wishing them all prosperity; and though in after-years he may exercise the parental right of giving advice, he will not attempt to coerce the action of those who have come to years of maturity. The tie is strongest when it is not of the letter but of the spirit. At the same time it is well to preserve certain outward and visible signs of descent,— well for the fatherland, better for the colonies, who draw from that fatherland their social and political traditions and their spiritual sustenance. At the moment South Africa is in a transition stage. Her public opinion is scarcely formed on any subject; she is full of vague aspirations, uneasy yearnings, and half-fledged hopes. She will develop either into the staunchest of allies in any imperial federation, or the most recalcitrant and isolated of colonies. She has enough and to spare of good men who desire nothing more than that the African nation, when it comes, should be a British people, and if she is trusted whole-heartedly, she will not betray the trust. She will even accept advice and reproof in proper cases, for, unless we drive her to ingratitude, she is not ungrateful for the blood and treasure which Britain has spent on her making. But she is like a young well-bred colt, whose mouth may be easily spoiled by over-bitting, and whose temper will be ruined by the bad hands or too hasty temper of its trainer.

Two important constitutional questions remain. One is the great policy of Federation, which looms as a background behind all sporadic constitutional forms. The second concerns that part of the imperial forces which is to be stationed in South Africa—a matter which is not only an army question but one deeply affecting colonial interests. To these the two succeeding chapters are devoted.

[30] Mr Bryce, in his 'Studies in History and Jurisprudence,' vol. i. pp. 430-467, has a valuable examination of the old Transvaal and Orange River Colony constitutions.

[31] Stray dogmas from the French Revolution had undoubtedly some share in the ferment preceding the Great Trek, but I cannot think that the voortrekkers carried any such baggage with them to the wilderness.

[32] The original *Grondwet* declared that no Roman Catholic Church, nor any Protestant Church which did not teach the Heidelberg Catechism, should be admitted within the Republic.

[33] There was no reason *in law* under the old Orange Free State Government why a native should not have the municipal franchise through ownership, and an Asiatic through occupation of town property. But in practice—a practice deduced from the spirit of the *Constitutie*—no such voters were registered.

CHAPTER XVII.

THE POLICY OF FEDERATION.

No South African problem is more long-descended than the question of Federation. It was a dream of Sir George Grey's in the mid-century, and it was a central feature in the policy of Sir Bartle Frere—that policy which, after twenty years of obscuration, is at last seen in its true and beneficent light. Nor was it held only by English governors. Local statesmen in Cape Colony saw in it a panacea for the endless frontier difficulties which tried their patience and their talents. The ultra-independent colonist, in whose ears "Africa for the Afrikanders" was beginning to ring, seized upon it as a lever towards a more complete autonomy. Men like Mr Rhodes, to whom Africa was an empire and its people one potential nation, looked on it as the first step towards this larger destiny. Every student of political history for the last fifty years, considering the physical situation of the different states and the absence of any final dividing line between them, confidently anticipated for South Africa, and under more favourable conditions, the development which Australia has already reached. But the movement shipwrecked on the northern republics. Old grievances and jealousies set the Transvaal and the Orange Free State in arms against the prospect, and, since the essence of federation is full mutual consent, the project failed at the first hint of serious opposition. Now all things are changed. The social and constitutional difficulties which would obviously arise from the inclusion of independent or all but independent states in a federation of colonies have disappeared with the independent states themselves. Now at last all South Africa save the Portuguese and German seaboards is under one flag.

The chief barriers have gone, but the need for federation is as insistent as ever. A common flag is a strong tie, but it does not in practice prevent many local jealousies and petty oppositions. Disunion is only justifiable among colonies of equal standing when there is some insuperable physical barrier between them or some radical disparity of interests. Providence is so clearly on the side of the larger social battalions, that an isolated state, though within a colonial system, is at a disadvantage even in matters concerning its own interests. The nationalism which rejoices in local distinctions, however recent in origin, is admirable enough in its way, and ought to be preserved; therefore the complete merging of several units in one is always to be regretted, even when justified by grave needs. The new state will never or not for a long time acquire the consistency and proud self-consciousness of the destroyed units. But federation shows another and a better way. The parts are maintained in full national existence, but in so far as their interests transcend their own boundaries they are united in one larger state. There is another advantage, often pointed out by American writers on the subject, which concerns a country like South Africa, whose boundaries cannot yet be said to be finally delimited. North of the Zambesi there is a vast vague region, partly under the High Commissioner, partly included in British Central Africa, which in time will become separate colonies, with interests wholly different from the states of the south. To add a new tract and a novel population to a state is always a difficult matter, for the existing *régime* may be most unsuited for such extension. But it is easy to include a new colony in a federation. In Mr Bryce's words, federation "permits an expansion, whose extension and whose rate and manner of progress cannot be foreseen, to proceed with more variety of methods, more adaptation of laws and administration to the circumstances of each part of the territory, and altogether in a more truly natural and spontaneous way than can be expected under a centralised government. Thus the special needs of a new *régime* are met by the inhabitants in the way they find best; its special evils are met by special remedies, perhaps more drastic than an old country demands, perhaps more lax than an old country would tolerate; while at the same time the spirit of self-reliance among those who build up these new communities is stimulated and respected."[34]

The need for federation in the case of South Africa is made greater by the fact that there are one or two burning questions common to all her states which cannot be satisfactorily settled save by joint action. Foremost stands the native problem. If there is not some sort of geographical continuity of policy in the treatment of natives, all our efforts will be unavailing. The natives of South Africa may be regarded, among other things, as a great industrial reserve; and if the policy outlined in another chapter is to be followed, different labour laws and different methods of taxation may work incalculable harm. If extravagant inducements to work are held out in the Transvaal, it will not be long before the labour market is ruined elsewhere. If an improvident system of taxation exists in Natal, it may unsettle and discontent other native populations, since it is highly probable that in the future natives will be less tied to localities, and will move through the whole country in search of work. The mining authorities have long recognised the necessity of a single policy, as is shown by such institutions as the Chamber of Mines and the Native Labour Association; and it would be odd if in political questions, where the need is equally urgent, the same truth should be neglected. In connection with natives the control of the sale of intoxicants is another matter of South African importance. It is a matter on which South Africa is now practically at one; but there are limits to the prescience of local legislation and local officials, and it may easily happen that an inadequate law inadequately administered in one colony may undo most of the good that an energetic administration is attempting in another. If identity of policy, again, is indispensable in relation to the subject races, the same identity is most desirable in those inter-racial questions between white men which will long have their place in South African politics. An unwise treatment of the Dutch population in the Cape will infallibly react on the new colonies. Any one who knows the way in which Cape precedents in this connection are quoted in the Transvaal, just as Transvaal precedents were quoted before the war in the Cape, will recognise the difficulty which the present disunion creates. In educational matters, such as the proportion of time devoted to the teaching of the Dutch language, while every colony must necessarily decide for itself, there is great need of one controlling authority to supervise and direct. There is, again, the question of permit law and the exclusion of undesirables, and the kindred matter of the position of the imperial forces. A lax permit law in one colony nullifies all the strictness of its neighbours. Army questions—whatever the future position of the South African force—will always have an intercolonial significance, for the different troops are under one commander-in-chief, they will meet for training and manœuvres, and they are part of one general scheme of imperial defence. In some questions an attempt at co-operation has already been made,—in railway conferences and customs unions,—but it is obviously a clumsy method which proceeds from conference agreements to ratification by the several legislatures; and many important and difficult questions will go on arising from day to day which will be decided in quite different ways by local authorities, to the confusion of all and the increase of unnecessary distinctions. Lastly, there are a number of lesser matters, of which veterinary and game regulations may be taken as the type, whose treatment, to be satisfactory, must be governed by a common principle and in the hands of a common executive.

Such are a few of the practical reasons for federation. There is a deeper reason based on the future of our colonial system. South Africa at the present moment is deeply cleft by gulfs of race, fiscal policy, imperial attachment. There will always be within her bounds a party, not perhaps a very important or very intelligent party, made up of those to whom the British tie is galling and the tradition of kinship mere foolishness. If the present particularism is allowed to remain unreformed, it may easily happen that in this colony or that some turn of the political wheel may give such a party an authoritative voice, and the result may be the beginning of endless misunderstandings, and in the end the creation of an impassable gulf. It is because South Africa as a whole is so unswerving in her loyalty that it is wise to create some united authority representing the whole land, and looking at this great question from a high standpoint, which can provide against the parochialism of a party and the accidental caprice of a state. This feeling is strong among the English inhabitants of the new colonies, and is, I believe, destined to grow in width and strength throughout the country, when the fever of reconstruction is at an end and South Africa has leisure to meditate on her political future.

If we examine present conditions we can discern, to borrow the common metaphor of writers on federation, both centripetal and centrifugal tendencies. To begin with, the constitutional framework exists. The head of a federation is already at hand in the High Commissioner, in whom is vested the government of all South Africa apart from the self-governing colonies. It was the custom formerly to combine this office with the governorship of the Cape: for the moment it is joined with the governorship of the Transvaal and the Orange River Colony. With the present narrow definition of the High Commissioner's duties, it is right that this should be so; but there is no constitutional reason why he should not be a separate official. It has never been a popular office with self-governing colonies, who dislike the idea that the governorship should have in one of its aspects powers over which the colony has no control; but this objection could not arise to the head of a federal government. By the letters patent of 1900 the High Commissioner is invested with the control of the South African Constabulary in the new colonies and the administration of the Central South African railways, and he is empowered to call together conferences of the self-governing colonies for the discussion of common problems. Here is already existing the administrative machinery of a federation. The rock on which many federal enterprises have split is the election of the supreme head, and in most systems it is the weakest point. But South Africa is saved this part of the problem. She has a supreme federal office, which has existed for more than twenty years, and with the slightest alteration of functions the High Commissionership could be transformed into a Federal Viceroyalty.

South Africa, again, is for all practical purposes a geographical whole. The vast tableland which makes up nine-tenths of it has almost everywhere uniform climatic conditions, and the strips of coast land have among themselves a comparatively uniform character, so that two types may be said to exhaust its geographical and climatic features. There is no distinction so radical as between the Atlantic states and Texas or between Nebraska and the Pacific seaboard. This physical harmony prevents any natural cleavages, such as impassable mountain-ranges or large navigable rivers; and it imposes upon the inhabitants uniformity in modes of travel, and in the simpler conditions of life. If we look at the people of the several states we find a common nationality—or rather a common admixture of nationalities. The English proportion may be much higher in Natal and the eastern province of Cape Colony, the Dutch in the western province and the Orange River Colony; but everywhere there is the same divided race, and in consequence kindred political problems. There is, further, one supreme Imperial Government for all, one constitutional tradition to provide, as it were, a background to local politics and a basis for federation. There are common dangers from invasion, against which all the colonies are protected by one navy. Subject to minor local differences, there is a common structure observable in the constitutions of the several self-governing colonies to which the Transvaal and Orange River Colony will no doubt in time approximate. Many of the most vital problems are the same for the whole of South Africa,—the control and the civilisation of the natives, the amalgamation of the two white races, the conservation of water, the protection against pests and stock diseases. Two of the most important administrative departments have already a common basis, if they are still far from complete union. All South African railway systems, now that the old Beira line has been relaid, have the same gauge, their rolling stock is interchangeable, officials pass readily from one system to another, and by means of railway conferences attempts have been made to arrive at a common understanding on railway policy. Finally, all South Africa is now united in one Customs Union.

But if the centripetal elements,[35] which make for federation, are numerous and potent, disjunctive and centrifugal forces also exist, though they create no difficulties which a patient statesmanship could not surmount. The obvious historical and racial differences between the colonies may be neglected, for, though on one side a force of separation, they are in another and more important aspect an agency for union, since they create a problem which in some form or other every colony has to meet. The primary disruptive force is economic. The interests, the material interests, of the population of each colony are widely different. In Cape Colony, on the whole, the farming interest predominates, though there, again, there is an internal distinction between the aims of the vine-growing and agricultural south-west and the pastoral north and east. Natal, so far as it is not a huge forwarding agency, is also based on agriculture. The Orange River Colony, though it has a respectable mining interest, is, and will doubtless remain, pre-eminently a pastoral state. The development of Rhodesia is not yet quite apparent, but it is probable that it will end by having a mining and a farming interest of about equal strength. But the Transvaal is overwhelmingly industrial both in population and prospects. In time, no doubt, Transvaal agriculture will play an important part, but the main asset of the colony must long be found in her mines, and the subsidiary industries created by them, which will be left as a legacy when the reefs are worked out to the last pennyweight. That is to say, in South Africa there are three colonies where the predominant interest is agricultural,—one in which the mining and farming interests are likely to be evenly matched, and one, the richest and therefore not the least important, in which the mining interest casts all others into the shade. It is obvious that economic policy will vary greatly in each, even in those general matters which would naturally fall under the survey of a federal government. The bias of the agricultural colonies is towards protection; the absolute necessity of Rhodesia and the Transvaal is free trade or a near approach to it. The industrial population of the Rand must have food at a reasonable price, else the labour bill will wipe off the profits of the mines, and to secure this cheap food, taking into consideration the long railway freights, entry at the coast free of duty is desired. So too with the raw material of mining: any taxation of such imports is directly inimical to the prosperity of South Africa's foremost industry. On the other hand, the coast farmers have good grounds to complain. They look to the Rand for their market, and unless they are to be secured from the competition of lands like the Argentine, where food-stuffs can be grown almost as a waste product, they will grumble against any rebate of coast duties.

The deadlock might be final were it not for the geographical position of the Transvaal. Had she a port of her own she might well decline any federation, and continue to import on her own terms, leaving the other colonies to make the best of it. But, as things stand, she has to bring in most of her imports through ports in the coast colonies, and for a large part of the distance over their lines of railway. Were this, again, a full statement of the case, the Transvaal might be at the mercy of the other colonies, and be compelled to accept their terms or starve. But fortunately the Transvaal, while not in a position to dictate absolutely, has a card of her own by which she can command reasonable treatment. She can import by the much shorter line from Delagoa Bay, and she is contemplating the construction of an alternative line to the same port. These two lines, when completed, will make her virtually independent of the coast colonies, provided—a provision which there seems no reason to doubt—a good understanding is maintained with Portugal. Clearly some *modus vivendi* must be arrived at if there is not to be an endless friction, which can only result in inconvenience to the interior colony and great financial loss to the coast.[36]

This chief centrifugal force, divergence of economic interests, becomes, therefore, in practice a powerful centripetal force, the chief lever of federation. Some kind of harmony must be attained; the only question is whether this agreement is to be partial and temporary or thorough and final. Federation, while on its practical side a familiar policy to all classes in South Africa, is still in its political aspect a little strange to men's minds, smacking somewhat of constitutional doctrinairedom. When we are dealing with self-governing colonies, there can be no question of imposing it as a mandate from above: to be effective and permanent it must come from within, a proposal based on a national conviction. There was, indeed, a time in the last year of the war when Cape Colony lay in the throes of disruption, and her wisest citizens were weary of the vagaries of her politics; when Natal was acquiescent, and when the new colonies were still a battlefield. It seemed to many that then a federation might have been imposed with the consent of most thinking men. But the moment passed; local politics were restored to their old activity, and the opportunity for imperial interference was gone. A federal movement must therefore advance slowly and circumspectly, and be content with small beginnings, lest any hint of coercion should drive the units still farther apart.

There is no argument so convincing as success, and a satisfactory federation in miniature would go far to prepare the way for the larger scheme. Fortunately we have one sphere where experiments towards federation can be given a fair trial. The Transvaal and the Orange River Colony are under one governor and the same system of government. Though they have many points of difference, they have also many common problems which are even now dealt with by one central authority. The South African Constabulary in the two colonies is one force under one Inspector-General. The Central South African railways, which control the whole railway system, are under one Railway Commissioner and one General Manager. Education is under one Director of Education. In addition to this departmental union, the two colonies are subject to one common debt, the Guaranteed Loan. The War Debt lies for the present wholly on the Transvaal;[37] but the loan for reconstruction is devoted to purposes common to both, and they are jointly and severally liable for its interest and redemption. If the Orange River Colony were to pay its fair share of the interest—having regard to the capital expenditure apportioned to it—it would be bankrupt tomorrow. It must either pay a great deal less than its due, or some arrangement must be arrived at by which there is no fixed apportionment of either interest or capital, but the whole debt is administered jointly, and charged upon certain common properties.

The method adopted has been fully explained in another chapter. Here it will be sufficient to point out the federal consequences of the arrangement. If the railways, the South African Constabulary, and all common services are to be charged to one common budget, and subjected to a common administration, then some kind of common council must be established with a share of both legislative and executive powers. It would be necessary to give this council, or some committee of it, the final decision in railway administration, to grant it power to operate upon railway profits, and to make grants for the services of the loan, and for other services placed under its authority, without reference to the councils of the separate colonies. Such powers have not been unknown in constitutional history, and Austro-Hungary furnishes an instructive precedent. There we find a common executive, not responsible to either of the two Parliaments, for such common interests as foreign affairs, the army, and imperial finance. On most matters connected with these common interests the separate Parliaments legislate; but the voting of money for common purposes and the control of the common executive is placed in the hands of the famous Delegations, which are appointed by the two Parliaments. The position is, therefore, that there is a common Ministry for Finance, War, and Foreign Affairs, controlled by the Delegations, and working on funds voted and appropriated by the Delegations. This power of appropriation without ratification by the separate colonies is the essence of the new council, which is thus, to continue the parallel, a compound of the Delegations and the Common Ministry of Austro-Hungary. Certain funds are ear-marked for its use, and its deficits, if any, will be met by contributions, in certain fixed proportions, from the treasuries of the two colonies; while its surplus, if it is ever fortunate enough to have one, will be divided, in whole or in part, between the two colonies, going as a matter of fact to assist in meeting the charges of the War Debt. It has an administrative control over all existing common services, and any other which may be subsequently put under its charge by the local legislatures.

Such a council obviously falls far short of a true federation. It is primarily a financial expedient to provide a simple and effective machinery for administering somewhat complicated finances. But it is a step, and a considerable step, in the right direction. Its executive functions are concerned with truly federal matters; and its powers of acting alone in questions of administration, and of voting and appropriating funds without reference to the separate legislatures, is a recognition of the central doctrine of federation. Indeed at the present moment the two new colonies have a *de facto* federal government. The grant to the new council of legislative powers on matters of common interest, and the corresponding limitation of the powers of the separate legislatures, would establish a complete *de jure* federation. There is no reason why this goal should not soon be reached. The two colonies are bound together by many ties,—above all, by that most stringent bond, a common debt. For three years they have been administered by one governor. Though there may be symptoms of local jealousy in both, there can be no real popular objection, as there is no logical reason, against their federation.

But while the new colonies present a simple problem, the extension of the policy to the self-governing colonies requires delicate and cautious handling. If the limited federation be a success, it will have the power of a good example, especially since there are many throughout South Africa to seize and emphasise the lesson. Meantime other agencies are at work for union. The Bloemfontein Conference of March 1903, which, in addition to settling a customs' tariff and recommending a preferential policy for British goods, passed resolutions on certain questions, such as native affairs, of wide South African interest, is the type of that informal advisory union which may well come into being at once. The appointment, further, of a South African committee to investigate some of the more vexed and obscure details of native policy, is another step in the same direction. The new colonies, which contain the chief motive force for South Africa's future, must give the lead. They hold in their hands the guide-ropes, for federation may be said to depend upon the development of two problems—the racial and the economic; and both reach their typical form in the new colonies. In these questions are involved the chief grounds of separation and the chief impulses towards union, and according as the new colonies settle them within their own bounds will arise the need and desire for a more comprehensive settlement.

The type of federation which South Africa may adopt will, no doubt, vary considerably from most historical precedents. It should in certain respects be more rigid, since, apart from a few outstanding troubles, there are no permanent differences between the parts. In certain respects, too, it should be more elastic, for a federated South Africa would be not only a substantive state, but a member of a greater system, and some of the old free colonial traditions which pertain to that system should be left to the federated units. It is a vain task at this stage to attempt the outlines of a scheme, since the foundations are not yet fully apparent. Needs which are now in embryo will be factors to be reckoned with when the time is ripe, and perhaps some of the forces which seem to us to-day to dominate all else will have disappeared or decreased in strength. There is a wealth of historical precedent for South African statesmen to follow; for, apart from the United States and sundry European parallels, there are two types of federation within the colonial system—the Dominion of Canada and the recently created Australian Commonwealth. Between them these two cases provide a most complete parallel for South Africa. In Canada there was a distinction of races not less marked than Dutch and English. There was, further, an imperfectly explored hinterland which the colonists looked to bring by degrees under the same constitution. In Australia there were grave intercolonial disputes on railways and customs and a wide divergence of economic interests. A keen jealousy was felt by the smaller for the larger states, and the scheme of federation had to be delicately framed to adjust state pride with federal requirements. On the whole, the difficulties which the framers of the federal constitution had to face in Canada and Australia were greater than we find in South Africa: in the United States, immeasurably greater. But often the probability of federation stands in inverse ratio to the ease with which it can be effected, and the very simplicity of this South African problem may delay its settlement. There are, however, forces which must between them hasten the end. One is the economic disparity, at least as great as in Australia and greater than in Canada, which makes itself felt so constantly in the daily life of the inland colonies, that they may find themselves compelled to push the matter in spite of the apathy of the coast. The other is the very real national sentiment which is growing to maturity in the country. The war has welded the English inhabitants into something approaching a nation. Having suffered so deeply, they are the less prone to local jealousies and the more attached to the ideal of imperial unity.

A scheme of South African federation, as has been said, will have to differ materially from any of the existing types. Though details are premature, certain principles may be accepted as essential. The first concerns the subjects relegated to the Federal Government. In the United States these are, roughly, foreign affairs, the army and navy, federal courts of justice, commerce, currency, the post office, certain general branches of commercial law, such as copyrights and patents, an oversight of the separate states to protect the inhabitants against any infringement of the fundamental rights granted by the constitution, and taxation for federal purposes. Several of these functions are needless in a federation of English colonies. Foreign affairs and army and navy questions assume a different form from what they present in a wholly separate community; and since there is no *Grondwet* known to English constitutional law, there is no need for an oversight of the separate states in case of its infringement.

That is already provided for by the ultimate right of the British Crown to annul legislation which may conflict with the chartered rights or limitations of a colony. But there are certain powers, not referred to in the American scheme, which are essential to a modern system. Railways, telephones, and telegraphs should come under the purview of the national Government, as also all customs tariffs and all bounties which may be granted on production. Powers must be given to the national Government to take over the existing debts of the separate states, and in times of financial distress to come to their assistance. On judicial and legal questions—the nature of the federal courts, the mechanism of appeal, the branches of law which are suitable for federal jurisdiction—it is impossible to speak; as it is premature to attempt an outline of the constitution of the federal Government, the form of its legislation, the functions of its executive. Such questions require long and careful consideration on the part of the South African colonies, and may happily take their colour, when the time arrives, from some accepted scheme of imperial federation. Two points only may be noted as even now obvious desiderata of policy. In Canada the state governors are appointed by the federal Ministry; in Australia they are nominated by the Crown in the same way as the Governor-General. Experience has shown that the Australian method is the superior one, since it allows a state governor and his ministers to communicate directly with the imperial Government, and so preserve a formal independence which is at once harmless and grateful to state pride. It is impossible to doubt that the Australian precedent should be followed in South Africa. The second point concerns the method of effecting federation. The Canadian scheme was based on resolutions drafted by a conference of delegates at Quebec. They were approved by the legislatures of the provinces, embodied in a bill drafted by a committee of Canadian statesmen, and passed by the imperial Government. Federation was thus, as in the United States, the work of conferences and legislatures alone. Australia, recognising that this was a question which deeply concerned the population of the colonies, followed a better plan. The federal constitution, after passing through a long period of conferences and examinations by state legislatures, was submitted to a direct popular vote, and a certain majority was prescribed for it in each state. Such a federation, secured by the consent of a whole people, has a stability against future attacks and captious emendation which belongs to no scheme sanctioned only by a legislative body. For though popular representation is in theory a representation for all things, yet a matter so vital in its application and so far-reaching in its issues deserves to be made the subject of a special mandate.

I have said that foreign affairs and army and navy questions do not, under the ordinary practice of the colonial system, have much connection with colonial governments, and therefore may be left out of most federal proposals. But though the technical last word may never lie with the Federal Government, yet a South African federation would have genuine foreign interests, and would keep a watchful eye on the movements of the colonising Powers of Europe. Had there been a federation, there would have been no German acquisition of Damaraland, nor would we have found imperial authorities refusing the offer of Lourenço Marques for a trifling sum. No colonist can ever quite forgive those memorable blunders, which prevented British South Africa from having that geographical unity from the Zambesi to the Cape which its interests demand. Thirty years ago it would have been easy for Britain to proclaim a Monroe doctrine for South Africa—for that matter of it, for East Africa also. The opportunity has passed, but a strong national Government could still exercise great influence on foreign affairs, and prevent encroachment upon Portuguese territories by that Power which twenty years ago saw in Africa material for a new German Empire and has never forgotten its grandiose dreams, as well as keep an eye upon that dangerous mushroom growth, the Congo Free State, and check its glaring offences against civilisation. Army and navy questions belong, in their broadest sense, to schemes of imperial federation, a discussion of which here would be out of place; but since there is already in South Africa a large military force under one commander-in-chief, certain army questions arise which may find their proper answer only in federation, but which even now require a provisional settlement. According as we treat the matter, it may become a unifying or a violently disjunctive force, a step towards federation or a movement towards a wider disintegration. The bearing of the army question on South African policy is the subject of another chapter.

[34] American Commonwealth, vol. i. p. 465.

[35] The grounds of Australian federation are a useful parallel for South Africa. I give Mr Bryce's list ('Studies in History and Jurisprudence,' vol. i. p. 478): "The gain to trade and the general convenience to be expected from abolishing the tariffs established on the frontiers of each colony; the need for a common system of military defence; the advantages of a common legislature for the regulation of railways and the fixing of railway rates; the advantages of a common control of the larger rivers for the purposes both of navigation and irrigation; the need for uniform legislation on a number of commercial topics; the importance of finding an authority competent to provide for old-age pensions and for the settlement of labour disputes all over the country; the need for uniform provision against the entry of coloured races (especially Chinese, Malays, and Indian coolies); the gain to suitors from the establishment of a High Court to entertain appeals and avoid the expense and delay involved in carrying cases to the Privy Council in England; the probability that money could be borrowed more easily on the credit of the Australian Federation than by each colony for itself; the stimulus to be given to industry and trade by substituting one great community for six smaller ones; the possibility of making better arrangements for the disposal of the unappropriated lands belonging to some of the colonies than could be made by those colonies for themselves."

[36] A provisional *modus vivendi* has been found in the new Customs Union.

[37] There is a contingent liability on the Orange River Colony to pay a sum of £5,000,000, as its special contribution, from any profit which may fall to its Government from the discovery of precious minerals.

CHAPTER XVIII.

THE ARMY AND SOUTH AFRICA.

The foremost political lesson of the late war was the solidarity of military spirit throughout the Empire. But this cohesion is only in spirit, and the actual position of colonial forces is that of isolated units, connected in no system, and subject to no central direction. For a student of military law, or that branch of it which concerns the relation of military forces to the civil power, a survey of the British colonies has much curious interest. Speaking generally, since 1868 there have been no imperial forces in any self-governing colony, since we have acted on the principle that when a colony became autonomous the defence of its borders, except by sea, must be left to its own government. Colonial troops are, therefore, militia and volunteer, who take different forms according to the needs of the colony. In some the militia, or a part of it, is to all intents a regular force, performing garrison duty and acting as a school of instruction for the other auxiliary forces. In Canada, for example, there were in 1902 a troop of cavalry, a troop of mounted rifles, two batteries of field artillery, two companies of garrison artillery, and a battalion of infantry, in which the men were enlisted for three years' continuous service. In New South Wales, to take one state of the Australian Commonwealth, provision was made for a permanent force, which included a half-squadron of cavalry, three companies of garrison artillery and one field battery, a company of infantry and various supplementary services, with men enlisted for five years. In New Zealand the enlistment for the permanent force, which consists of artillery and submarine miners, is for eight years, three of which may be passed in the reserve. Next comes the militia proper on the home model, where the men are partially paid and are subject to a certain amount of annual training. Lastly there is a wide volunteer organisation, stretching from fully organised companies of infantry and mounted rifles down to small local rifle clubs. In certain colonies where there is an aboriginal or unsettled population, such as Canada, Cape Colony, and Natal, there is also a permanently embodied police force, which may rank with the permanent militia as a sort of colonial regulars. All such forces are under the full control of the Colonial Governments, whether, as in the Australian Commonwealth and Canada, under the Federal Ministry of Defence, or, as in Cape Colony, under the department of the Prime Minister. An imperial officer may be lent, as in Canada and Australia to-day, for the command of the colonial force, but as soon as he enters upon his command he becomes a servant of the Colonial Government. To that Government alone belongs the power of raising new forces, of changing the status of existing troops, of ordering their distribution, of regulating their rates of pay, and of lending them for service beyond the colony. A strong general officer commanding may have great influence in all such decisions, but technically he is merely an adviser who receives his orders from the local authorities.

This is one chief type of the organisation of our over-sea imperial force. The other is furnished by India. There we have a native Indian army, and a large number of imperial troops, all of whom are under the authority of the commander-in-chief in India, who in turn is under the control of the Indian Government. When imperial troops are stationed in any other part of the Empire they are commanded by an officer who is directly subject to the War Office; but in India, as soon as a battalion lands it takes the status of the local forces and passes under the authority of the local government. The War Office retains certain powers, but for all practical purposes the Indian command is wholly decentralised.

South Africa affords the spectacle of a confusion of the two types. It is made up partly of Crown colonies and dependencies and partly of self-governing states. At this moment it is occupied by imperial troops whose numbers, for the purpose of this argument, may be put at 30,000. Such troops are stationed in Cape Colony and Natal as well as in the new colonies, and the command has been unified and vested in one commander-in-chief, who is subject only to the War Office and has no responsibility to the local governments. We have, therefore, the anomalous case of an autonomous colony occupied by imperial troops, a policy which is out of line with English practice. When self-government is given to the Transvaal and the Orange River Colony, the South African general will command what will be neither more nor less than an alien army of occupation. At the same time, wholly apart from the regular forces, there are police troops in Natal, Cape Colony, the new colonies, and Rhodesia; and a large number of volunteer regiments, who are directly under the control of the local governments. The South African military organisation is thus split in two by a deep gulf, and unless some method of union is found, we shall be confronted with a system alien to the tradition of our colonial policy and in itself clumsy and unworkable. But this question is intimately bound up with others—the desirability of the retention of imperial troops, the organisation of such troops in relation to the imperial army, indeed the whole question of that branch of imperial federation which is concerned with the defence of the Empire. It involves certain problems of military reform which are violently contested by good authorities. In this chapter it is proposed, as far as possible, to consider the matter of the South African army solely from the standpoint of South African politics, referring to the military aspect only in so far as may be necessary at points where South African politics are merged in wider schemes of imperial unity.

The first question concerns the policy of keeping imperial troops in South Africa at all. The size of the force depends, of course, on the duties which it is intended to perform, but for the retention of some troops there seems to be every justification. Few people believe that there is much likelihood of another outbreak, but after a war of the magnitude of that which we have recently gone through it would seem scarcely provident to leave the peace of the country solely to the care of the police. In a country, again, where British prestige is a plant of recent growth, it is well to provide the moral support of regular battalions. If useful for no other purpose, they serve as a memento of war, a constant reminder of the existence of an imperial power behind all local administration. We have also to face the fact that we have committed ourselves to some kind of occupation force by undertaking a large preliminary expenditure on cantonments, which will be money wasted if the scheme is dropped. For this purpose we have spent between two and three millions, and unless we are to be held guilty of causeless extravagance, we must abide by the plan to which this outlay has committed us.

The original scheme was for a garrison force. For this purpose 30,000 men are too many if our forecast be correct, and far too few if it be wrong. Half the number would be ample for any peace establishment, and we may be perfectly certain that as soon as self-government is declared in the new colonies there would be many attempts to cut down the number or do away with the force altogether. Alien garrison troops will be always unpopular, and, as has been said, they are foreign to British policy with regard to autonomous colonies. A force on the garrison basis would find itself with little to do, the general commanding would be exposed to the jealousy of the colonial troops, and involved in constant difficulties with the colonial governments, and, save in the unlikely event of a rebellion, would have no very obvious justification for the existence of his command.

If South Africa is to remain a station for any considerable number of imperial troops, some mode of co-operation must be discovered with the local governments. This co-operation would be possible between the colonial administration and a garrison force; but it would be infinitely more satisfactory if the whole status of the imperial troops were changed. For a garrison establishment makes it difficult, if not impossible, not only to bring the general commanding into touch with the governments, but to bring the local troops into line with the regular, and both unions must be accomplished before any satisfactory settlement can be given to the problem. The simplest solution was to treat the South African force, not as a garrison, but as part of the regular army on the home establishment, sent there for the purpose of training, and liable to be utilised at any moment for active service in any part of the Empire. There are certain objections to the scheme, plausible enough though not insuperable, from the military standpoint; but for the present we may limit our argument to those points which concern South Africa, and those difficulties which spring from the nature of the country—difficulties which are far more real to the soldiers who are directly concerned than the wider question of the present scheme of military organisation.

The advantages are sufficiently obvious. There are few finer manœuvring grounds in the world than the great Central South African tableland. There is sufficient cover to make scouting possible and not enough to make it easy, and the intense clearness of the air and its singular acoustic properties will train a man's senses to a perfection unknown in other armies and impossible to acquire in the restricted areas of a populous country. The soldier will have to face the rudiments of war in a far more difficult country than he is likely to be used in. He will learn to shoot, or rather to judge ranges correctly under unwonted conditions, which is rarer and more vital than mere accurate marksmanship. He will learn the real roughness of campaigning in long manœuvres; and from the same cause regiments will acquire that elasticity and cohesion which come from constant working together. If we except enteric, caused by bad sanitation, which has been the curse of the war, but is not a speciality of the country, the veld is almost exempt from diseases. Life there will not only train the senses and the intelligence, but will give health and physical stamina. A year of such training will make a man of the young recruit from the slums of an English city. Physique is the final determinant in war, and with our present system of recruiting and training there is no guarantee for its existence. Lastly, our soldiers trained on the veld will become natural horse masters, which few even of the cavalry are at present. They will learn that care of their horses which every Boer has as a birthright, that simple veterinary skill and common-sense whose lack has cost us so many millions. South Africa is a natural horse-breeding country, and in co-operation with Government stud-farms a breed of remounts could be got which would unite the merits of the Afrikander pony with the weight and bone required for army work. Instead of having to ransack foreign countries for our horses, we should breed all we wanted for ourselves under the eye of our imperial officers, and breed them too in a place which is the best centre in the Empire for distribution to any possible seat of war.

The objections to the scheme are partly of sentiment and partly of technical difficulties. South African service, it is said, is at present unpopular. Our army has recently concluded a long and arduous war, fought under conditions of extreme discomfort. Small wonder if troops who have been kicking their heels for eighteen months in remote blockhouses should have little good to say of the pleasures of the life. For the officers there have been dismal quarters, a cheerless dusty country, heavy expenses, little sport, and no society; and the lot of the men, though relatively less hard, has been equally comfortless. The proper answer to such a contention is to ignore it. It is the objection of the non-professional officer, and cannot be entertained. The forces in South Africa are sent there for training, not for garrison life, and if the place is a good training-ground, the question of congenial society and interesting recreation has nothing to do with the matter.[38] But there is no reason why South African life for the future should be unattractive. An English society is rapidly arising, English sports are becoming popular, the cantonments can easily be made comfortable homes, and there are a thousand ways, such as the allotting to each soldier who desires it a small patch of land to cultivate, in which the men can be made to feel an interest in the country. For the officers there is a sporting hinterland as fine and as accessible as the Pamirs to the Indian sportsman. Living is undoubtedly more costly, and there will have to be special allowances for South African service; but with a proper canteen system, such as existed during the war, the cost of luxuries might be kept low enough for all. There is a future, too, for the reservist which he cannot look for at home. Even as an unskilled workman he can command wages which are unknown in England; and the men who, at the end of their three years' service, would join the South African reserve, would be young enough to begin civil life in whatever walk they might choose.

The chief technical difficulties, exclusive of sea-transport, which is outside our review, are the extra cost, the difficulty of recruiting, and the delays in bringing reservists from home in case of active service. The last will be met in a little while by the creation of a South African reserve; but in the meantime there are many ways in which it might be surmounted. Battalions might be brought up to fighting strength by the inclusion of men from local forces. It would be an easy matter to introduce into the terms of enlistment of the South African Constabulary a condition of foreign service, and to keep from 1000 to 2000 men in readiness. It would be possible also to enlist 1000 men of the Transvaal volunteer force for special foreign service, paying to each man a bonus of £12 per annum. The real solution of this difficulty is bound up, as we shall see later, with the whole theory of a colonial army; but even on the present system it is easy to provide a working expedient. The question of extra cost—for each man would require an extra 6d. per day, or £9, 2s. 6d. per annum—is answered by pointing out that such a force being on the home establishment would do away with the necessity of linked battalions, and would effect a saving of twenty-four battalions and six regiments of cavalry, so that even if the extra cost were 50 per cent, the total saving would far outbalance it.[39] The recruiting difficulty is unlikely to be a serious one. We may lose to the army a little of the loose fringe of half-grown boys from the towns,—stuff which, as history has shown, can be transformed into excellent fighting men, but which at the same time does not represent the last word either in moral or physical qualities. But many of the best of our young men, whose thoughts turn naturally to the colonies, would gladly seize the chance of three years' service there, in which they would gain experience of the new lands, and be able to judge, when their turn came for entering reserves, which line of life promised most. No Emigration Bureau or Settlement Board would be so effective an agency in bringing the right class to the country. But, further, such a system would throw open to us the vast recruiting-grounds of our colonies. It is difficult for one who has not been brought face to face with it to realise the military enthusiasm which the war has kindled not only among the more inflammable, but among the coolest and shrewdest of our younger colonists. They know—none better—the joints in our armour; but they have paid generous tribute to the solidarity of spirit, the gallantry of our leaders, the unbreakable constancy of our men. A few fanciful war correspondents have done a gross injustice to our colonial soldiers by painting them as a race of capable braggarts, who laughed at our incompetence in a game which they understood so vastly better. It is safe to say that in the better class there was no hint of such a spirit; and the way in which irregular horse, with fine records of service, have traced the source of victory in the last resort to the stamina of the British infantry, does credit both to their judgment and their chivalry. They have become keen critics of any organisation, looking at war not only with the eyes of fighting men but of professional soldiers. All the details of the profession are of interest to them, and an imperial force in South Africa could draw largely both for officers and men upon the local population. The benefit of such a result, both to the colonies and to ourselves, is difficult to over-estimate. A common profession would do much to smooth away the petty differences which are always apt to widen out gulfs. The army would become a vast nursery of the true imperial spirit, and a school to perpetuate the best of our English traditions; and would itself gain incalculably by the infusion of new and virile blood, and the weakening of prejudices, both of class and education, which at present are a grave menace to its efficiency.

If the imperial Government accept the retention of a South African Army Corps as part of the home establishment, it is worth while considering how best this new departure in army policy can be used to further the interests of South Africa herself, and those wider imperial interests which are daily taking concrete shape and casting their shadow over local politics. Leaving for a moment the question of imperial forces, we find in South Africa a local military activity which, though less completely organised than in some of the older colonies, is yet well worth our reckoning with. The war brought into being a large number of irregular corps, most of which have now disappeared. In Cape Colony the permanent force is the Cape Mounted Rifles, which has an average strength of 1000 men, enlisted for five years, and sworn to "act as a police force throughout the colony, and also as a military force for the defence of the colony." Since the war the town guards and district mounted troops, the former limited to 10,000 and the latter to 5000 men, have been placed on a permanent footing. They are loosely organised volunteer forces, enlisted for no fixed period, and bound to serve in the one case in the neighbourhood of the towns, and in the other within their own districts. There are also a number of ordinary volunteer corps, composed chiefly of mounted infantry, and field and garrison artillery, and a number of mounted rifle clubs for local defence. All types of corps included, there are probably not less than 20,000 men undergoing some kind of military training and pledged to some form of service in Cape Colony alone. Natal presents a very similar picture. Her regulars are the Natal Police Force, with a strength, including the Zululand Police, of between 500 and 600 men, enlisted for three years, and including both mounted and foot divisions. There is a considerable volunteer force, with artillery, infantry, and mounted rifles, two companies of naval volunteers, and a number of rifle clubs with a strength of over 2000. We may put the defensive strength of Natal, which, considering her size, is remarkable, at a little under 5000 men. The British South African Police, which is stationed in Southern Rhodesia, has a strength of a little over 500, and the Southern Rhodesia Constabulary and volunteers increase the forces of that district to nearly 2000 men. In the new colonies the chief force is the South African Constabulary, with a nominal strength of 6000 men, of which two-thirds are stationed in the Transvaal. It is an expensive force, each man costing on an average £250 per annum; but there is reason to believe that the figure may soon be reduced to £200, or even less. In the Transvaal a volunteer force has been organised of nine regiments. No ultimate strength has been fixed, but 10,000 may be taken as a fair estimate. In April 1903 the force numbered fully 3000, and as the country becomes more populous there is little reason to doubt that the maximum will be reached.[40]

There is thus a force of over 40,000 men engaged in local defence throughout South Africa, and of this the 8000 police are for all practical purposes regular troops. At the present moment the command of this force is split up among the different colonial governments and is wholly dissociated from any connection with the command of the imperial regulars. We have seen that the situation is full of grave difficulties for the regulars themselves, since there is no place in colonial policy for an alien garrison force. But the strongest argument in the present system lies not in the difficulties which it involves but in the advantages which it forgoes. We have in South Africa a population which, to use Napier's famous distinction, is not only bellicose but martial, with a natural aptitude for soldiering and a keen interest in all details of military organisation. Until the regular command is brought into line with the local forces this genius will expend itself on casual volunteering, and when we next call for colonial aid we shall have the same haphazard units, instead of colonial regiments drilled and manœuvred on one system and forming a part of some regular division. The arguments for a federation of the whole South African command are difficult to meet, and there is little danger of opposition from the local governments. The danger lies in the fact that it would necessarily involve some reconstruction of our whole military system, and military conservatism is slow to depart from the traditions of the elders.

If imperial defence means anything it must include the provision in every great colonial unit, in Canada, Australia, South Africa,—particularly in South Africa,—of a force on the lines of the Indian army, with an elastic organisation, embracing both imperial regulars and local troops. Granted the sanction of the imperial Government, there is no special difficulty in the machinery required to create it. If South Africa were federated it would be simplicity itself. All that would be wanted would be to bring the general officer commanding the imperial troops, since his command has been unified, into relation with the Federal Ministry of Defence, and unite in his person the functions which Sir Neville Lyttelton now exercises in South Africa and those which at present belong to Lord Dundonald in Canada. But, pending federation, we must have recourse to one of those intercolonial representative bodies which form the thin end of the federal wedge. The general commanding would be given the command of local forces by an act of the local legislature, subject in all questions of policy, finance, and organisation to the authority of an intercolonial committee of defence.[41] Each colony would elect two or more representatives, on the lines of the present Intercolonial Council of the Transvaal and Orange River Colony; the council thus formed would be empowered by the legislatures which elect it to decide what share of the cost was to be borne by the separate colonies, to arrange for combined manœuvres, to supervise appointments, and, in case of local wars, to decide what force should be sent to the front, and in the event of an imperial war, to say what local forces should be lent for service. The general commanding would be responsible to the War Office for moving imperial troops, subject to its direction, and for the internal discipline and organisation of the imperial divisions. There would, thus, be clearly defined limits of authority for both the imperial and local Governments, and at the same time every inducement to co-operation. In so far as he was in command of the whole of the South African forces, the general commanding would be subject in South African matters to the defence committee; while, in so far as he was in command of imperial troops, he would take his orders on imperial questions, such as a foreign war, from the Home Government. The present officers in command of colonial police and volunteers would, of course, come under his authority precisely on the same basis as officers of regulars.

The advantages of such a scheme are many, both from the standpoint of policy and of military efficiency. It would please the colonies, who would have an army of their own, drilled on regular lines and affiliated to the imperial army, and at the same time would feel that they had a share in the control of the forces and the military policy of the Empire. It would ensure the efficiency of local troops, and would prepare them for co-operation with the regulars,—not the clumsy partnership of troops tagged on to a division which cannot use them, but the true co-operation which follows on absorption in a larger unit with which they have been trained. It would provide an easy means for the transfer of colonial officers to imperial regiments, and would act as a magnet for colonial recruiting. In the case of local wars, as I have said, the whole force would be ready to take the field under the orders of the general commanding. In the case of a foreign war the imperial Government would direct the distribution of the regulars, and it would be for the committee of defence to say what local troops should be lent for foreign service.[42] Beyond this, the only duties of the War Office would lie in the selection of staff officers and the general commanding—a matter in which the concurrence of the colonial governments might be obtained as a matter of courtesy. On the financial side it is probable that the scheme would considerably lessen the burden of defence. The only way in which the colonies can ever be expected to contribute to the cost of imperial defence is by providing armies and navies of their own. To pay for that which does not directly concern you is a form of tax, and so hostile to the letter and spirit of our colonial traditions. But if local governments are given a direct interest in an imperial army in which their own troops are subsumed, and whose policy they largely control, I do not think they will be ungenerous. There is no reason why they should not meet the cost of the general and his staff, and contribute part, if not the whole, of the extra pay which the regular troops in the South African command must receive, and the bonus to the volunteer corps which are held ready for foreign service. Such payments, once the federation were effected, would no doubt come as a spontaneous offer. Decentralisation and centralisation are, by way of becoming catchwords, repeated without understanding to justify the most diverse schemes. But every true policy must include both, since in certain matters it is well to decentralise, and in others unification is imperative. Such a scheme as has been sketched combines the sporadic colonial forces in one effective unit of organisation, and at the same time relieves the tension at imperial headquarters by relegating detailed administration to the local authorities, who are best fitted to supervise.

The military is, as a rule, the most difficult aspect of a federation, but in our circumstances it is likely to be the simplest. We have a federal nucleus in the imperial command, and a strong impulse in the fact that the local volunteer and police forces have already served side by side with regulars in the field, and are inspired with a military spirit which may soon disappear unless fostered and utilised. A federation of local forces exists in Canada and in the Australian Commonwealth; a union of the imperial forces exists in South Africa. The problem is to federate the local forces in advance of a political federation, and to unite them with the imperial command in a system which, though a new departure in military policy, contains no detail which has not been somewhere or other already conceded. If the scheme in itself is worth anything, the practical difficulties are small. It is unlikely that the colonial governments will offer any opposition; and so far as South African interests are concerned, the foundations would be laid of a true federation. From the point of view of imperial politics the step would have an even greater significance, for a type would be created of a new army organisation which would provide for a federated imperial defence; and the precedent having once been created, the other colonies would readily follow suit.

[38] The final answer to this objection would be the reorganisation of the militia—the only force for home defence—and the release of the present regular army for service over-sea.

[39] I have thought it unnecessary to recapitulate in detail the financial argument used by advocates of this policy. Roughly it is as follows: The present Army Corps system provides for 78 battalions at home, 66 in India, and 12 in South Africa—a total of 156. The proposed

system provides for 42 at home, 24 in South Africa, and 66 in India—a total of 132. There is thus a saving of 24 battalions, besides 6 regiments of cavalry.

In figures, 24 battalions at £64,000 = £1,536,000

And 6 cavalry regiments at £45,000 = £270,000

A total of, £1,806,000

Including supplementary expenses, the total reductions would be over £2,000,000.

[40] The details of the force may be of interest. In April 1903 it consisted of two regiments of the Imperial Light Horse, one regiment of the South African Light Horse, one regiment of the Johannesburg Mounted Rifles, one regiment of the Scottish Horse, one regiment of the Central South African Railway Volunteers, one regiment of the Transvaal Light Infantry, one regiment of Transvaal Scottish, one regiment of Railway Pioneers, a medical staff corps, and a headquarters' staff. The names of some of the most famous irregular corps are thus perpetuated. A new regiment—the Northern Rifles—has recently been formed at Pretoria.

[41] A committee of defence has been formed in Natal, consisting of the officers commanding the imperial and the local forces and representatives of the local government.

[42] This scheme would involve a departure from the present military organisation on the basis of army corps. We cannot expect to get an army corps for each colonial district, and the advantages disappear if such reinforcements are to be distributed to make up the strength of the army corps drawn from the whole Empire. The unit must be smaller—something in the nature of a division of, say, three brigades with one brigade of mounted troops. In South Africa we could have several divisions of regulars and several of local troops. The system would have the merit of harmonising with the organisation of the army in India, where reinforcements are most likely to be required.

CHAPTER XIX.

THE FUTURE OUTLOOK.

The problems discussed in the foregoing chapters have been concerned chiefly with the new colonies, for it is to them that we must look for the motive force to expedite union. They must long continue to be the most important factor in British South Africa, partly from their accidental position as the late theatre of war, and more especially from their wealth, the intricacy of their politics, the high level of ability among their inhabitants, the splendid chances of their future, and the delicacy of their present status. Union, if it comes, will come chiefly because of them; and in any union they will play a great, if not a dominant, part. Whither they pipe, South Africa must ultimately follow. But this is not because there can be any differentiation in value between the states, since all are self-subsistent and independent, but because in the new colonies the problems which chiefly concern South Africa's future are already naked to the eye and focussed for observation. The Transvaal will be important because within it the fight which concerns the whole future of the African colony will be fought to a finish. It will add to the problem some features which concern only itself, but the general lines it shares with its neighbours. The economic strife, the amalgamation of races, the native question, the movement towards federation, with all its many aspects, and, last but not least, the intellectual and political development of its citizens,—this is the problem of the Transvaal, and in the gravest sense it is the problem of South Africa's future.

In the preceding pages the separate questions have been briefly considered. But here we may note one truth which attaches to them all—the settlement of no single one is easy. Each will defy a supine statesmanship, and in each failure will be attended with serious disaster. Patience and a lithe intelligence can alone ensure success, and it is doubtful if that happy Providence which has now and then taken charge of our drifting and muddling will interfere in this province to save us from the consequences of folly. Every question stands on a needle-point. Mining development—if the wealth of the country is to be properly exploited—must continue as it has begun, utilising the highest engineering talent, and straining every nerve to extend the area over which profits can be made. The labour question requires tact and patience, prescience of future interests, a recognition of the needs of the complex organism of which it is but one aspect. The native question shows the same narrow margin between success and failure, and demands a degree of forethought and statesmanship which would be an exorbitant requirement were it not so vital a part of the social and economic future. Agriculture and settlement can only be made valuable by a close study of facts, and an intelligence which can correctly estimate data and bring to bear on them the latest results of experimental science. Finally, in its financial aspects the problem has a near resemblance to the most complicated of recent economic tasks, the re-settlement of Egypt.

Burdened with a heavy debt, the country is speculating on its future and living on its capital. For the next few years it will in all likelihood achieve solvency; but the margin may be small, and the result may be secured only by the retention of certain revenue-producing charges at an unnatural figure. A considerable part of the debt will be applied to services which will make a good return in time, but for a little while revenue may barely cover disbursements. In finance, above all other provinces, there is need of a severe economy, coupled with a clear recognition of the country's needs and a judicious courage. It is a gamble, if you like, but with sleepless and ubiquitous watchfulness the odds are greatly in our favour. The very forces which fight against us, the complexity of economic and social interests, will become our servants, if properly understood, and will solidify and preserve our work, as the house fashioned of granite will stand when the building of sandstone will crumble. The shaping force of intelligence remains the one thing needful. Of high and just intentions there can be little doubt, but in the new South Africa we are more likely to be perplexed by the fool than the knave. Will the result, as Cromwell asked long ago, be "answerable to the simplicity and honesty of the design"? Neither to the one nor the other, but to that rarer endowment, political wisdom.

So much for administrative problems. A country whose future is staked upon the intelligence of its Government and its people is an exhilarating spectacle to the better type of man. England has succeeded before on the same postulates and in harder circumstances. But there are certain subtler aspects of development, where the same high qualities are necessary, but where the end to be striven for is less clear. There is the fusion of the two races, an ideal if not a practical necessity. As has been said, a political union already exists after a fashion. There seems little reason to fear any future disruption, for on the material side Dutch interests are ours, and all are vitally concerned in the common prosperity. Administrative efficiency will make the Boer acquiesce in any form of government. But that which Lord Durham thought far more formidable, "a struggle not of principles but of races," may continue for long in other departments than politics, unless we use extraordinary caution in our methods. The very advance of civilisation may militate against us by vivifying historical memories and rekindling a clearer flame of racial resentment. The Dutch have their own ideals, different from ours, but not incompatible with complete political union. Any attempt to do violence to their ideals, or any hasty and unconsidered imposition of unsuitable English forms, will throw back that work of spiritual incorporation which is the highest destiny of the country. They have a strong Church and a strong creed, certain educational ideas and social institutions which must long remain powers in the land. And let us remember that any South African civilisation must grow up on the soil, and must borrow much from the Dutch race, else it is no true growth but a frail exotic. It will borrow English principles but not English institutions, since, while principles are grafts from human needs, institutions are the incrusted mosses of time which do not bear transplanting. It is idle to talk of universities such as Oxford, or public schools like Winchester, and any attempt to tend such alien plants will be a waste of money and time. South Africa will create her own nurseries, and on very different lines. If we are burdened in our work with false parallels we shall fail, for nothing in the new country can survive which is not based on a clear-sighted survey of things as they are, and a renunciation of old formulas. Let us recognise that we cannot fuse the races by destroying the sacred places of one of them, but only by giving to the future generations some common heritage. "If you unscotch us," wrote Sir Walter Scott to Croker, "you will find us damned mischievous Englishmen," and it will be a very mischievous Dutchman who is coerced into unsuitable English ways and taught sentiments of which he has no understanding. When a people arise who have a common culture bequeathed from their fathers, and who look back upon Ladysmith and Colenso, the Great Trek and the Peninsular War, as incidents in a common pedigree, then we shall have fusion indeed, a union in spirit and in truth. Nothing which has in it the stuff of life can ever die, and there is something of this vitality in the Dutch tradition. Our own is stronger, wider, resting on greater historical foundations, and therefore it will more readily attract and absorb the lesser. But the lesser will live, transformed, indeed, but none the less a real part of the spiritual heritage of a nation where there will be no racial cleavage. The consummation is not yet, and, maybe, will be long delayed. It will not be in our time; perhaps our sons may see it; certainly, I think, our grandchildren will be very near it. Such a development cannot be artificially hastened, and all that we can do is to see that no barriers of our own making are allowed to intervene. Meantime we have a *de facto* political union to make the most of.

What manner of men are the citizens of this new nation to be? They will have the vigour which belongs to colonial parentage, the freshness of outlook and freedom from old shibboleths. But they should have more. They start as no colony has ever started, with the echoes of a great war still in their ears, with a highly developed industry and the chances of great wealth, and with a population showing as high a level of intelligence as any in the world. The nature of their problem will compel them to remain intellectually active, and as the eyes of the world are on them they will have few temptations to lethargy. They may take foolish steps and be beguiled into rash experiments, but I do not think they will stagnate. And for this people so much alive there is the chance of an indigenous culture, born of the old, when they have leisure to make it theirs, and the freshening influences of their new land and their strenuous life. South Africa cannot help herself. She must play a large part in imperial politics; her views on economic questions will be listened to by all the world; a political future, good or bad, she must accept and make the most of. But behind it all there is the prospect of that intimate self-development, that progress in thought, in the arts, in the amenities of life, which, like righteousness, exalteth a nation. The finest of all experiments is to unite an older civilisation with the natural freshness of a virgin soil, and she, alone among the colonies which have ever been founded, has the power to make it. Not only is it a new land, but it is Africa, a corner of that mysterious continent to which the eyes of dreamers and adventurers have always turned. The boundaries of the unknown are shrinking daily, and where our forefathers marked only lions and behemoths on the map, we set down a hundred names and a dozen trading stations. The winds which blow from the hills of the north tell no longer of mystic interior kingdoms and uncounted treasures. We know most things nowadays, and have given our knowledge the prosaic form of joint-stock companies. But the proverb still justifies itself.[43] Africa is still a home of the incalculable, not wholly explored or explorable, still a hinterland to which the youth of the south can push forward in search of fortune, and from which that breath of romance, which is the life of the English race, can inspire thinkers and song-makers. Girdled on three sides by the ocean, and on the fourth looking north to the inland seas and the eternal snows of Ruwenzori—I can imagine no nobler cradle for a race. I have said that a structure built with difficulty is the most lasting. Her complex problems will knit together the sinews of intelligence and national character, and the great commonplaces of policy, so eternally true, so inexorable in their application, will become part of her creed, not from lip-service but from the sweat and toil of practical work. If to these she can add other commonplaces, still older and more abiding, of civic duty, of the intellectual life, of moral purpose, she will present to history that most rare and formidable of combinations, intellect and vitality, will and reason, culture guiding and inspiring an unhesitating gift for action.

There is already a school of political thought in South Africa, a small school, and thus far so ill-defined that it has no common programme to put before a world which barely recognises its existence. It owes its inspiration to Mr Rhodes, but its founder left it no legacy of doctrine beyond a certain instinct for great things, a fire of imagination, and a brooding energy. Its members are very practical men, landowners, mine-owners, rich, capable, with nothing of the ideologue in their air, the last people one would naturally go to for ambitions which could not be easily reduced to pounds sterling. But they are of the school: at heart they are pioneers, the cyclopean architects of new lands. It is one of South Africa's paradoxes that there should exist among successful and matter-of-fact men of business a hungry fidelity to ideals for which we look in vain among the doctrinaires who do them facile homage. And they are also very practical in their aims. Mr Rhodes never desired a paper empire or that vague thing called territorial prestige. What filled his imagination was the thought of new nations of our blood living a free and wholesome life and turning the wilderness into a habitable place. He strove not for profit but for citizens, for a breathing-space, a playground, for the future. The faults of his methods and the imperfections of his aims, which are so curiously our own English faults and imperfections, may have hindered the realisation of his dreams, but they did

The African Colony

not impair that legacy of daimonic force which he left to his countrymen. You may find it in South Africa to-day, and if you rightly understand it and feel its hidden movements you will be aghast at your own parochialism. It is slow and patient, knowing that "the counsels to which Time hath not been called Time will not ratify." But with Time on its side it is confident, and it will not easily be thwarted.

Excursions in colonial psychology are rarely illuminating, lacking as a rule both sympathy and knowledge; but on one trait there is a singular unanimity. The two chief obstacles to imperial unity, so runs a saying, are the bumptious colonial and the supercilious Englishman. I readily grant the latter, but is the first fairly described? A colonist is naturally prone to self-assertion in certain walks of life. If he creates an industry alone and from the start in the teeth of hardships, having had to begin from the very beginning, he is apt to lose perspective and unduly magnify his work. If he owns a bakery, it is the finest in the world, at any rate in the British Empire. He compares his doings with his neighbours' within his limited horizon, and he is scarcely to be blamed if he brags a little. His bravado is only ridiculous when taken out of its surroundings, and at the worst is more a mannerism than an affection of mind. But on the intellectual side he is, in my judgment, conspicuously humble, a groper after the viewless things whose omnipotence he feels dimly. To the home-bred man history is a commonplace to be taken for granted; to the colonist who has shaped a workaday life from the wilds, it is a vast mother of mystery. Traditions, customs, standards staled to us by the vain emphasis of generations, rise before him as revelations and shrines of immortal wisdom. What to us is rhetoric is to him the finest poetry; and for this reason in politics he is prone to follow imaginative schemes, without testing them by his native caution. Our somewhat weary intellectual world is a temple which he is ready to approach with uncovered head. It is not mere innocence, but rather, I think, that freshness of outlook and optimism which he gathers from his new land and his contact with the beginnings of things. Truth and beauty remain the same: it is only the symbols and the mirrors which grow dim with time; and to the man who is sufficiently near to understand the symbols, and sufficiently aloof to see no flaw or tawdriness, there is a double share of happiness. The superficial assurance, the "bumptiousness" of the saying, is surely a small matter if behind it there is this true modesty of spirit.

A national life presumes union, but South African federation is simply a step to a larger goal. It may be objected that in the foregoing chapters the cardinal problem is treated as less the fusion of the two races than the development of South Africa on certain lines within our colonial system. Such has been the intention of the book. The Dutch have accepted the new *régime*; they will fight, if they fight, on constitutional lines under our ægis and within our Empire, and in a sense it may be said that racial union on the political side already exists. But the further political development of the country, as self-consciousness is slowly gained—that, indeed, is a matter on which hang great issues, good or bad, for the English people. Because the furnace has been so hot, the metal will emerge pure or it will not emerge at all. A new colony, or rather a new nation, will have been created, or another will have been added to the catalogue of our infrequent failures, and the loose territorial mass known as South Africa will become the prey of any wandering demagogue or aspiring foreign Power. Our late opponents will take their revenge, if they seek it, not by reviving the impossible creed of Dutch supremacy, but by retarding South Africa from what is her highest destiny and her worthiest line of development. Her future, if she will accept it, is to be a pioneer in imperial federation: a pioneer, because she has felt more than any other colony the evils of disintegration, the vices of the old colonial system, the insecurity of government from above, and at the same time is in a position to realise the weakness of that independence which is also isolation. This is not the place to enter upon so vast a question. To many it is the greatest of modern political dreams. Without it imperialism becomes empty rhetoric and braggadocio, a tissue of dessicated phrases, worthy of the worst accusations with which its enemies have assailed it. Without it our Empire is neither secure from aggression nor politically sound nor commercially solvent. Within it alone can any true scheme of common defence be realised. Moreover, it is the glamour needed to give to colonial politics that wider imaginative outlook which England enjoys in virtue of a long descent. Colonial politics tend to become at times narrow and provincial;

in a federation they would gain that larger view and ampler pride which a man feels who, believing himself to be humbly born, learns for the first time that he is the scion of a famous house. Their kinship, instead of the long-remembered sentiment of a descendant, would become the intimate loyalty of a colleague. And home politics also would lose the provincialism, equally vicious, if historically more interesting, which lies somewhere near the root of our gravest errors, and in relinquishing a facile imperialism find an empire which needs no rhetoric to enhance its splendour.

But before South Africa can become an ally in federation she must make her peace with herself. If it is difficult to exaggerate the need for untiring intelligence in the making of this peace, it is even harder to overestimate the profound significance which her success or failure in the task of self-realisation has for the prestige of our race. Our colonial methods are on trial in a sphere where all the world can watch. And while our aim is a colony, the means must be different from those which we have hitherto used in our expansion. A nascent colony was neglected till it asserted itself and appeared already mature on the political horizon. But in the growth of this colony England must play a direct part, since for good or for ill her destinies are linked with it, and supineness and a foolish interference will equally bring disaster. There is one parallel, not indeed in political conditions, but in the qualities required for the shaping of the country. If we can show in South Africa that spirit of sleepless intelligence which has created British India, then there is nothing to fear. For, as I understand history, India was made by Englishmen who brought to the task three qualities above others. The first was a wide toleration for local customs and religions—a desire to leave the national life intact, and to mould it slowly by those forces of enlightenment in which sincerely, if undogmatically, they believed. The second was the extension of rigorous justice and full civil rights to every subject, a policy which in the long-run is the only means of bringing a subject race into the life of the State. Last, and most vital of all, they showed in their work a complete efficiency, proving themselves better statesmen, financiers, jurists, soldiers, than any class they had superseded. This efficiency is the key-note of the South African problem, so far as concerns British interests. If the imperial Power shows itself inspired with energy, acumen, a clear-eyed perception of truth as well as with its traditional honesty of purpose, South Africa will gladly follow where it may lead. But she will be quick to criticise formalism and intolerant of a fumbling incapacity.

Sed nondum est finis. We stand at the beginning of a new path, and it is impossible to tell whither it may lead, what dark fords and stony places it may pass through, and in what sandy desert or green champaign it may end. Political prophecy is an idle occupation. American observers on the eve of the French Revolution saw England on the verge of anarchy and France a contented country under a beloved king. Even so acute a writer as de Tocqueville assumed that America would continue an agricultural country without manufactures, and that the fortunes of her citizens would be small. If philosophers may err, it is well for a humble writer to be modest in his conclusions. In the past pages an effort has been made neither to minimise the difficulties nor to over-estimate the chances of South African prosperity. "Whosoever," said Ralegh, "in writing a modern history shall follow truth too near the heels, it may haply strike out his teeth." I can ask for no better fate than to see all my forecasts falsified, the dangers proved to have no existence, the chances shown a thousandfold more roseate. But whatever may be the destiny of this or that observation, there can be no dispute, I think, upon the gravity of the problem and the profound importance of its wise settlement. And when all is said that can be said it is permissible to import into our view a little of that ancestral optimism which has hitherto kept our hearts high in our checkered history, for optimism, when buttressed by intelligence, is but another name for courage. There is an optimism more merciless than any pessimism, which, seeing clearly all the perils and discouragements, the hollowness of smooth conventional counsels and the dreary list of past errors, can yet pluck up heart to believe that there is no work too hard for the English race when its purpose is firm and its intelligence awakened. With this belief we may well look forward to a day when the old unhappy things will have become far off and forgotten, and South Africa, at peace with herself, will be the leader in a new and pregnant imperial policy; and the words of the poet of another empire will be true in a nobler and ampler sense of ours, "They who drink of the Rhone and the Orontes are all one nation."

[43] "Out of Africa comes ever some new thing" is generally quoted in the Latin of Pliny, but it is probably as old as the first Ionian adventurers who sailed to Egypt or heard wild Phœnician tales. It is found in Aristotle: Λέγεταί τις παροιμία ὅτι ἀεὶ φέρει Λιβύη τι καινόν (Hist. Anim., viii. 28).

www.ingramcontent.com/pod-product-compliance
Lightning Source LLC
Chambersburg PA
CBHW031323230426
43670CB00006B/221